Dedicated

To

John C Barrett & Lorene Hopkins Barrett

Copyright © 2015 Dr. John C. Barrett Jr. PH-D
SOS Publications West Plains, Missouri U.S.A. Printed in U.S.A.

Dr. John C. Barrett Jr. is the coordinator of Support Outreach Services = SOS. Dr. Barrett is dedicated to publishing self-help books on helping you help yourself. It is our hope that this book will help guide your own life and help you meet the needs of others. **SOS ministries / revivals**:

Conferences - Seminars & Work Shops & Training Manuals

4 Bible Studies

How Does God Answer Pray?

We are Ambassadors for Christ.

Opening the Door to Christian Psychology.

Applying Christian Principles

All Scripture quotations, unless otherwise noted, are taken from the (KJV).

Support Outreach Services (SOS) LLC

1122 W Cass Ave West Plains, MO 65775

(417) 204-8022 – drbarrettphd@yahoo.com www.sosselfhelpbooks.info

Cover design By Dr. John C Barrett Jr. PH-D

ISBN-10 1541116852

ISBN-13 9781541116856

OPENING THE DOOR TO CHRISTIAN PSYCHOLOGY

Defining the differences between man's view and God's view

Bible Study in the book of Romans

Support Outreach Services =

SOS Publications / Self-Help (BOOKS)

SOS Life Enhancement

SOS Self Improvement

SOS New Beginnings

Let us help you climb your mountain!

(Book) FACING THE REAL ME

Author: John C. Barrett Jr. B.S/ M.A/PH-D

Clinical Psychologist,

Counselor, / Analysis

Table of Contents

Index of our study: .... **P. 3**

PREFACE .... **P. 6**

SUPPORT OUTREACH SERVICES .... **P. 13**

Chapter 1 .... **P. 22**
HUMANISTIC VIEW OF PSYCHOLOGY

Chapter 2 .... **P. 56**
THE BRAIN'S CHARACTERIZED RESPONSES

Chapter 3 .... **P. 82**
THE PHYSIOLOGICAL FUNCTION OF THE BRAIN

Chapter 4 .... **P. 114**
LIFE LINE PRACTICAL AXIOMS & EVALUATIONS

Chapter 5 .... **P. 122**
HUMAN NATURE ROMANS CHAPTERS 1-8

Chapter 6 .... **P. 166**
GOD'S PROMES IN ROMANS CHAPTERS 9-16

Chapter 7 .... **P. 230**
HUMAN NATURE AND EMOTIONS

Chapter 8 .... **P. 272**
THE IMPACT OF RELATIONSHIPS

Chapter 9 .... **P. 292**
HOW A PERSON THINKS & FEELS ABOUT THEMSELVES

Chapter 10 .... **P. 312**
BURNOUT, DEPRESSION, & STRESS

Chapter 11 .... **P. 344**
SELF - ACTUALIZATION & DISCIPLINE

Chapter 12 .... **P. 382**
SOS PROGRAMS & SERVICES

Appendix A .... WEB REFERENCES .... **P. 393**

Appendix B .... DEFINITIONS .... **P. 394**

Appendix C .... BIBLE REFERENCES .... **P. 395**

Index of our study:

Preface, by Dr. John Barrett PH-D / author / speaker / minister

The Modern Age Psychotherapy & Drugs

The psychology of man from a Biblical point of view

The modern age of the humanistic view point

C. S. Lewis sets the tone for modern Christian psychology.

Carl Rogers Personal Centered Approach.

1. Profile of self will, image, esteem, and worth

Comparing the modern age of psychology and The Scriptural view of psychology

A. Self-will exposes your true motives

B. The Scriptural views self-will

C. Self-love theory to loving yourself

Christian Psychology

My Christian Testimony:

Demonstration Chart I Formula Plus & Minus

The Life Cycle

Human Nature in the Life Line

Demonstration Chart II Axiom (1) Normal Reaction

Demonstration Chart II Axiom (2) Normal Highs & Lows (1)

Demonstration Chart II Axiom (3) Normal Breakdown

Demonstration Chart II Axiom (4) Long term Breakdown

Demonstration Chart II Axiom (5) Short term Breakdown

Demonstration Chart II Axiom (6) Struggle & Breakdown

Axiom (6) Short term Breakdown

Axiom (6) Struggle &

Personal observation & conclusion on Breakdowns
Demonstration Chart III A Studies, Profiles, and Information
Study in the book Romans
The natural conflicts, struggles, & warfare!
    a. Control – Controlled – Controlling – Out-of-Control,
    b. Co-dependency/Addictions/Abuse =
Alcoholism-Drugs-Pills-Smoking & Sexual-addictions/Adultery.
    c. Anxiety, Depression, Bipolar, & Weight problems!
      (a. **Hurt** (b. **Anger** (c. **Bitterness** (d. **Hostility** (e. **Pain** (f.
Disappointments (g. **Guilt**
    The modern age of methodology terms and The Scriptural
view of each
    A down-hill-spiral could exposes the weaknesses in
Christian's.
    Downhill / Christian point of view
    Burnout - Depression - Anxiety

    Life is about Christian discipline, Self-control, motives, and
attitudes

PREFACE

The Bible is probable the best book on psychology because it tells of man's failures, how to deal with them, how to live with them. It helps a person understand themselves, and gain knowledge as to who we are. I would like to talk about the successes in a person's life, the biggest influences comes from a person's failures.

I have dealt with 36 plus boys, personal counseling with them and did groups sessions every mouth. The success stories are the ones who get into church / youth group / group sessions. I call it replacement behavior modification and those who believe God is the answer to a better life. We want to train people to become mentors.

The Bible says God gave man the knowledge and ability to live with others and rule at the same time. The same is true in a sense as He accepts people who are willing to change, look at history and the nations that have fallen throughout the centuries. There is no doubt the Bible gives us examples of the human concepts of love and also the values of knowing good from evil.

We will look at psychology from the Bible, and its insights about people in the Bible. From the very beginning God shows how men and women are responsible to live and understand there are consequences for their actions. We can go through history and find people who have succeeded, the results of their accomplishments. In contrast how does God deal with a person that is what we are going to discover in this study. I believe the combination of both forces will give us the best answers to why and how people react.

Christian Psychology and Therapy adds another domination as to how the mind works; the Bible also gives us answers to the body and mind, as we look into the soul, and into the heart of a person. The mind and heart is the mental make-up of a person, the soul has to do with our relationship to God also fit into who we are?

That is one of the reasons for the study of Romans in this book. To those Christians who enjoy Bible studies it helps them grow in their relationship with God and to understand the scriptures. Many consider the book of Romans to be one of the key books in the New Testament, it outlines the plan of salvation clearly and thoroughly. It is because of God's goodness and patience God is able bring people to repent and turn from their sin. **Romans** *7 teaches us valuable lessons about ourselves our helplessness condition and sinfulness our inability to please God without believing in Christ. May we never forget these lessons? God-intended Christian to live life free from captivity and the bondage of sin.*

The key is God's love in Romans (Christians) who are called with a purpose. He also explains what it means to be a child of God which can lead us into understanding we become the "Sons of God!" Those who live by the Spirit are after the things of the Spirit, having put away the desires of the flesh and the death contained therein, and live anew in Christ We as Christians, are the "first fruits of the Spirit," The theme of the Bible is the truth of God's word!

"Who shall deliver me?" In this cry for a Deliverer, notice what a person says, not say: WHAT SHALL I DO? or HOW SHALL I DELIVER MYSELF? No, this person has come to the end of them self. Dependence on SELF can and does led to defeat and failure. They render themselves powerless and helpless, at this point they are without hope. Finally, a person cries out for deliverance, how can they do this outside them self.

In our relationships in Romans chapter 5. Once we have entered into this relationship with God, through faith in Jesus Christ, we discover a whole new world of blessings we had not anticipated. His love shows up in our hearts.

This same love assures us of the hope we have in God's future promises being fulfilled.

A person can become an enabler and empower each other by helping each other, the opposite is true when the enabler aids a person's addiction.

Our <u>motto</u> is found in Galatians 6:1, 2 "Bearing one another's burdens"... "lest we be taken in a fall and restoring one another." In other words being there for the other person, we have to be careful when a person becomes an enabler in their faults or addiction. That is why we proclaim, "Tough love techniques in helping others, they have to learn how to help themselves stand on their own.

Defining the differences between man's view and God's view Mark 8:35:

"Whosoever will save his *life* shall lose it, and whosoever will lose his life for my sake and the gospel's, the same shall save it."

There are two other aspects of a person in this verse, Mark speaks of a person's *life* and of his or her soul is linked to our human behavior. It speaks of the *physical* aspects of salvation. In the humanistic view they don't take into account the spiritual aspects of a person, how do we deal with the physical aspects, the Scriptures takes into account both the physical and spiritual.

Parable, Christ is talking about His death, if the grain of wheat die it shall live again and those that follow Him:

John 12:24-27   (1)

V-24 "Verily, Verily; I say unto you, Except a corn of wheat fall into the ground and die, it abideth alone: but if it die, it bringeth forth much fruit.

8

V-25 He that loveth his life shall lose it: and he that hateth his life in the world shall keep it unto life eternal

V-26 If any man serve me, let him follow me; and where I am, there shall also my servant be: if any man serve me, him will *my* Father honour.

V-27 Now is my soul troubled; and what shall I say? Father, save me from this hour: but for this cause came I unto this hour."

There are **3 Parts** of our study on is the **Introduction to Christian psychology** and they go hand and hand with the Bible, I like to think of how a glove covers the hand. Now I want you to get the total picture as we take on this study.

Sometimes we just need help and help can come when a person goes through the situation and circumstances. The journey is the important part of the healing process, the answer is somewhere, if we're not sure we are not likely going to be able to deal with a situation, in that case doubts and fears will take over.

Help may come from the most unlikely sources. We can feel we need or want a change of direction, if the answer is not there or we can't see it. We may be going through a crisis that is the time a person usually calls on God. If we can only get you to stop before that next step is taken.

The answer is there if we could only see it. Prayer comforts in the meantime. We need to make good decisions/choices and keep trying to find the best solutions possible. That is where counseling comes into play putting both of them together.

• The search may be the answer and our faith in ourselves will be tied to the limits of the mind and body.

• The problem maybe that we cannot see the real problem and we may not want to accept the answer.

- We can get confused about this time, it is always much more difficult when a person is going through a crises or problem, as we are looking at the darkest hour,
- We may not be able to see the light for the darkness.

There is always hope when we let God help!

People may not be able to see the light as they look through the tunnel, but we know there is an end somewhere we want to help people find the light that is the reason we are writing this book. We know what others have gone through and how we have helped them at the same time the same can be said in my own life. At this point it can look pretty germ when a person is engulfed by the darkness, the journey must continue because there is always hope.

Another thing we want to point out we can't always see what seems obvious to others, someone else may be able to shade some light at that point. They can help a person see the light at the end of the tunnel. Now there is hope when a person sees the light at the end of the tunnel. We may be trying to go through the mountain as person tries to deal with their problems. Remember the short cut is going through the mountain, it would probable much harder when a person is going up the mountain, remember to stay calm don't panic, or get overwhelmed at any point and time.

In my case I was able to find myself and harness the power in me that power was in God. It takes a great deal of care and understanding of both sides of the human spirit and mind. The human side and spiritual side of a person doesn't always agree at any given time. I had been dealing with the human side I got frustrated at times. I am going to show you how I have dealt with this human aspect and make up. There are many different avenues and channels that go through our life and life system (body) this can leave a lasting impression on how to deal with the next problem. We have stated the need to look at both sides of the coin if we're going to understand ourselves/me.

In Paul writes throughout the New Testament he uses the term old man and the new man, putting away foolish things.

Ephesians 4:20-24 (2)

V-20 "But ye have not so learned Christ;

V-21 If so be that ye have heard him, and have been taught by him, as the truth is in Jesus:

V-22 That ye put off concerning the former conversation the old man, which is corrupt according to the deceitful lusts;

V-23 And be renewed in the spirit of your mind;

V-24 And that ye put on the new man, which after God is created in righteousness and true holiness."

That is what this study about becoming a better person we will use over 60 passages of scriptures that a person can understand how to deal with the changes that will help a person.

Part I

Why do we act the way we do and make the choices/decisions we make?

Life is about making adjustments during the journey, trying to understand one's self, the meaning of *how,* and the *why's* of life in relation to the challenges in any given situation. Certainly the degree of **emotion** and **feelings** largely has to do with our actions and reactions taking place in any given situation. What else transpires during any given situation? The cause and effect of course is very important in the situation. The most over looked factor is their relationships, the people involved in the situations, and certainly the outcome of any situation is important too.

Our journey begins in "Part One". There are new discoveries about the **brain's architecture** relating a person's **emotions**.

Here are some explanations as to some of the most baffling moments in our life is when our **feelings overwhelm** us and our rationality has been set aside for a brief span of time.

Understanding the interplay of our **emotions** and how the **brain structures** work may give us some insights into how and why we act the way we do. In some cases the **brain** will give us clues into fear or passion, but for beyond that there may be grief or joy taking place in an **emotional situation**.

There is much to be learned from our **emotional makeup**, understanding how the **brain** works will guide in determining why things went wrong, even our best intentions don't always work, to the undermining of our best intentions. Things can subdue our **emotions** and **control** them at the time while revealing destructive tendencies, such as our **selfishness, self-will,** when our **emotional impulses** take over in a situation, such as anger, frustration, or joy and happiness.

What is ticking, or clicking in the Brain?

Our emotions **can cause us to rise or fall in a given situation.** I do not believe that the brain has grown over millions of years, the knowledge of the brain workings has grown over the years, especially the last fifty years. We're going study the brains functions with the insight of the knowledge of its working how to feed information into the working mind the psychology of what happens.

SUPPORT OUTREACH SERVICES
(Introduction)

Dr. John Clinton Barrett Jr, PH-D, **I am the Program Coordinator**, Support **O**utreach Services **SOS LLC.** Author, Publisher, & Creator of Self Help and Healing Network. Since 1997, I have been providing a referral service Community Outreach Sessions in West Plains, MO. We will profile particular situations free of cost to the person, our internet www.sosselfhelpbooks.info. Profiling my study guides which deals with specific problems, requests and questions. We will try to address the different needs, desires, and wants in a person's life by using these self-help profiles and information. Email us at drbarrettphd@yahoo.com

In conjunction, **SOS** publications has 4 Bible studies, (Book) "HOW DOES GOD ANSWER PRAYER? **SOS** offers Support = outreach "Prayer Partners", Services = Matching-Profiles, Conferences & Seminars, (Book), "WE ARE AMBASADORS FOR CHRIST". (Manual) "Mentoring & Coaching", (Book) "OPENING THE DOOR TO CHRISTIAN PSYCHOLOGY" (Manual) "The Road to Recovery" (Book) "APPLYING CHRISTIAN PRINCIPLES" (Manual) "Leadership Training" Our Services and Programs = our Healing Network Links. Support **O**utreach Services **SOS** Self Help and Healing Network.

Part II
What is ticking, or clicking in our Bible studies?
The Biblical view of sin and human behavior
The psychology of man From a Biblical point of view.

13

Dr. John C Barrett Jr. B/S, M/A, PH-D
My Testimony is like, "the woman at the well"!

My Testimony

"The road back was not an easy task. My heart had been broken a number of times. I was filled with hurt and anger toward those who had hurt me. Yes, I was disappointed in myself. Why did all of this happen to me, as a Christian? I became rebellious, angry, and disappointed those feelings took over my life. I did not take into consideration my responsibility in all of this. I thought it would all work itself out over time, it didn't. Was I ever wrong, I thought I was happy the farther away I got from God?

Until, I experienced the, *"Grace of God in a real way"*. I have had that peace since 1988, when dealing a near death situation brought me to my keens. I had been dealing with heart and health problems since 1982. That led me into prayer, and "the very presence of God", I was so excited.

The Holy Spirit led me at that time and laid a challenge on my heart to write about the things that was going to happen. I did not obey or take my destiny seriously at that the time. I went on with my life expecting a miracle, a sign, or earth-shaking event, but it didn't happen.

Not until 1997, when God spoke to me again and reaffirmed my destiny. This experience started the greatest change in my life, but only since 1997.

I committed to the calling since then God has given me with a vision as to what needed to be done. Since then God has blessed me with intercessory prayer and spiritual warfare for others. I have seen miracles, victories, and Satan defeated in many cases. Lives restored; families reunited I have seen joy and victory in my own life.

The proof comes as God is still in my life, the fact that I have gotten my Masters Degree in Counseling and a PH-D Doctorate Degree in Psychology. I don't like to read, but I became a good student. I'm definitely not considered a writer. The evidence is very crucial, because Support Outreach Services is still in progress.

Early on, in 1993, or 4, I got into a Sunday school class which gave me support and later became a singles group. My fellowship, Bible study, sharing my problems with others has helped me to see where I was, and how far I had to go to get back to where I was as a Christian. A church home, the prayers of Christian friends and family were there for me. My personal prayer life, and devotion to God helped me to make the changes needed in my life.

May I talk to you on a personal level? I became a Christian at the age of 13 and spent my life trying to know God. However, I didn't know how to *communicate* or *fellowship* with God as young Christian. "*How sad*". My life and testimony had gotten so mixed up because of divorce; it almost destroyed me in the process, this is the way Satan influences a person.

I attended several Group Sessions during this time Christian teaching helped restore the joy in my life and gave me a purpose for living. My salvation means so much more to me now than it ever did before. I hope my testimony will help others.

May I continue by using three illustrations out of the Bible? I am like the woman at the well I felt very insignificant as a divorcee. I had to deal with the stigma of divorce and the Bible helped me understand what Christ said to the women at the well I have been divorced. In **John 4:4-42**. Christ used this woman to bring a city to Him. I am very much like that woman at the well. I've been divorced, and remarried; that really left a stigma to deal with. This left me with low **self-esteem** and guilt. <u>If God can use me He can use anyone</u>.

I am like the prodigal son:

It is God's forgiveness that we need, as this story makes clear, our Father has not condemned us. It is our own forgiveness that is needed, we have to be aware and experience of His Love. We receive the gifts of forgiveness as we are willing to extend forgiveness to our brother.

The challenge of our healing journey is twofold—for we are like *both* the prodigal son, the self-righteous son in this parable.

Like the prodigal, I needed to recognize and find fulfillment, happiness, safety, and find peace. For all the misdirected ways I sought my own way for a while. I found my treasure only by remembering who I was, by coming back to God. This was my deepest longing, my true heart's desire. Even in the midst of my pain, I lost my way and found my way back to God. I remember how bad I felt, I can hear Him calling me by the longing of my heart, then I decided to come back to God. In that instant I made a decision, this is still an ongoing journey. We must learn that whenever happens we do not want to deny a brother his rightful place in God's Son, to do this we also deny things for ourselves.

Luke 15:11-32 (3)

V-11 "And he said, A certain man had two sons:

V-12 And the younger of them said to *his* father, Father, give me the portion of goods that falleth *to me*. And he divided unto them *his* living.

V-13 And not many days after the younger son gathered all together, and took his journey into a far country, and there wasted his substance with riotous living.

V-14 And when he had spent all, there arose a mighty famine in that land; and he began to be in want.

V-15 And he went and joined himself to a citizen of that country; and he sent him into his fields to feed swine.

V-16 And he would fain have filled his belly with the husks that the swine did eat: and no man gave unto him.

V-17 And when he came to himself, he said, How many hired servants of my father's have bread enough and to spare, and I perish with hunger!

V-18 I will arise and go to my father, and will say unto him, Father, I have sinned against heaven, and before thee,

V-19 And am no more worthy to be called thy son: make me as one of thy hired servants.

V-20 And he arose, and came to his father. But when he was yet a great way off, his father saw him, and had compassion, and ran, and fell on his neck, and kissed him.

V-21 And the son said unto him, Father, I have sinned against heaven, and in thy sight, and am no more worthy to be called thy son.

V-22 But the father said to his servants, Bring forth the best robe, and put *it* on him; and put a ring on his hand, and shoes on *his* feet:

V-23 And bring hither the fatted calf, and kill *it*; and let us eat, and be merry:

V-24 For this my son was dead, and is alive again; he was lost, and is found. And they began to be merry.

V-25 Now his elder son was in the field: and as he came and drew nigh to the house, he heard musick and dancing.

V-26 And he called one of the servants, and asked what these things meant.

V-27 And he said unto him, Thy brother is come; and thy father hath killed the fatted calf, because he hath received him safe and sound.

V-28 And he was angry, and would not go in: therefore came his father out, and intreated him.

V-29 And he answering said to *his* father, Lo, these many years do I serve thee, neither transgressed I at any time thy commandment: and yet thou never gavest me a kid, that I might make merry with my friends:

V-30 But as soon as this thy son was come, which hath devoured thy living with harlots, thou hast killed for him the fatted calf.

V-31 And he said unto him, Son, thou art ever with me, and all that I have is thine.

V-32 It was meet that we should make merry, and be glad: for this thy brother was dead, and is alive again; and was lost, and is found.

I feel like the women caught in adultery

John 1:7-11 (4)

V-7, "*and said unto them, He that is without sin among you, let him first cast a stone at her.*"

V-10, "*When Jesus had lifted up himself, and saw none but the*

woman, he said unto her, Woman, where are those thine accusers?
  hath no man condemned thee?
V-11 *"She said, No man, Lord. And Jesus said unto her, Neither do*
  I condemn thee: go, and sin no more."

It was hard to gain my feeling of self-respect! This is one of the hardest things I've ever done. It exposed my PRIDE & SELF-WILL. How did I change things? What is happens? It really starts in the heart, mind and the human spirit. It took a conscience effort to change my attitude toward myself and life. The first step is commitment and then I use these **3 D's Dedication, Determination, & Discipline**.

There are the inside and outside influences there can be an internal conflict from within.

First and for-most is God! Second is us! Third, are the many avenues within a person?

Who would have thought with four years of Bible College and twelve years of Christian service would have prepared me for anything, but it didn't! I am in the same position as anyone else. I had to find my own way back. The last 3 chapter in our (Family Biography) is about the journey, and a way back to God AGAIN.

Prayer is one of the key elements in my life was "To know God is my Testimony". Then reconciliation means a personal relationship with "God the Father, God the Son and God the Holy Spirit".

I found that reconciliation within was the key to success and happiness, I wasn't any worse or better than anyone else, in God's eyes. In fact it has given me a better understanding of life. I certainly have no room to criticize anyone else. It has given me a love and compassion for others. Please remember me in your prayers, as I pray for you!

May I use the second (illustration) and take my testimony a step farther, I was like this woman; in **John 8:7-11**. The woman was supposedly caught in sin, what did Christ say to her *"neither do I condemn you: Go and sin no more"*. "This truly happened to me". I do not have to carry the weight of my past problems around with me anymore, isn't that great! God truly forgives I'm free of GUILT.

I had to learn how to forgive myself <u>reconcile</u> and realize what God had done. I had to quit beating myself to death for what had happened. Believe it or not I had to make peace with myself and turn it over to God and believe God will answer my prayers that is bases for the change in my prayer life. That had to happen before I could forgive others. Now I am truly FREE. I am the happiest I've have ever been knowing God has freed me from my sin.

I do not have to be a minister to do God's work or will. Anyone can share in God's love and what He has done in their lives. Christ said, *"what ever you have done unto the least of these my brethren, you have done unto me"*; **Matt. 25:40. Matt. 25:45, 46** says (if we don't, we will not be apart of heaven or His Kingdom). This is truly one of God's answers in my life and sharing this with someone else.

Part III
The Pictorial View and Brake Down of the Brain.
The physical make-up of the body and brain.
The Life Line = Breaking down of Chart I

(Poem) In His Hands

'Twixt gleams of joy and clouds of doubt
Our feelings come and go;
Our best estate is tossed about
In ceaseless ebb and flow.
No mood of feeling, form of thought
Is constant for a day;
But thou, 0 Lord, thou changest not:
The same thou art alway.

I grasp thy strength, make it mine own,
My heart with peace is blest;
I lose my hold, and then comes down
Darkness, and cold unrest.
Let me no more my comfort draw
From my frail hold of thee,
In this alone rejoice with awe—-
Thy mighty grasp of me.

Out of that weak, unquiet drift
That comes but to depart,
To that pure heaven my spirit lift
Where thou unchanging art.
Lay hold of me with thy strong grasp,
Let thy almighty arm
In its embrace my weakness clasp,
And I shall fear no harm.

Thy purpose of eternal good
Let me but surely know;
On this I'll lean—let changing mood
And feeling come or go—
Glad when thy sunshine fills my soul,
Not lorn when clouds o'ercast,
Since thou within thy sure control
Of love dost hold me fast .
—John Campbell Shairp

Chapter 1
HUMANISTIC VIEW OF PSYCHOLOGY

May I admonish you to do the same by going to church or getting into a Christian organization? You may want to be a part of **Support Outreach Services** "One to one common ground". We can share each other's burden with others.

The last thing about my testimony I have a relationship with all three parables, the 99 sheep that were safe in the fold at one point I was that lost person. Two, I was like the women having 10 pieces of silver and lost one piece again. That is what our ministry is about finding and helping people who have lost their way.

Luke 15:1-10   (5)

V-1 "Then drew near unto him all the publicans and sinners for to hear him.

V-2 And the Pharisees and scribes murmured, saying, This man receiveth sinners, and eateth with them.

V-3 And he spake this parable unto them, saying,

V-4 What man of you, having an hundred sheep, if he lose one of them, doth not leave the ninety and nine in the wilderness, and go after that which is lost, until he find it?

V-5 And when he hath found *it*, he layeth *it* on his shoulders, rejoicing.

V-6 And when he cometh home, he calleth together *his* friends and neighbours, saying unto them, Rejoice with me; for I have found my sheep which was lost.

V-7 I say unto you, that likewise joy shall be in heaven over one sinner that repenteth, more than over ninety and nine just persons, which need no repentance.

V-8 Either what woman having ten pieces of silver, if she lose one piece, doth not light a candle, and sweep the house, and seek diligently till she find *it*?

V-9 And when she hath found *it*, she calleth *her* friends and *her* neighbours together, saying, Rejoice with me; for I have found the piece which I had lost.

V-10 Likewise, I say unto you, there is joy in the presence of the angels of God over one sinner that repenteth."

In **Gal. 6:1, 2** *"Helping each other is God's way of helping us heal and bear our Burdens"*. I feel that our greatest influence can be in helping others deal with the same situations that we have faced. We can share in that responsibility and the blessing of helping others, you can receive support on our web site www.selfhelpbooks.info and be a blessing by sharing and participating in **SOS** studies, surveys and evaluations.

I have profiled my testimony, and our services. I hope we can help you, I have gone through some of my experiences and how I dealt with the turmoil of divorce as a Christian. I have had several health crises and crippling arthritis. I have dealt with heart problems in the past, faced a heart tack and won the battle. Also, I given you some idea how I dealt with the human-will, human-spirit, **low-self-esteem** in our books and studies.

That is why **SOS** studies and programs were developed in the process of dealing with my life. I'm happy to say that good can come out of bad situations even triumph in the end.

Let me give a great illustration from Thomas Edison, he had so many successes, there were many failures, one was the invention of the light bulb.

Almost every famous person has had to face some unkind remarks by their critics. They believe in themselves and ignore their critics. Some people ridicule others to make themselves feel important at another person's expense, sometimes it makes them look bad because of what they have done to someone.

Think about Galileo and look at what happened to Jesus. *Quotation: "Progress is made* only *by those who are strong enough to endure being laughed at"* Solutions are often new ideas greeted with laughter, contempt, or both from the scoffer. That is just an unpleasant fact, so make up your mind not to let it bother you. Ridicule should be viewed as a badge for the innovative thinker.

Thomas Edison, in his search for the perfect filament for the incandescent lamp, tried anything he could think of, including whiskers from a friend's beard. In all, he tried about 1800 things. After about 1000 attempts, someone asked him if he was frustrated at his lack of success. He said something like, *"I've gained a lot of knowledge I now know a thousand things that won't work."*

Fear of failure is one of the major obstacles to creativity and problem solving. The cure is being able to change your attitude about failure. Failures along the way should be expected and accepted; they are simply learning tools that help you focus the way toward success. Not only is there nothing wrong with failing, but failing is a sign of action and struggle, an attempt is much better than inaction. The go-with-the-flow types may never have any problems they may feel they have never failed, they are essentially at a loss for new ideas, nor can they ever enjoy the feeling of accomplishment that comes after a long struggle.

Suppose you let your fear of failure hold you back and your risk taking, if it doesn't bother you, you have never fail. If you try three things in a year and you accomplish three things. At the end of the year the score is: 3 Successes, 0 Failures. Now suppose the next year you don't worry about failing, you try a hundred things, you fail at 70 of them. At the end of the year, the score is 30 successes, but most people are not able to deal with 70 failures. Which would you rather have three successes or 30 times as many? Just think of what 70 failures will have taught you if you can look at the positive aspects of your failures. A proverb: *"Mistakes aren't fun, but they sure are educational."*

Others may want to know more how the process was created and that might be the best way to help you. Example, when I needed help, at first I didn't want any help. My pride was there, I can say pride stood in the way, then pride did help at times because I never gave-up, my goal was to reach a balance. Pride is an advantage, or disadvantage in motivation, depending on how it affects you and how you deal with a situation. I thought I could handle anything, I guess you could call that pride in away; I made some mistakes along the way because of the trials and errs.

I found that writing about my problems, (Diary or Journal) helped me deal with the mental and physical. Writing about the actual experiences helped and being able to talk to others about what had happened helped me. I felt it was my fault or was it? I didn't know what to do or how I was going to escape the inevitable. Instead I kept it inside and didn't want expose my weakness, I felt safe, because nobody really knew what was going on inside. I really didn't want anybody to know how I felt. I was afraid of the consequences I really didn't want to know how bad off I was, I was hurting inside.

Much was accomplished in those early days of stumbling around I thought I was going to die.

I did one of the worst things anyone could do, I did nothing. Don't feel alarmed this is a normal reaction in most cases. In my case I was going to a doctor, but he wasn't much comfort. He said I was doing just fine I knew better.

This is a good example of a normal reaction to a situation. In the sequence of health problems I was getting weaker and weaker by the day, and weeks where passing; I got to the point I had no strength. I couldn't walk from the living room to the bathroom without getting dizzy. I thought I would live the rest of my life helpless and probably dye an early death. I felt, I was in real trouble at this time.

There was some good that came out of all of these catastrophes. Usually things start to look up when a person is at the bottom, a person either looks up or looks down. The problem is when the slide still is going down. In my case this was the beginning of the end of my down-hill-slide. It wasn't all down-hill as some would think, in their quest for success and happiness. Mine was a series of downs, after every up there was a down again. Kind of like taking "one step forward and two backward", as some people put it.

As you can see I have not gone into a lot of the details at this time it would take a long time to fill in the whole story, I do this in our book, "FACING THE REAL ME - Run John Run" our family biography I relate some of my feelings about our European and Indian heritage. I have three volumes of **Self Helps Books**. That makes it easier to understand not every situation will fit into very person's life.

Now I want to build on this study how Christian Psychology fits into what the Bible says about person's human nature, as it relates to psychology. We will start with the humanistic view of psychology.

Part I
Introduction:
Why do we act the way we do & make good choices/decisions?

The Bible itself proclaims it is the WORD FROM God.
2 Peter 1:19-21   (6)

V-19 "We have also a more sure word of prophecy; whereunto ye do well that ye take heed, as unto a light that shineth in a dark place, until the day dawn, and the day star arise in your hearts:
V-20 Knowing this first, that no prophecy of the scripture is of any private interpretation.
V-21 For the prophecy came not in old time by the will of man: but holy men of God spoke *as they were* moved by the Holy Ghost."

Defining the differences between man's view and God's view

Different authoress with the same beliefs, they used the irrigational manuscripts to write The New Testament, it was written in "Greek", The Holy Spirit guided the writers to write what He wanted them to write. Every word has a private interoperation because of the translation from the "Greek" to the many langue's of the world. Therefore, the best way to describe the Bible it did not originate with man, God used man to write and instilled the thoughts **John 16:1-16** calls the Holy Spirit the "Spirit of truth."

27

The Holy Spirit caused men to write the absolute truth. They were "carried along" by the "Spirit of truth." The Bible, therefore, is truth and can be trusted.

John 16:1-16   (7)

V-1 "These things have I spoken unto you, that ye should not be offended.

V-2 They shall put you out of the synagogues: yea, the time cometh, that whosoever killeth you will think that he doeth God service.

V-3 And these things will they do unto you, because they have not known the Father, nor me.

V-4 But these things have I told you, that when the time shall come, ye may remember that I told you of them. And these things I said not unto you at the beginning, because I was with you.

V-5 But now I go my way to him that sent me; and none of you asketh me, Whither goest thou?

V-6 But because I have said these things unto you, sorrow hath filled your heart.

V-7 Nevertheless I tell you the truth; It is expedient for you that I go away: for if I go not away, the Comforter will not come unto you; but if I depart, I will send him unto you.

V-8 And when he is come, he will reprove the world of sin, and of righteousness, and of judgment:

V-9 Of sin, because they believe not on me;

V-10 Of righteousness, because I go to my Father, and ye see me no more;

V-11 Of judgment, because the prince of this world is judged.

V- 12 I have yet many things to say unto you, but ye cannot bear them now.

V-13 Howbeit when he, the Spirit of truth, is come, he will guide you into all truth: for he shall not speak of himself; but whatsoever he shall hear, *that* shall he speak: and he will shew you things to come.

V- 14 He shall glorify me: for he shall receive of mine, and shall shew *it* unto you.

V-15 All things that the Father hath are mine: therefore said I, that he shall take of mine, and shall shew *it* unto you.

V- 16 A little while, and ye shall not see me: and again, a little while, and ye shall see me, because I go to the Father."

2 Timothy 3:16 we learn that the Bible is

V-16 *"given by inspiration of God"* or God-Breathed."

The Bible is truth and can be trusted it tells us how to be saved by our personal faith in Jesus Christ. All other supposed ways of salvation will lead in deception to one's self. The importance of God's word as a measurement of truth in one's self.

(Proverbs 14:12).

V-12 "There is a way which seemth right unto man, but the end tereof are the ways of death."

The Holy Scripture are able to make thee wise unto salvation through faith which is in Christ Jesus. The authority of the Bible it is reliable an absolute authority because it is truth.

2 Timothy 3:14-17   (8)

V-14 "But continue thou in the things which thou hast learned and hast been assured of, knowing of whom thou hast learned *them*;

V-15 And that from a child thou hast known the holy scriptures, which are able to make thee wise unto salvation through faith which is in Christ Jesus.

V-16 All scripture *is* given by inspiration of God, and *is* profitable for doctrine, for reproof, for correction, for instruction in righteousness:

V-17 That the man of God may be perfect, thoroughly furnished unto all good works."

Romans 8:28 "And <u>we know that all things work together for good to them that love God</u>, <u>to them who are called according to</u> <u>*his* purpose."</u>

The humanistic view point by:

C. S. Lewis modern Christian psychology. [1]

"Every time you make a choice you are turning the central part of you, the part of you that chooses, into something a little different from what it was before. Taking your life as a whole, with all of your innumerable choices, all your life long you are slowly turning this central thing either into a heavenly creature or into a hellish creature; either into a creature that is in harmony with God, and with other creatures, and with self, or else into one that is in a state of war and hatred with God, and with its fellow creatures, and with itself."

By C.S. Lewis

Carl Roger's Personal Centered Approach TO PSYCHOLGY

Pages 1 – 2   [2]

THE PERSON-CENTRED APPROACH

Excerpted from John Rowan's Bibliography

"This is the approach developed by Carl Rogers, and is sometimes for that reason called Rogerian counseling or therapy, although Rogers himself never approved of that title.

What it says is that if we approach another person in a certain way, we can enable them to grow and develop and work through any problems they may have. And the suggestion is really that any approach which is genuinely going to help people must involve working in that same way. Well, what is this way? It entails three qualities.

The first quality is empathy.

Many people believe that this is the single quality which is most important in all forms of therapeutic listening. It means getting inside the world of the person who comes for therapy (usually called the client, though some people not in this group prefer other words such as patient or consulter) so that that person feels accepted and understood.

Two things are important about this:

(1) that the empathy be accurate,

(2) that the empathy be made known to the client.

Both of these are learnable skills, they do make a huge difference to the relationship between client and counselor.

The second quality is genuineness.

If empathy is about listening to the client, genuineness is about listening to myself - really tuning in to myself and being aware of all that is going on inside myself. It means being open to my own experience, not shutting off any of it. Again it means letting this out in such a way that the client can get the benefit of it. Genuineness is harder than empathy because it implies a lot of self-knowledge, which can really only be obtained by going through one's own therapy in quite a full and deep way.

It is only a fully-functioning person (Rogers' word for the person who has completed at least the major part of their therapy) who can be totally genuine.

The third quality is non-possessive.

It means that the client can feel received in a human way, which is not threatening. In such an atmosphere trust can develop, the person can feel able to open up to their own experiences and their own feelings.

It may be noticed here that these three qualities are really what we would hope for from any human being. Anyone who would not be capable of exhibiting these qualities would not be much of a human being. So there is a lot in this approach about learning how to be a human being. It is one of the paradoxical and exciting things about the humanistic approach generally that it assumes that everyone is capable of being fully human.

In a therapeutic situation where these qualities are operating, Rogers found, clients go through a sequence of stages which more and more closely approach being fully functioning persons, able to take charge of their own lives and really be themselves.

Rogers later extended his work to basic encounter groups (small groups where the same principles operate), to organisational work on several different levels (for example, working with a class in school, with the school itself, with the whole school district), and to work with cross-cultural groups to improve international understanding. He saw his work as having political implications: for him personal power and political power were closely connected."

http://www.ahpweb.org/articales/rogers.html   3/11/05

Key Theorists in Psychology –CARL ROGERS, 1902-1987

Page 1 of 3   [3]

"Carl Rogers was an American psychologist, born in Oak Park, Ill. In 1930, Rogers served as director of the Society for the Prevention of Cruelty to Children in Rochester, New York. He lectured at the Univ. of Rochester (1935–40), Ohio State Univ. (1940–44), and the Univ. of Chicago (1945–57), where he helped to found a therapeutic counseling center. After teaching at Univ. of Wisconsin until 1963, he became a resident at the new Center for Studies of the Person in La Jolla. A prominent figure in the humanistic school of psychology, Rogers is best known for his client-centered therapy, which suggested that the client should have as much impact on the direction of the therapy as the psychologist. His works include Client-Centered Therapy (1951) and On Becoming a Person (1961)."

http://www.psy.pdx.edu/Psi/KeyTheuries/Rogers.html

1/11/2000

Association for Humanistic Psychology Pages 4-8   [4]

"Throughout history many individuals and groups have affirmed the inherent value and dignity of human beings. They have spoken out against ideologies, beliefs and practices which held people to be merely the means for accomplishing economic and political ends. They have reminded their contemporaries that the purpose of institutions is to serve and advance the freedom and power of their members. In Western civilization we honor the times and places, such as Classical Greece and Europe of the Renaissance, when such affirmations were expressed.

Humanistic Psychology is a contemporary manifestation of that ongoing commitment. Its message is a response to the denigration of the human spirit.

That has so often been implied in the image of a person drawn by behavioral and social sciences.

During the first half of the twentieth century, American psychology was dominated by two schools of thought: behaviorism and psychoanalysis. Neither fully acknowledged the possibility of studying values, intentions and meaning as elements in conscious existence. Although various European perspectives such as phenomenology had some limited influence, on the whole mainstream American psychology had been captured by the mechanistic beliefs of behaviorism by the biological reductionism and determinism of classical psychoanalysis.

Ivan Pavlov's work with the conditioned reflex (induced under rigid laboratory controls, empirically observable and quantifiable) had given birth to an academic psychology in the United States led by John Watson which came to be called "the science of behavior" (in Abraham Maslow's later terminology, "The First Force"). Its emphasis on objectivity was reinforced by the success of the powerful methodologies employed in the natural sciences and by the philosophical investigations of the British empiricists, logical positivists and the operationalists, all of whom sought to apply the methods and values of the physical sciences to questions of human behavior. Valuable knowledge (particularly in learning theory and the study of sensation and perception) was achieved in this quest. But if something was gained, something was also lost:

The "First Force" systematically excluded the subjective data of consciousness and much information bearing on the complexity of the human personality and its development.

The "Second Force" emerged out of Freudian psychoanalysis and the depth psychologies of Alfred Adler, Erik Erikson, Erich Fromm, Karen Horney, Carl Jung, Melanie Klein, Otto Rank, Harry Stack Sullivan and others.

These theorists focused on the dynamic unconscious - the depths of the human psyche whose contents, they asserted, must be integrated with those of the conscious mind in order to produce a healthy human personality. The founders of the depth psychologies believed (with several variations) that human behavior is principally determined by what occurs in the unconscious mind. So, where the behaviorists ignored consciousness because they felt that its essential privacy and subjectivity rendered it inaccessible to scientific study, the depth psychologists tended to regard it as the relatively superficial expression of unconscious drives.

Carl Rogers, 1962

By the late 1950's a "Third Force" was beginning to form. In 1957 and 1958, at the invitation of Abraham Maslow and Clark Moustakas, two meetings were held in Detroit among psychologists who were interested in founding a professional association dedicated to a more meaningful, more humanistic vision. They discussed several themes - such as self, self-actualization, health, creativity, intrinsic nature, being, becoming, individuality, and meaning - which they believed likely to become central concerns of such an approach to psychology.

In 1961, with the sponsorship of Brandeis University, this movement was formally launched as the American Association for Humanistic Psychology. The first issue of the Journal of Humanistic Psychology appeared in the Spring of 1961.

In 1964, at old Say brook, Connecticut, the first invitational conference was held, an historic gathering that did much to establish the character of the new movement. Attendees included psychologists, among whom were Gordon Allport, J.F.T. Bugental, Charlotte Buhler, Abraham Maslow, Rollo May.
Gardner Murphy, Henry Murray and Carl Rogers, as well as humanists from other disciplines, such as Jacques Barzun, Rene Dubos and Floyd Matson.

The conferees questioned why the two dominant versions of psychology did not deal with human beings as uniquely human nor with many of the real problems of human life. They agreed that if psychology were to become more than a narrow academic discipline limited by the biases of behaviorism, if it were to study human attributes such as values and self-consciousness that the depth psychologists had chosen to de-emphasize, their "Third Force" would have to offer a fuller concept and experience of what it means to be human.

By this time the term "human psychology" was in general use. It reflected many of the values expressed by the Hebrews, the Greeks, the Renaissance Europeans, others who have attempted to study those qualities that are unique to human life that make possible such essentially human phenomena as love, self-consciousness, self-determination, personal freedom, greed, lust for power, cruelty, morality, art, philosophy, religion

Abraham Maslow, Carl Rogers and Rollo May, who had participated in the conference at Old Say brook, remained the movement's most respected intellectual leaders for the decades that followed. Maslow developed a hierarchical theory of human motivation which asserted that when certain basic needs are provided for, higher motives toward self-actualization can emerge.

Rogers introduced person-centered therapy, which holds that intrinsic tendencies toward self-actualization can be expressed in a therapeutic relationship in which the therapist offers personal congruence, unconditional positive regard and accurate empathic understanding.

Thus, Maslow and Rogers embraced self-actualization both as an empirical principle and an ethical idea. Their vision of human nature as intrinsically good became a major theme of the "human potential" movement, but was criticized by some other humanistic psychologists as an inadequate model of the human e
xperience.

Humanistic psychology expanded its influence throughout the 1970s and the 1980s. It's impact can be understood in terms of three major areas:

1) It offered a new set of values for approaching an understanding of human nature and the human condition.

2) It offered an expanded horizon of methods of inquiry in the study of human
behavior.

3) It offered a broader range of more effective methods in the professional practice of
psychotherapy.

The Humanistic View of Human Behavior

Humanistic psychology is a value orientation that holds a hopeful, constructive view of human beings and of their substantial capacity to be self-determining. It is guided by a conviction that intentionality and ethical values are strong psychological forces, among the basic determinants of human behavior. This conviction leads to an effort to enhance such distinctly human qualities as choice, creativity, the interaction of the body, mind and spirit, the capacity to become more aware, free, responsible, life-affirming and trustworthy.

Sense there is much difficulty involved in inner growth, humanistic psychologists often stress the importance of courageously learning to take responsibility for oneself as one confronts personal transitions. The difficulty of encouraging personal growth is matched by the difficulty of developing appropriate institutional and organizational environments in which human beings can flourish. Clearly, societies both help and hinder human growth. Because nourishing environments can make an important contribution to the development of healthy personalities, human needs should be given priority when fashioning social policies. This becomes increasingly critical in a rapidly changing world threatened by such dangers as nuclear war, overpopulation and the breakdown of traditional social structures.

Many humanistic psychologists stress the importance of social change, the challenge of modifying old institutions and inventing new ones able to sustain both human development and organizational efficacy. Thus the humanistic emphasis on individual freedom should be matched by a recognition of our interdependence and our responsibilities to one another."

http://www.ahpweb.org/aboutahp/whatis.html   3/11/05

Aristotle's Challenge: Pages 1-2 [5]

There is a need to pay attention to the psychological science of the body, soul, and mind, and new ideas that influence the mechanics of **emotions** that transforms some life in the most delicate moments into happiness or under despair.

As Aristotle's premise, "To be angry with the right person, to the right degree, at the right time, for the right purpose, and in the right way". (Readers who are not drawn to neurological detail may want to proceed directly to this section).

The Modern Age Psychotherapy & Drugs

People have become users of mood drugs for the treatment of bipolar disorders / depression. All drugs cause serious side effects; and close monitoring is necessary. For instance Lithium can cause tremors, diarrhea, thirst, memory problems. Depakote can cause drowsiness, upset stomach, diarrhea, tremors, hair thinning, and liver and pancreatic irritation.

The main concern has been the cost of these second-generation drugs and another is weight gain and blood-sugar has become a problem and other experienced changes in their EKG's.

Antia anxiety Medications

Including antidepressants, beta blocking, and anxiolyyics. Beta blockers are cardiovascular drugs that block adrenaline (beta) receptors thus preventing many of the physical symptoms of anxiety. Integral (proranolol)

Side effects include fatigue, dizziness, and worsening of asthma. BuSpar (buspirone)

Psychostimulants for AD and ADHD

> Ritalin (methylphenidate)
>
> Concerta (sustained release methylphenidate)
>
> Dexedrine (dextroamphetamine)
>
> Adderall (four amphetamine salts)
>
> Cylert (pemoline)"

Enforced by the U. S. Drug Enforcement administration.

Most of these drugs are short time acting and can produce rebound quickly and ware off in a short time and the symptoms of ADHD come back. The drug has to be used on a daily basis and when needed."

Copied   11/03/05

Part II

What is ticking, or **clicking in the Brain?**

CLEAR MIND CENTER

Creating EEG Sensory Solution's

Re-training abnormal brainwaves   [6]

"Patterns often eliminates or improves symptoms of the following disorders:

ADD/ADHD

Addictions

- Anxiety/Depression /OCD
- a Autism / Asperses Syndrome
- Chronic Fatigue/ Fibromyalgia
- Head Injuries
- Memory Loss

- Migraines
- Post Traumatic Stress Disorder
- Sleep Disorders
- Stroke Completion

Announcing the Latest Technology in Brainwave Therapy for Mental Fitness

That is reason new ideas have had be incorporated to combat the drug use. Most people don't get enough exercise, however few understand the need to exercise their brain:

Just as lifting weights can produce bigger biceps, training your brain into normal patterns can give you improved emotional and physical stability. Imagine a brain work-out center that guides your brain into working more efficiently and improving the way you feel. Properly balanced rhythms result in optimal brainwave patterns. Our emotions are a reflection of the rhythms in our brains:

Excess beta can produce anxiety, too much frontal alpha could result in depression, or elevated theta could produce ADD. Training your brainwaves into efficient patterns allows your central nervous system to learn how to self-regulate, directing it away from debilitating, painful, destructive disorders, into effortless processing and optimal functioning.

WHEN PASSIONS OVERWHELMS REASON

It was a series of errors and reactions in response to fourteen-year-old Matilda Crabtree thinking she would play a practical joke on her father. She jumped out the closet and yelled "Boo" as her parents where coming home from some friends.

Hearing the noise Bobby Crabtree reached for his .357 caliber pistol and went to Matilda bedroom not knowing she had not stayed all night at friend's house, so he went to investigate. As she jumped from the closet he shot her in the neck. She died twelve hours later.

One emotional reaction is fear and the instinct to survive and protect one's self and family. Mr. Crabtree was motivated at that time by fear and to some degree probably over reacted to the situation. Automatic reactions are already set in the mind in this kind of situation. If someone comes into our home we are allowed by law to protect our self and family. But in this case his emotions was not a safe guide. But what if it had been burglar then his actions would have been justified.

The civilized world has given us laws and moral laws such as "the Code of Hammurabi and the Ten Commandments. Despite these social constraints, passion and far overwhelm reason time and time again.

In terms of biological design the basic neural circuitry of emotion, has worked for centuries. For better or worse aptitude and responses to human encounters are not only based rational judgments but also emotional judgments at the time.

Impulses to action

As the author was driving in Colorado, a snowstorm hit and blotted out his vision of the car a few lengths ahead. The feeling of fear took over and his foot was on the brake without him really thinking about it. His anxiety had built to fear. He pulled over to the side of the road until the snow let up to where h could see. Only to be stopped down the road by an ambulance crew helping a passenger in a car that rear-ended a slower plow.

42

He said he would have probably hit them if he had keep going. I was overwhelmed by the internal state that compelled me to stop and take heed to the danger ahead.

Sociobiologists point to the preeminence of the heart and mind over intelligence at such crucial moments when they conjecture about why evolution has given emotion such a central role in human psyche.

We should not ignore the power of emotion in human nature. As we know from experience when decision-making dictates our actions, feelings count every bit as much –if not more-then the thought process. We need to emphasis the value of rational thinking as well as IQ.

All emotions are in sense impulses to act, like the animal kingdom, emotions are at the root of impulses and actions. The repertoire of each emotion plays a roll by their distinctive biological signatures.

Research has found new ways to peer into the body and brain, discovering more physiological details of how emotion prepares the body and mind for different kinds of responses.

The central brain circuitry triggers interact with the emotional experience. The brain reacts also, to create reflex reactions. When the blood flows to certain parts of the body it makes the heart beat faster and also, creates energy to that part of the body causing the body and muscles to react. There is also another part of the body system that goes into action the, which is equally as important the Adrenal glands create additional energy to the body system and needs to be accounted for in the situation or problem.

Which brings about emotions like happiness and/or depression. An increase in activity in the brain center can bring about positive feelings and increase available energy, and quieting anxiety.

There is likely not going to be any physiological shift or recover caused by an emotional upset, but it does give the mind and body a chance to quitting down.

The body and mind needs general rest and well-being to handle the tasks ahead with enthusiasm, striving toward vitally and reaching goals.

The biological makeup of psychology has to with happiness, joy, fear, love, surprise, and sadness, hurt, anger, disgust, bitterness, and guilt, remorse.

The biological properties of mankind have advanced significantly in the past hundred years because of agricultural advancements and medical advances. Thus advancing the life expectancy of mankind specially in the United States and other developed nations.

Our two Minds

I have head this story many times of a women going through a painful divorce because their husband falls in love with a younger women. Months of bitter wrangling over the house, money, and custody of the children follow. It is a very emotional experience for the one who has loss of a husband.

Never-the-less this is good example one the act of emotional mind and the rational mind being put through an extreme test. In a real sense we have two minds, one that thinks and ones feelings. These are two fundamentally different ways of knowing interaction in the mental, Psychic phenomena. Along side is another system of knowing impulsive and sometimes the illogical makeup of the emotional mind set.

The emotional/rational is the distinction between the "heart and mind"; knowing something is right "in your heart", conviction rather than thinking with your rational mind. There is a reasoning process when it comes to rational-to-emotional control over the mind-set. The more intense the feelings the more dominant, the emotional mind set becomes, the more ineffectual the rational mankind gets. There are some that believe having emotion and intuition have a great influence the decisions we make sometimes they do over rule our rational thinking.

There is even more to our two minds, of emotion and rational, operate in harmony for the most part. Ordinarily there is balance between emotion and the rational mind. The emotional feelings feeding input into the situation while the rational mind is refining the input. Sense the brain circuitry interconnected to interactions of emotions there is going to be glands acting to sucret chemicals into the bodies energy and nerve system. In some cases causing emotional and chemical imbalances.

HOW THE BRAIN (WORKS)

I do not believe that the brain has grown over millions of years but rather the knowledge of the brain workings as grown over the years especially the last fifty years. So we're going study the brains functions with the insight of knowledge of it's working to feed information into working mind set.

The most primitive part of the brain, is shared with all species that have more than a minimal nervous system. The brainstem is found at the top of the spinal cord. The root brain regulates basic life functions like breathing and the metabolism of the body's other organs, as well as controlling stereotyped reactions and movements.

The primitive brain cannot be said to think or learn; rather a set of preprogrammed regulators that keep the body running and reacting in away that ensures survival. The brainstem is merged with the emotional centers.

The fact that the thinking brain grew from the emotional reveals much about the relationship of thought to feeling.

The olfactory lobe, the cells take in and analyze smell. Our emotional life is also influenced by smell every living entity, be it as it may nutritious, poisonous, sexual partner, predator, or pray. Each has a molecular signature that is carried in the wind. The olfactory lobe centers for emotion that evolve, eventually growing large enough to encircle the top of the brainstem. The olfactory center is composed of little thin layers of neurons gathered to analyze smell. One layer of cells take what has been smelled and sorts it into relevant categories: edible or toxic, sexual availability, enemy or meal. A second layer of cells send reflexive massages throughout the nervous system telling the body what to do.

How Does Counseling Work?

Creating a clear mind and the unique groundbreaking approach in counseling using the Bible in connection with counseling. The stimulation of the mind is a powerful technique for encouraging the brain to produce specific frequencies, through the well-documented entrainment process. This combines the mind and brain into the proper balanced state. Our unique system of counseling combines counseling with a Biblical view to achieve a rapid improvement in mental and physical statues, yielding powerful long-lasting results.

Taking the Shame Out Of Mental Illness

The brain is becoming more and more of an open book that can be read through the use of noninvasive imaging techniques. Recent developments in computer technology have opened the way to examine brain functions safely. Many abnormalities can be addressed and normalized with Biblical Counseling. For example, depressed clients may feel that they are to blame for their condition because of being weak-willed or lacking in personal fortitude. However, many depressed clients have an abnormal pattern of EEG showing in the anterior left hemi-sphere that has been with them since birth. Therefore, having depression is not a cause for shame or guilt. Depression often relates to brain dynamics. More importantly is training people to do something about those dynamics. Clients can be empowered to change brain metabolism and reduce or even eliminate medications. The brain can heal itself—or at least improve—without the aid of medication.

Counseling has been shown to be a Very Powerful Technique for improving the Brain Functions

Counseling works through a mechanism known as operant conditioning. When a part of the brain is operating at an abnormal frequency (too fast or too slow), the brain can learn to normalize the activity of that area. **The brain is a learning machine.** If you tell it what it needs to do it will react to what it has learned, give it a reward for doing it, it can learn to make less of the abnormal activity and more of the normal activity. As the brain gets better at making the normal activity, the threshold for getting a reward is raised. Eventually the brain gets so good at making the normal activity feel better and that it is no longer needs the feed-back, and is able to make the normal activity to respond when-ever it is required. The mechanism is thought to be through reorganization of functional pathways in the brain. This is a new and exciting wave of the 21st century—advances continue to be made the area of counseling.

My Brain, My Pain

If you are tired of only being offered drug treatment (which is often only mildly effective), the exciting news is that "Christian Counseling has the ability to retrain the brain. This now provides an important alternative to medication for safely modifying how the brain works. Chemical imbalances in the brain can lead to mood problems, anxiety and a host of ailments, and yet most doctors who are specialists treat complaints without considering the brain as the source of both the ailment and its cure.

In some individuals, anxiety may also be associated with a brain pattern of excessive fast beta brainwave activity. It is as if the brain is idling too fast and the individual finds it difficult to relax. Patients with this pattern usually have generalized anxiety; worry, ruminate excessively, and have difficulty turning off their minds and falling asleep. Alcoholics and children of alcoholics, as well as individuals with Obsessive Compulsive Disorder also show a similar high beta pattern. They may especially be attracted to alcohol, marijuana, tranquilizers or pain-killers because these drugs increase relaxed brainwave activity. They are essentially seeking to self-treat their own brain abnormality.

How I resolved troubling Issues, & Bad Habits

My life was **out of control** and I could function and I was constantly reaching for something to make me feel better-coffee, food, alcohol, and pills. After a while I would promise myself it was the last time, but instead I found myself quitting my self-destructive habits. My mood was changing the highs were **short-lived** and the **lows seemed** to last forever, leaving me feeling hopeless, depressed and anxious. I had a constant, unexplainable underlying tension, putting me on perpetual edge. During these group sessions I felt calm I was able to release deep unconscious feelings about myself that had been haunting me for years. As these sessions progressed, I found myself less reactive, the constant ruminations had finally stopped, I felt more grounded in myself. This new feelings allowed me to step away from destructive looping patterns that had at once dominated my life and gave me the ability to create a new, happier and healthy way of well-being.

When The Brain Works... The Body Responds!

Research and clinical studies show many cognitive situations that are unresponsive to medication or counseling therapy can be resolved within the sessions. Chronic, longstanding emotional and physical issues, including those even complicated by substance abuse, can show marked improvement after counseling.

The second part of this counseling relies on biblical answers as to why a person may react to certain situations how and why they think about themselves."

Notes from session by Dr. John C Barrett PH-D

Brain School 101   [7]
Notes: (9/8/2008)
Dr. Parker

"I am going to present the brain in context of biology in recommending behavior modification and the useful functioning of the brain. The brain is an atomic structure, function and therefore can be seen in hot and cold areas and presents a landscape of the brain. Inclusive of the systematic hot and cold kinsidic in nature and biological make up of the brain. Photons are like visible light structures.

There is a new way of being able to compute axial topographical views of the brain X-Rays, MRI's, and Hydrogen atomic Magnetic Cat Scans.

• View neuron MRI

• By being able to mirror neurons structures

• Therapists can arouse behavior change by mirroring the actions and change behaviors

• Ganglia Gyrus cells 9x the # of neurons to the 10th trillion.

The brain actions cause impulsive reactions which causes metabolic reactions which can lead to addictions.

It is not a single function when using the image techniques can be slices in the cell levels by the topographical view of the brain. This is done by using 3-D cameras with 3 different views of the brain. When the brain surface is smooth there little or no problems, the more pronounced the deeper the craters' become.

The left side of temporal lob may result in decreased recall of verbal and visual content, including speech perception. The right temporal lob may result in decreased recognition of tonal sequences and many musical abilities can also effect recognition of visual content (recall of faces).

The prefrontal cortex involves intellect, actions and thinking:

INTELLECT,
ATTENTION SPAN
PERSEVERANCE
PLANNING
JUDGMENT

ACTIONS,
IMPULSE CONTROL
ORGANIZATION
SELF-MONITORING AND SUPERVISION

THINKING
EXECETIVE THING
CRITICAL THINKING
FORWARD THINKING
PROBLEM SOLVING
LEARNING FROM EXPERIENCE AND
MISTAKES
ABILITY TO FEEL AND EXPRESS EMOTIONS
INFLUENCES THE LIMBIC SYSTEM
EMPATHY
INTERNAL SUPERVISION

The ADHD hyper active person can result in:

- Thinking, thinking within their action
- They are acting out what they are thinking
- Highly emotional relationships can be hard to deal with

The ADD person is:

- Social they are not adjusted
- Impulsive in actions and thinking
- Low attention span and do not finish projects

They can be hot like the ring of fire and increased temporal lobes activity. The healthy left temporal lobes help a person to use control emotion in a situation. The hot and cold functions at the same time are creating deregulation. In such functions of moodiness, anxiety, and fear. The hot and cold also gives insight into addictions. The singular gyrus is unpredictable based on the time of the activity and the adjustment of the temporal lobes.

The prefrontal cortex has some function in remembering the emotional level and memory. For the most part it is factual memory – relating to the hippocampus left temporal lobes.

The cortical hyper-fusion is related to the ring of fire hot temporal lobes and the singular gyrus bring about the impulsive observation in the actions and thinking process. The impulsive actions equates to the cingulate gyrus of worry and hypertension, and obsessive behaviors creating a hot singular cyrus.

The limbic activity is related to cognitive profile: apathy / attention with an objective attitudes may create sadness, whimpering, or crying. This can lead to minor or deep depression, and result in being able to regulate and being able to control the depression.

The cognitive depression may also relate to the thinking, feeling, and acting process. The basal ganglia also relates to worried about self and the right temporal lobe relates to self while the left is about others. Cognitive worry also can be associated with the thinking, feeling and acting, thinking without acting.

In conclusion

A person with ADD depression:

I feel good, but is out of touch with the real world.

A healthy cerebellum is good when it is hot. The cerebellum controls motor control and creates organization in the body and mind. Cold cerebellum limits and creates disorganization, poor judgment and can take heed to sadness or mood swings.

PTSD (Post Traumatic Stress Disorders)

• Increase in interior cingulate

• Increase in the basal ganglia

• Increase in the thalamus

• Increase in the right cortex

• Increase in the left temporal lobe

This will show up in the singular gyrus toward the center of the brain. Impulsive behavior is bipolar disorder and number of other things can also show up in the singular gyrus."

End of session I.

Life Bridge
DIAGNOSTICS

"There is increasingly more need for brain scans and one of these is image of the biological factors. The brain is the network that process input into mind, body, and spirit. The brain patterns are trace through neuron paths and by the use of neural transmitters.

This can be done by developing a comprehensive history of behavior patterns. Neuro scans are helpful in depicting the neuro paths in the brain.

The prefrontal cortex is critical in diagnosing bipolar disorders. Given the PFCs historical and theoretical relevance to adaptive social behavior, it is not surprising that this region was among the first to be examined in anti-social and violent populations. By using the structural brain imaging to show an 11% reduction in PFC grey matter in patients with anti-social personality disorders. The amygdala has been a major focus of attempts to understand the poor empathy and fear responses observed using functional magnetic resonance imaging (fMRI). The prefrontal–amygdala connections are disrupted, leading to deficits in contextual fear conditioning, regret, guilt, and affects the regulation of the singular gyrus.

How a person thinks, feels, and acts in relation to God. The big question is *who are you*? The cerebellum in at the base of the brain structure and is important when it comes to brain injures. The brain is very soft, but the skull is very so it can protect the brain.

How can a person stop what *they are doing* and change things. The hippocampus is an emotion and memory are very closely related. You know this from your experience going to a party, and meeting a bunch of new people.

Which faces are you going to remember? The woman who made you laugh, the man who made you feel embarrassed, and your new boss -- the ones who had an emotional impact.

EMDR is a therapeutic technique in which the patient moves his or her eyes back and forth, hither and thither, while concentrating on the problem. It is claimed that EMDR can help with phobias, generalized anxiety, paranoid schizophrenia, learning disabilities, eating disorders, substance abuse, and even pathological jealousy, but its main application has been in the treatment of posttraumatic stress disorder **(PTSD)**.

The Hyperbaric oxygen therapy exposes a person to increase pressure and allows a greater absorption of oxygen to reach the cells and within the brain. The oxygen enables the body's ability to heal. You can see good increasing the oxygen in heal and fitness will help the healing process."
www.lifebridgedianostics.com

Out-Of-Date Neural Alarms

One drawback of such neural alarms there is an urgent message, goes through the **amygdala** sends **out-of-date** or **not so relevant messages**. The emotional memory the amygdala scans the experience, comparing it to what has happened in the past to now. The response may be mild, but close enough to cause the brain to send an alarm. The trouble maybe charged with **emotional memories** that triggers a crisis.

During this early period of life, other brain structures, particularly the **hippocampus, which is circuital for narrative for memories,** and **the neocortex is the seat of rational thought**.

The memory, the amygdala and hippocampus work hand and hand; each stores retrieve information independently. The early childhood can be triggered by wordless blueprints before an infants has words to express them, these emotional memories are triggered. It can be an emotional response to a past situation or event.

Harmonizing Emotions And Thoughts

The connections between **the amygdala (**and **related limbic structures)** the **neocortex** is the hub of battles or cooperative treaties struck between head and heart, thought and feeling. This circuitry explains why emotions are so crucial to affective thoughts, making wise decisions simply allowing a person to think clearly.

Chapter 2

THE BRAIN IS CHARACTERIZED BY ITS RESPONSES

Part III

The Pictorial View and Brake Down of the Brain.   [8]

"A **response** can be different then a **reaction,** however, both being triggered by a person's **response**. A **response** may not be a reaction, but a **reaction** always takes place when a person takes action. The **response** is also the result of an **evaluation**, or **command** given by another person or by the person's inner-being, the **brain** takes on some form of action, but a person has brought it about by some kind of **feelings**.

Chart I   Anatomy of the brain

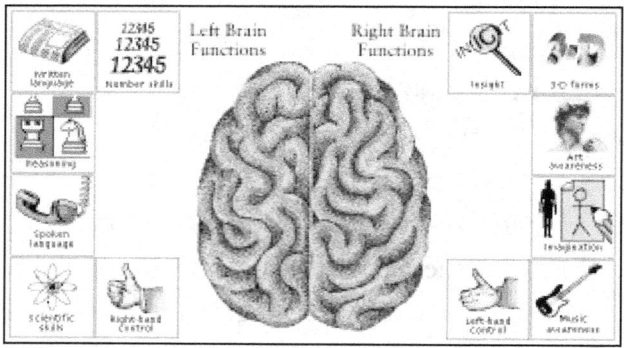

BRAIN HEMISPHERE FUNCTION

"The technical terminology and viewing the brain image is the outside of the brain, showing the major lobes (frontal, parietal, temporal and occipital) the brain stem structures (pons, medulla oblongata, and cerebellum).

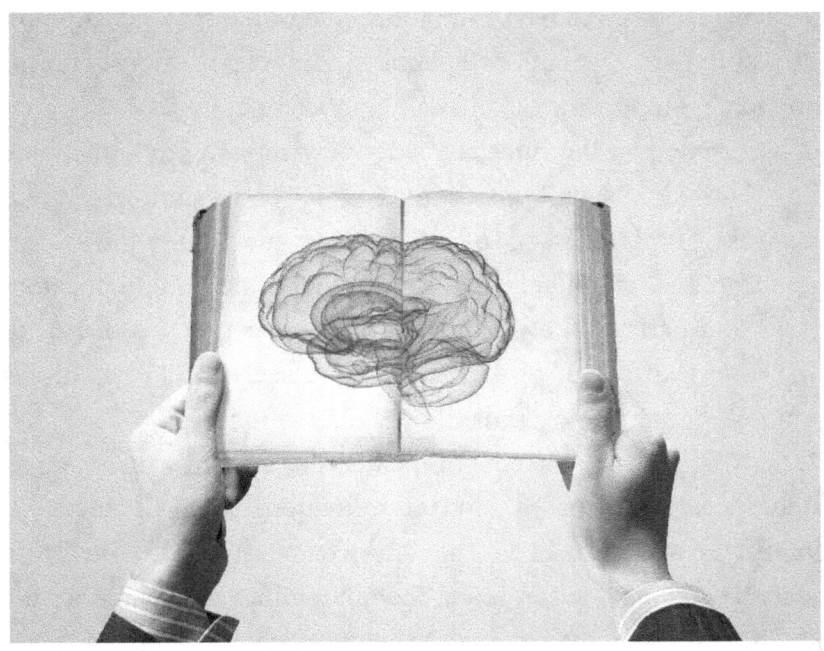

The second is viewed from the inside of the brain terminology the "Limbic System" (thalamus, cingulate gyrus, fornix, amygdale, hippocampus, and parahippocampal gyrus).

The image on the right is a side-view showing the location of the "Limbic System" inside the brain. The "Limbic System" consists of a number of structures, including the fornix, hippocampus, cingulated gyros, amygdale, the parahippocampal gyrus and parts of the thalamus. The hippocampus is one of the first areas affected by Alzheimer's disease. As the disease progresses, damage extends throughout the lobes.

The brain is also the core of the nervous system where thought, memories, sensation, motor coordination, and all metabolic control is accomplished. The brain can be divided into three general sections: the forebrain, the hindbrain, and the midbrain.

The forebrain, which contains the prefrontal cerebral cortex, is the region where most of the higher processes such as memory, logical thought, consciousness, and reasoning are carried out. The cerebral cortex and cerebrum are divided into right and left hemispheres. These hemispheres, which are separated by a band of transverse nerve fibers called the corpus callosum, have their own level of specialization. The forebrain also contains important switching centers and metabolic regulatory centers like the hypothalamus and pituitary gland.

The memory bank is another aspect that a person doesn't want to over look. It is just as important to the function of the brain. What a person thinks of when the word memory enter their mind.

I can remember, when having an argument, all of the past arguments and old flair ups were brought up, as the years passed, the longer the disagreement lasted because all the past faults had to be brought up again whether it related or not.

Nothing ever got settled because the first problem was always apart of the present argument, a classic (illustration) of the memory bank. I understand it's hard to forget, in some cases they say, "I'll never forget" because the memory brings back horrible memories in a present situation, but a person should remember the good memories are stored there too.

This is a crucial part of our human-make-up, the memory. People have a tendency to remember the bad, or blot out things they don't want to remember from the past, that is (selective memory). One of the worst parts of the memory is that it remembers the bad and seams to forget the good. The hurt, anger, bitterness, and pain leave a lasting memory with very strong emotions and feelings. Therefore, a person has a tendency to dwell on the past mistakes and problems, this is really bad; in either case it can cause serious problems in dealing with the now/present in a person's life.

The **hind brain**, which is separated from the **forebrain** by the **midbrain**, is located at the junction of the spinal cord and cerebrum. This region contains the more primitive structures of the brain from an evolutionary standpoint, but they function to regulate some of the most vital processes in the body. Breathing, heart rate, and muscle coordination are controlled here and sensory impulses are filtered and routed at this point.

Terms for an Anatomy of the brain
- Amygdala – limbic structure involved in many brain functions, including emotion, learning and memory. It is part of a system that processes "reflexive" emotions like fear and anxiety.

Cerebellum – governs movement.

• Cingulate gyrus – plays a role in processing conscious emotional experience.

• Frontal lobe – helps control skilled muscle movements, mood, planning for the future, setting goals and judging priorities.

• Hippocampus – plays a significant role in the formation of long-term memories.

• Medulla oblongata – contains centers for the control of vital processes such as heart rate, respiration, blood pressure, and swallowing.

• Limbic system – a group of interconnected structures that mediate emotions, learning and memory.

• Occipital lobe – helps process visual information.

• Parahippocampal gyrus – an important connecting pathway of the limbic system.

• Parietal lobe – receives and processes information about temperature, taste, touch, and movement coming from the rest of the body. Reading and arithmetic are also processed in this region.

• Pons – contains centers for the control of vital processes, including respiration and cardiovascular functions. It also is involved in the coordination of eye movements and balance.

• Temporal lobe – processes hearing, memory and language functions.

• Thalamus – a major relay station between the senses and the cortex (the outer layer of the brain consisting of the parietal, occipital, frontal and temporal lobes)."

http://www.ahaf.org/alzdis/about/AnatomyBrain.html   1/23/07

Chart I Brain Basics: Know Your Brain: National Institute of Neurological and Struck Pages 1-3   [9]

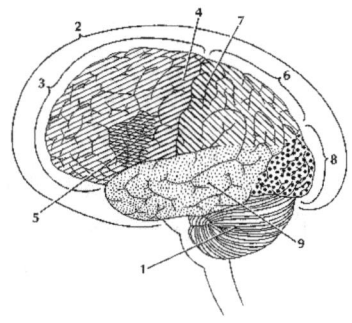

"The brain is the most complex part of the human body. This three-pound organ is the seat of intelligence, interpreter of the senses, initiator of body movement can control behaviors. Lying in its bony shell and washed by protective fluid, the brain is the source of all the qualities that define our humanity. The brain is the crown jewel of the human body.

For centuries, scientists and philosophers have been fascinated by the brain, but until recently they viewed the brain as nearly incomprehensible. Now, however, the brain is beginning to relinquish its secrets. Scientists have learned more about the brain in the last 10 years than in all previous centuries because of the accelerating pace of research in neurological and behavioral science, the development of new research techniques. As a result, Congress named the 1990s the Decade of the Brain. At the forefront of research on the brain and other elements of the nervous system are the National Institute of Neurological Disorders and Stroke (NINDS), which conducts and supports scientific studies in the United States and around the world.

This fact sheet is a basic introduction to the human brain. It may help you understand how the healthy brain works, how to keep it healthy, and what happens when the brain is diseased.

The Forebrain --- The Midbrain --- The Hindbrain
The Architecture of the Brain

The brain is like a committee of experts. All the parts of the brain work together, but each part has its own special properties. The brain can be divided into three basic units: the **forebrain**, the **midbrain**, and the **hindbrain**.

The hindbrain includes the upper part of the spinal cord, the brain stem, and a wrinkled ball of tissue called the **cerebellum (1)**. The hindbrain controls the body's vital functions such as respiration and heart rate. The cerebellum coordinates movement and is involved in learned rote movements. When you play the piano or hit a tennis ball you are activating the cerebellum. The uppermost part of the brainstem is the midbrain, which controls some reflex actions and is part of the circuit involved in the control of eye movements and other voluntary movements. The forebrain is the largest and most highly developed part of the human brain: it consists primarily of the **cerebrum (2)** the structures hidden beneath it (*see* "The Inner Brain").

When people see pictures of the brain it is usually the cerebrum that they notice. The cerebrum sits at the topmost part of the brain and is the source of intellectual activities. It holds your memories, allows you to plan, enables you to imagine and think. It allows you to recognize friends, read books, and play games.

The cerebrum is split into two halves (hemispheres) by a deep fissure. Despite the split, the two cerebral hemispheres communicate with each other through a thick tract of nerve fibers that lies at the base of this fissure. Although the two hemispheres seem to be mirror images of each other, they are different. For instance, it seems to lie primarily in the left hemisphere, while the right hemisphere seems to control of the abstract reasoning skills.

For some as-yet-unknown reason, nearly all of the signals from the brain to the body and vice-versa cross over on their way to and from the brain. This means that the right cerebral hemisphere primarily controls the left side of the body, the left hemisphere primarily controls the right side. When one side of the brain is damaged, the opposite side of the body is affected. For example, a stroke in the right hemisphere of the brain can leave the left arm and leg paralyzed.

The Geography of Thought

Each cerebral hemisphere can be divided into sections, or lobes, each of which specializes in different functions. To understand each lobe and its specialty we will take a tour of the cerebral hemispheres, starting with the two **frontal lobes (3)**, which lie directly behind the forehead. When you plan a schedule, imagine the future, or use reasoned arguments, these two lobes do much of the work. One of the ways the frontal lobes seem to do these things is by acting as short-term storage sites, allowing one idea to be kept in mind while other ideas are considered. In the rearmost portion of each frontal lobe is a **motor area (4)**, which helps control voluntary movement. A nearby place on the left frontal lobe called **Boca's area (5)** allows thoughts to be transformed into words.

When you enjoy a good meal—the taste, aroma, and texture of the food—two sections behind the frontal lobes called the **parietal lobes (6)** are at work. The forward parts of these lobes, just behind the motor areas, are the primary **sensory areas (7)**. These areas receive information about temperature, taste, touch, and movement from the rest of the body. Reading and arithmetic are also functions in the repertoire of each parietal lobe.

As you look at the words and pictures on this page, two areas at the back of the brain are at work. These lobes called the **occipital lobes (8)**, process images from the eyes and link that information with images stored in memory. Damage to the occipital lobes can cause blindness.

The last lobes on our tour of the cerebral hemispheres are the **temporal lobes (9)**, which lie in front of the visual areas and nest under the parietal and frontal lobes. Whether you appreciate symphonies or rock music, your brain responds through the activity of these lobes. At the top of each temporal lobe is an area responsible for receiving information from the ears. The underside of each temporal lobe plays a crucial role in forming and retrieving memories, including those associated with music. Other parts of this lobe seem to integrate memories and sensations of taste, sound, sight, and touch.

The Cerebral Cortex

Coating the surface of the cerebrum and the cerebellum is a vital layer of tissues. It is called the cortex, most of the actual information processing in the brain takes place in the cerebral cortex. When people talk about "gray matter" in the brain they are talking about this thin rind. The folds in the brain add to its surface area therefore increase the amount of gray matter and the quantity of information that can be processed.

The Inner Brain

Deep within the brain, hidden from view, lay structures that are the gatekeepers between the spinal cord and the cerebral hemispheres. These structures not only determine our emotional state, they also modify our perceptions and responses depending on that state, allows us to initiate movements that you make without thinking about them. Like the lobes in the cerebral hemispheres, the structures described below come in pairs: each is duplicated in the opposite half of the brain.

The **hypothalamus (10)**, about the size of a pearl, directs a multitude of important functions. It wakes you up in the morning, and gets the adrenaline flowing during a test or job interview. The hypothalamus is also an important emotional center, controlling the molecules that make you feel exhilarated, angry, or unhappy. Near the hypothalamus lies the **thalamus (11)**, a major clearinghouse for information going to and from the spinal cord and the cerebrum.

An arching tract of nerve cells leads from the hypothalamus and the thalamus to the **hippocampus (12)**. This tiny nub acts as a memory indexer—sending memories out to the appropriate part of the cerebral hemisphere for long-term storage and retrieving them when necessary. The **basal ganglia** (not shown) are clusters of nerve cells surrounding the thalamus. They are responsible for initiating and integrating movements. Parkinson's disease, which results in tremors, rigidity, and a stiff, shuffling walk, is a disease of nerve cells that lead into the basal ganglia.

Making Connections
(No image for **13 – 16**)

The brain and the rest of the nervous system are composed of many different types of cells, but the primary functional unit is a cell called the neuron. All sensations, movements, thoughts, memories, and feelings are the result of signals that pass through neurons. Neurons consist of three parts. The **cell body (13)** contains the nucleus, where most of the molecules that the neuron needs to survive and function are manufactured. **Dendrites (14)** extend out from the cell body like the branches of a tree and receive messages from other nerve cells. Signals then pass from the dendrites through the cell body and may travel away from the cell body down an **axon (15)** to another neuron, a muscle cell, or cells in some other organ. The neuron is usually surrounded by many support cells. Some types of cells wrap around the axon to form an insulating **sheath (16)**. This sheath can include a fatty molecule called myelin, which provides insulation for the axon and helps nerve signals travel faster and farther. Axons may be very short, such as those that carry signals from one cell in the cortex to another cell less than a hair's width away. Or axons may

Scientists have learned a great deal about neurons by studying the synapse—the place where a signal passes from the neuron to another cell. When the signal reaches the end of the axon it stimulates tiny **sacs (17)**. These sacs release chemicals known as **neurotransmitters (18)** into the **synapse (19)**. The neurotransmitters cross the synapse and attach to **receptors (20)** on the neighboring cell. These receptors can change the properties of the receiving cell. If the receiving cell is also a neuron, the signal can continue the transmission to the next cell.

Some Key Neurotransmitters at Work

Acetylcholine is called an *excitatory neurotransmitter* because it generally makes cells more excitable. It governs muscle contractions and causes glands to secrete hormones. Alzheimer's disease, which initially affects memory formation, is associated with a shortage of acetylcholine.

GABA (gamma-amino butyric acid) is called an inhibitory neurotransmitter because it tends to make cells less excitable.

It helps control muscle activity and is an important part of the visual system. Drugs that increase GABA levels in the brain are used to treat epileptic seizures and tremors with Huntington's disease.

Serotonin is an inhibitory neurotransmitter that constricts blood vessels and brings on sleep. It is also involved in temperature regulation. Dopamine is an inhibitory neurotransmitter involved in mood and the control of complex movements. The loss of dopamine activity in some portions of the brain leads to the muscular rigidity of Parkinson's disease. Many medications used to treat behavioral disorders work by modifying the action of dopamine in the brain.

Neurological Disorders

When the brain is healthy it functions quickly and automatically. But when problems occur, the results can be devastating. One in five—suffer from damage to the nervous system. The NINDS supports research on more than 600 neurological diseases. Some of the major types of disorders include: neurogenetic diseases (such as Huntington's disease and muscular dystrophy), developmental disorders (such as cerebral palsy), degenerative diseases of adult life (such as Parkinson's disease and Alzheimer's disease), metabolic diseases (such as Gaucher's disease), cerebrovascular diseases (such as stroke and vascular dementia), trauma (such as spinal cord and head injury), convulsive disorders (such as epilepsy), infectious diseases (such as AIDS dementia), and brain tumors.

The National Institute of Neurological Disorders / Stroke

Since its creation by Congress in 1950, the NINDS has grown to become the leading supporter of neurological research in the

United States. Most research funded by the NINDS is conducted by scientists in public and private institutions such as universities, medical schools, and hospitals. Government scientists also conduct a wide array of neurological research in the more than 20 laboratories and branches of the NINDS itself. This research ranges from studies on the structure and function of single brain cells to tests of new diagnostic tools and treatments for those with neurological disorders."

For information on other neurological disorders or research programs funded by the National Institute of Neurological Disorders and Stroke, contact the Institute's Brain Resources and Information Network-(BRAIN)-at:

www.ninds.nih.govTop

Prepared by:
Office of Communications and Public Liaison
National Institute of Neurological Disorders and Stroke
National Institutes of Health
Bethesda, MD 20892
NINDS health-related material is provided for information purposes only and does not necessarily represent endorsement by or an official position of the National Institute of Neurological Disorders and Stroke or any other Federal agency. The treatment or care of an individual patient should be obtained through consultation.
All NINDS-prepared information is in the public domain and may be freely copied. Credit to the NINDS or the NIH is appreciated.
NIH Publication No.01-3440a
Last updated December 08, 2005
http://www.ninds.nih.gov/disorders/brain_basics/know_your_brain
.html   1/23/07

The Central & Peripheral Nervous System

Brain-Anatomy

By: Nick V.

Neurons

"Your brain is full of billions of microscopic cells. Many of these cells are special messengers called neurons. Neuron means "nerve cell." We have about 100 billion neurons in our body. To picture the size of a neuron, think about the fact that 30,000 neurons can fit on the head of a pin! Neurons carry special signals back and forth throughout your body. Billions of neurons are chained together in a network of nerves. Nerves are a large amounts of neurons linked together in a small place. Your nerves send tiny electronic signals through your body to the brain stem and   to   the   main   brain.

The neurons inside your brain have three basic parts. Every tiny neuron consists of a cell body, an **axon**, and a **dendrite**. Neurons "talk" to each other by sending chemicals to each other across a very tiny space called a **synapse**. Learning happens when two neurons "talk" to each other. As the brain makes connections, it actually grows dendrites and makes stronger synapses. That means that the more you learn, the **heavier** your brain gets! So that means you really can "grow" a better brain. Your brain is full of billions of microscopic cells. Many of these cells are special messengers called neurons. Neuron means "nerve cell." We have about 100 billion neurons in our body. To picture the size of a neuron, think about the fact that 30,000 neurons can fit on the head of a pin! Neurons carry special signals back and forth throughout the body. Billions of neurons are chained together in a network of nerves.

The neurons inside your brain have three basic parts. Every tiny neuron consists of a cell body, an **axon**, and a **dendrite**.

The Neurons "talk" to each other by sending chemicals to each other across a very tiny space called a **synapse**. Learning happens when two neurons "talk' to each other. As the brain makes connections, it actually grows dendrites and makes stronger synapses. That means that the more you learn, the **heavier** your brain gets! So that means you really can "grow" a better brain.

Do people loose brain cells as they get older? Yes, you lose brain cells every day because of decay and disuse. Scientists aren't sure how many you lose each day but you don't need to worry. You have enough to last for your whole lifetime.

Some people think that your brain can never grow new neurons. That isn't true. Scientists have found that one area of the brain called the hippocampus can grow new neurons. There is research to see if there are other areas of the brain that regrow neurons.

Glial Cells

You've probably never heard of a glial cell. That's because when people talk about brain cells, they usually only think of neurons. But did you know that without glial cells you're the neurons wouldn't work? So without gill cells we wouldn't have working neurons, without neurons there would be no point of gill cells. About 90 percent of your brain cells are gill cells (the other 10 percent are neurons) which mean that we have about 1,000 billion of them. Did you know that gill means "glue?" These cells are called gill or "glue" because they act like little ropes for neurons to hold on to when the brain is being formed. Otherwise, scientists think they act like housekeepers for neurons. Gill cells attach themselves to neurons and feed them. Unlike neurons, they are able to reproduce, so your brain can make as many as it needs.

Do you know what famous scientist had a whole lot of gill cells in his brain? The answer is Albert Einstein. The scientists who studied his brain found a huge number of gill cells in a specific area of his brain, " (…)

http://library.thinkquest.org/J002391/functions.html   1/23/2007

Definition: HOMEOSTASIS?   {1}

"Descartes' account of behavior focused on the external environment, the stimuli that impinge on our senses and the reactions that are triggered in our muscles."

Defining Emotions and Feelings

"Some emotional reactions and emotional memories can be formed without any conscious decision, cognitive predication at all. The amygdala houses memories and response repertoires that enacts without realizing why we did something the shortcut from the thalamus to the amygdala completely bypasses the neocortex.

Other research has shown that in the first few milliseconds of our perceiving something we not only unconsciously comprehend what it is, can decide whether we like it or not; the "**cognitive conscious**", presents awareness with just the identity of what we see, an opinion about it. Our **emotions** have a **mind** of their own, which can hold views quite independently of our rational mind.

The specialist in emotional memory
Referenced from the anatomy of the hippocampus:

Those **unconscious opinions are based on emotional memories**; their storehouse is the **amygdala**. The **hippocampus, which has been considered the key structure of the limbic system**, is more involved in registering and making sense of

perceptual patterns than with emotional reactions. The hippocampmus - main input is in proving what is going on in the memory of the **context**, vital for emotional meaning; it is the hippocampus that recognizes the differing significance.

While the hippocampus remembers the dry facts, the amygdala retains the emotional flavor that goes with those facts. If we try to pass a car on a two-lane road and narrowly miss a head on crash the **hippocampus retains the specifics**, like what stretch of road it was, who was with us, what the other car looked like. But the **amygdala will send a surge of anxiety** through a person whenever they try to pass a car in the feature.

The hippocampus is circuital to recognizing a face, amygdala adds that you really don't like about a person.

Under stress (or anxiety, or presumably the intense excitement of joy), a nerve running from the brain to the **adrenal glands atop the kidneys triggers a secretion** of the **hormones epinephrine and norpinephrine,** which surge through the body priming it for an emergency. These hormones activate receptors as they regulate the heart; it also carries signals back into the brain, triggered by **epinephrine** and **norepinephrine**.

Out-Of-Date Neural Alarms

One drawback to such neural alarms is the urgent message, the **amygdala sends what is called an out-of-date** or **not so relevant** message like what's wrong with the world we live-in. The emotional memory the amygdala scans the experience, comparing what has happened in the past to the now. The response may be mild, but close enough to alarm, the amygdala.

A few spare elements of the situation may bring back old memories similar to some dangerous situation in the past. The trouble it may be charged with **emotional memories** that triggers a pasted crisis response and can be equally out dated. The emotional brain and memories can go back to their childhood.

During this early period of life other brain structures, particularly the **hippocampus, which is circuital for narrative memories, and the neocortex, is the seat of a rational thought**.

At this point we going to use an illustration of **amygdala** in action when I heard a noise around three in the morning. I thought the ceiling had fallen, when I heard a big crash in the corner of our bedroom. I got out of bed realizing I was safe, I cautiously peered back in the bedroom to see what had caused the crash only to find some books had fallen in the bedroom.

The direct route has vast advantages in the brains, which is reckoned with in thousandths of a second. The amygdala's response to a perception in as little as twelve milliseconds-twelve thousandths of a second. The route from the thalamus to the neocortex to the amygdala takes about twice as long.

Some emotional mistakes are based on feelings prior to the thought process which are called "**precognitive emotions**", a reaction based on neural bits and pieces of sensory information that have not been fully sorted out and intergraded into a recognizable object. It's a very rare form of sensory information, something like a neural, "*name that tone*", where instead of a snap judgment of the melody instead being based on just a few notes, a perception is grasped on such little information. If in the case of the amygdala senses a sensory pattern of importance emerging, it jumps to a conclusion, triggering its reactions before there is any full conformation-or any confirmation is reached.

Small wonder we have little insight into our more explosive emotions, especially when they still have a grip on a person's memory. The amygdala can and does act and react delirium of rag before the cortex knows what is going on because such raw emotion is triggered independent of, and prior to the thought process.

The emotional manager

The **prefrontal lobes react** while the amygdala is at work in priming an anxious moment, impulsive reactions are another part of the emotional brain, which allows for more fitting corrective response. The **brains damper switch** for the amygdala and amygdala's surges appears to lie at **the other end of a major circuit to the neocortex, in the prefrontal lobes** just behind the forehead.

The **prefrontal cortex** seems to be at work when someone is fearful or enraged, but is stifled, when a person is trying to control their feelings, they are ordered to deal with something, the more effective they are as they deal with the situation or when reappraisal calls for a completely different response, like a mother worried about her baby or something said over the phone.

The **neocortex area of the brain brings a more analytical** or **appropriate response** to our emotional impulses, modulating the **amygdala** and other **limbic areas**.

Ordinarily the **prefrontal area** governs our emotional reactions from the start. **The largest sensory information comes from the thalamus**, remember, it does not go through the amygdala, but straight to the neocortex.

The **prefrontal lobes**, then orchestrates a reaction. If in the process an emotional response is called for, the **prefrontal lobes** dictate a response, working hand-in-hand with the **amygdala** and other circuits in these **emotional response to the brain**.

The neocotex is slower because of the circuitry it is also more judicious and considered, sense more thought precedes actions.

Emotional hijacking presumably involves two dynamics, **triggering the amygdala** and failure to activate the **neocortex** process that usually keeps **emotional response** in balance. At these moments the **rational mind** could be swamped by the **emotion**. One way the **prefrontal cortex** acts as an efficient manager of **emotion-weighing of the reactions** before acting it is by dampening the signals for activation sent out by the **amygdala** and other **limbic centers**. It is like a parent grabbing and asking a child properly (or wait) for what they want.

The "off switch", for depressing emotion seems to be the **left prefrontal lobe**. One of the tasks of the **left frontal lob** is to act as a neural thermostat, regulating unpleasant emotions. The **right prefrontal lobes** are a thermostat of negative feelings, while the **left lobes** keep those raw emotions in check, probably by inhibiting the **right lobe**.

Harmonizing Emotions and Thoughts

The connections between **the amygdala (and related limbic structures)** the **neocortex** are the hub of battles or cooperative treaties struck between the mind and heart, and feeling. This circuitry explains why emotion is so crucial to affective thinking, making wise decisions allowing a person to think clearly.

The emotions of a person has power to disrupt the thinking process. Neuroscientists use the term **"working memory"**, for the capacity of attention that holds the facts essential for completing a given task when one seeks a house while looking for another or eliminates of reasoning while taking a test.

The prefrontal cortex is the brain region responsible for the **working memory**. The circuits from the **limbic process of the brain** to the **prefrontal lobes** that signals a **strong emotion**, anxiety, anger, can create neural sabotaging. The ability of the **prefrontal lobe** to maintain **working memory**. That is way a person is emotionally upset, they "**can't think straight**", and why they are in continual emotional distress. The real deficits in a person's intellectual abilities, crippling their capacity to learn.

These deficits are more subtle not always measured by IQ testing, they show-up more in neuropsychological testing as well in a child's continual aggressive and impulsive behaviors. For example boys who have above-average IQ scores were doing poorly in school via the neuropsychological tests in some case it has impaired the frontal cortex functioning. They were also impulsive, anxious, and often disruptive, in trouble suggesting a faulty prefrontal control over their limbic urges.

These physical changes give the body added strength and energy. They prepare the body for dealing with stressful events such as giving a speech, aiding an accident victim, or fighting or fleeing from an attack. When stress is dealt with in a positive way, the body restores itself and repairs any damage caused by the stress. However, most of the time, people don't deal with stress in a positive way. Thus, stress-related tension builds up with no outlets, it takes its toll on the body.

PAIN

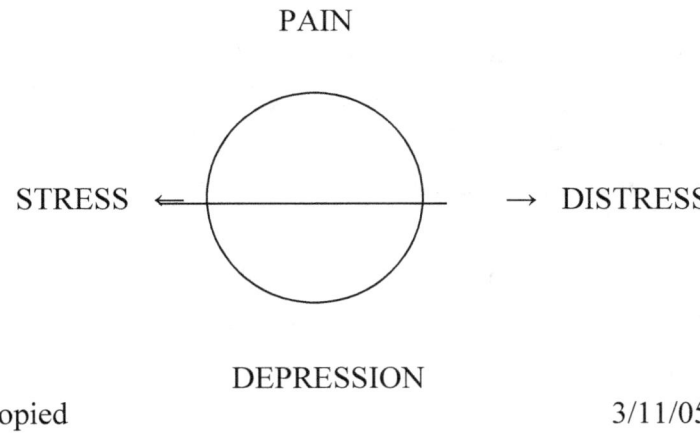

STRESS ⟵ ⟶ DISTRESS

DEPRESSION

Copied   3/11/05

Break the vicious cycle

The mind's reaction to stress is harder to predict. These mental reactions vary according to the situation and the person. They may include feelings of anger, fear, anxiety, annoyance or frustration. A small amount of stress can help people perform their best--during an exam, an athletic event, or on stage. With too much stress, people may become accident-prone, may not be able to function. Stress can be compared to a violin string. If the string is too loose (not enough stress), it won't produce music. If the string is too tight (too much stress), it will break of stress is necessary to function properly.

Realize everyone responds in different ways to events and situations. Some people like to be busy, with lots of activity. Others may prefer a slower pace, with less activity. What one person finds relaxing may be stressful to another.

The Bible has a lot say on the same subject and what a person thinks of themselves in fact that is the reason God had the Bible written, and how we apply Scriptures there in, to the subjects that relates to man are defiantly there for man, him or herself. I want to approach man as "**self**" from this stand point in our study. If you believe God made man to sin I don't believe that, we need God's grace to cover the sin question; that is a result of the fall of man.

77

You only have to go Genesis chapters 1-3 to find out what happened; we will do later. You will have to come to some conclusion about why man was created, and for what purpose it has in our study. We will do our best to get a better understanding of this position between God and man, and clear up some miss conceptions about "**self**".

Let's take a look at the fall of Satan and his Angles; if anyone tells you that life is not a battle, you had better beware of that person.

Paul said in:

Phil. 3:14

"I press toward the mark for the prize of the high calling of God in Christ Jesus."

I think Paul may be saying, I have a goal to fellow Christ's we need to understand his teachings and how they can help a person. Then, Paul said to Timothy in

II Timothy 4:6-8   (9)

V-6 "For I am now ready to be offered, and the time of my departure is at hand.

V-7 I have fought a good fight I have finished *my* course, I have keep the faith:

V-8 Henceforth there is laid up for me a crown of righteousness, which the Lord, the righteous judge, shall give me at that day: and not to me only, but unto all them also that love his appearing."

Then, Paul said I accomplished my goal "I finished my course".

Christ made it very clear we have to get the first commandment right. The commandments and **the word of God** pertains to the laws of the heart & mind, and, soul & body of a Christian's, We have a "spiritual **will**" and a physical **will,** it is important how we are able to **love one another.**

78

Daniel Goleman

"Another key pathway linking **emotions** and the **immune system** is via the influence of the release of **stress**. The *adrenaline glands*, *cortical, prolactin*, and the *neural opiates* are all released during **stress arousal**, each has a strong impact on the **immune cells**.

In this includes (broad categories these diseases). In *distressing emotions*, found that this is in order of magnitude relates to that of smoking, or high cholesterol are for heart disease, just as significant in major health problems."

Signs and symptoms of stress

Managing stress begins with learning the signs and symptoms of stress.

- Tiredness/exhaustion
- Muscle tension
- Anxiety
- Indigestion
- Nervousness/trembling
- Sleeplessness
- Cold, sweaty hands
- Loss of or increased appetite
- Grinding teeth/clenching jaws
- General body complaints, such as weakness, dizziness, headache, stomachache, or pain in the back or muscles.

Usually feeling depressed depends on how a person deals with events in their life, whether they are real or imagined. If you believe you're a helpless victim of depression, a person probably won't do anything to overcome it. Here are some tips to help you manage depression:

- Realize that you are responsible for how you feel. If you are aware that your state of mind is up to you, then you are more likely to take an active approach to improving your mood.
- Take care of yourself. You're special--so pamper yourself. Try something good to eat, take a leisurely bath, or buy something nice for yourself.
- Be a "doer." When you're sad or lonely, go to an event. Get involved in neighborhood or volunteer organizations. Don't forget the joy of giving.
- Find new activities to replace old ones so you can continue to grow and develop. Discover new creative outlets, such as hobbies, skills or interests.
- Remember that it's all right to cry. A good cry can be a healthy way to relieve tension.
- Keep in touch with family and friends, by phone if you can't get out. Don't let your arthritis set you apart from others.
- Try to discover what set off your depression and learn to avoid those events in the future.
- Be alert for signs of depression that last for more than two weeks. If you continue to have signs such as eating or sleeping too much or too little, or feeling hopeless, forgetful, restless, or more tired than usual, tell your doctor. Sometimes this type of depression is caused by a change or an imbalance in the body's chemistry. Often certain drugs can correct such an imbalance.

Relaxation techniques:
Learning how to relax is one of the most important ways to cope with stress in a positive way.
- To begin with, try to set aside time in a quiet place, away from people, TV, radio and other distractions

• Close your eyes. Slowly tense and then relax muscles that feel tense. Begin with your feet and work up to your neck.

• Sit in a comfortable chair with your feet on the floor and your arms at your sides. Close your eyes.

Chapter 3

THE PHYSIOLOGICAL FUNCTION OF THE BRAIN

The physical make-up of the body and brain.

The physiology of man is much more complicated because man is influenced by (his or her) surroundings and relationships. Where does the physical and emotional begin and end, or takeover in a situation, or does the circumstances take over the situation?

We cannot discuss and study the **physiology** and **psychology** of man without including the actual working of the brain and its functions, adrenal glands, the systems make-up the enter (man/woman0. Much like the Atom, which is made up of energy and mass, are two fold. The body is made of energy and mass as it functions in relation to the physiology and the psychology of a person.

Definition of **Physiology**: *Noun*   {2}
Latin *physiologyia* natural science
> **1 a :** a branch of biology that deals with the functions
> and activities of life or of living matter
> (as organs, tissues, or cells) and of the physical and
> chemical phenomena involved – compare
> anatomy.
> **2** : the organic process and phenomena of an organism
> or any of its parts or of a particular bodily process

Merriam-Webster's Collegiate Dictionary Eleventh Edition 2/15/04

Breathe in, saying to yourself, "I am . . . 7' then breathe out saying" . . . relaxed."

Continue breathing slowly, silently repeating to yourself something such as: "My hands are.. warm; my feet.. . are warm; my forehead . . . is cool; my breathing . . . is deep and smooth; my heartbeat is . . . calm and steady; I am . . . happy; I feel calm . . . and at peace."

• Light a candle, and focus your attention on the flame a few minutes. Then close your eyes and watch the image of the flame for a minute or two.

• Imagine a white cloud floating toward you. It wraps itself around your pain and stress. Then a breeze comes. It blows away the cloud, taking your pain and stress with it.

• Think about a place you have been where you once felt pleasure or comfort. Imagine it in as much detail as possible how it looks, smells, sounds and feels. Recapture the positive feelings you had then and keep them in your mind. Don't make any room for negative thoughts, stress or pain.

• Imagine that you've put all your concerns, worries and pain in a helium filled balloon. Let the air out and watch it float away.

Three parts of the body system that interact with the psychology.

1. The Adrenalin, Thyroid, and Pituitary Glands Sucrets Chemicals into the body's energy and nerve system.

2. The central nerve system reacts to these Chemicals usually creating a balance or imbalance in the health, and mental well-being of a person.

3. The Brain is the Head Quarter that interlocks these glands, systems, and through the central nerve system to the emotional control and well-being of a person.

Definition of **Psychic** : *Noun*   {3}
Function: *adjective*
  1 : of or relating to the *psyche* : PSYCHOGENIC
  2 : lying outside the sphere of physical science or
        knowledge
      : immaterial, moral, or spiritual in origin or force
  3 : sensitive to nonphysical or supernatural forces and
        influences
      : marked by extraordinary or mysterious sensitivity,
        perception, or understanding.
Merriam-Webster's Collegiate Dictionary Eleventh Edition 2/15/04

A person should be able to look at **physiology** and be able to distinguish between the physical aspects of **physiology**. The mental aspects of the conscious and subconscious **mental** aspects.

There may be imbalances that are created in the *psychogenesis*, such as patterns of hostility and rage also manifests in a person's outward expressions of emotion of anger and outrages.

The opposite can lead to subdued inter-personal-introvertedness. Low self-esteem and depression, in these cases of counseling and supporting the person is very important in leading them in the direction that is best suited for them and the situation.

Definition of psychology : *noun*   {4}
  1 : the science of mind and behavior
  2 a : the mental or behavioral of an individual or group
    b : the study of mind and behavior in relation to a
          particular field of knowledge of
  3 a : theory or system of psychology
Merriam-Webster's Collegiate Dictionary Eleventh Edition 3/20/05

In some cases a person is going to need more than counseling and support. They may need to be under the direct care of a Clinical Psychologist for the proper behavior medication they may need the guidance of a therapist.

This may also interact with the **soul/heart** of a person, which is made up from the inner workings of the brain. The proper understanding of one's self or at least working with someone who understands the inner workings of the brain. There is that aspect of a (man or woman) which cannot be understood without proper knowledge of the inner working of the human spirit.

Definition of soul : *noun*   {5}

1   : the immaterial essence, animating principle, or
            actuating cause of an individual life

    a : the spiritual principle embodied in human beings,
            all rational and spiritual beings, or the universe

    b : God

3   : a person's total self

4 a : an active or essential part

    b : a moving spirit : leader

5 a : the moral and motional nature of human beings

    b : the quality that arouses emotion and sentiment

    c : spiritual or moral force

        : person

6 a : personification, <she is the soul of integrity>

7 a : a strong positive feeling
            (as of intense sensitivity and emotional fervor)

Definition of heart : *noun*   {6}

    1 : the motional or moral as distinguished from the
        intellectual nature:

    a : generous disposition;

    b : love, affection, courage, and adore

      : one's innermost character, feelings, or inclinations

    2 a : the central or innermost part : center

    b : the essential or most vital part of something

Merriam-Webster's Collegiate Dictionary Eleventh Edition 3/22/04

The spirit of a person is made of the human spirit and will of a person and the Psychic inner linking with the person to God. There is a difference between the heart and soul?

To be certain if a person is without the proper balances and controls of their triune being. It could be causing multiple problems and even health problems physically, mentally are affecting the human spirit.

Emotions are impulses of energy that relate to the physical body, **physiologically make up** and **physiological** reactions go through the brain circuitry. The results reflect in the mental aspect such as choices/decision-making in a given situation.

We love things of value or of worth usually that is the case in point in God's love "unworthy" man even after the fall. Why didn't God offer the same opportunity to Satan and his angles? We have to understand Satan and his powers to be able to understand the heart and mind of God. They are eternal spirits and we are not affected by the physical death. People experience a physical death, but we also experience the "self" in us, and how our **will** plays a role in our life.

Definition of self- and will, {7}
Self
Main Entry: **self**
Function: *noun*

1 a : the entire person of an individual
   b : the realization or embodiment of an abstraction
2 a : (1) an individual's typical character or behavior
       <her true *self* was revealed>
     : (2) an individual's temporary behavior or
       character <his better *self*>
   b : a person in prime condition
       <feel like my old *self* today>
   3 : the union of elements (as body, emotions,
       thoughts, and sensations)
       that constitute the individuality and identity of
       a person
4 **:** personal interest or advantage
5 **:** material that is part of an individual organism
       <ability of the immune system to distinguish *self*
       from nonselfs

Will {8}
Main Entry: will
Function: *verb*

     : DESIRE, WISH <call it what you will>
1 **:** used to express desire, choice, willingness,
       consent, or in negative constructions refusal
       <no one *would* take the job>
     <if we *will* all do our best>
     <*will* you please stop that racket>
2 **:** used to express frequent, customary, or habitual

action or natural tendency or disposition
<*will* get angry over nothing>
<*will* work one day and loaf the next>

3 : used to express futurity
<tomorrow morning *I will* wake up in this first-class hotel suite --Tennessee Williams>

4 : used to express capability or sufficiency
<the back seat *will* hold three passengers>

5 : used to express probability and often equivalent to the simple verb **usage** see SHALL - **if you will**
: if you wish to call it that <a kind of preoccupation, or obsession *if you* Louis Auchincloss>

http://unabridged.meniam- bbster.com/cgi-bin/Third?book=Dictionary&will   3/5/2005

Free+will+problem - Merriam-Webster   Page 1 of 1 {9}

"**Free will** arises from the apparent inconsistency between causal determinations in to choose and making decisions with a capacity to choose alternatives in (his or her) life, to act freely in certain situations or all situations, thus does that mean acting independently of God's directive, to choose from a social point of view, or chose the divine intervention of God. God's significance derives from the fact that man is free moral agent and the will generally is consider to be a part of man's choice. The necessary presupposition of moral responsibility for their actions, or is it totally God's preemptive power over man, which determines everything (at least until the advent of quantum mechanics) has been regarded as a necessary presupposition of natural science.

Arguments for free-will are based on the subjective experience of freedom of choice, on sentiments of guilt, and on the

supposition of responsibility for personal actions that underlies the concepts of the laws of man, but is God the reworded or does He punish the bad things that happen, and is that the incentive to do good. In theology, the existence of free will must be reconciled with God's foreknowledge, with divine omniscience of God knowing everything and His goodness (in allowing man to choose good or evil), it can be explained by knowing God's divine grace, which allegedly is necessary for any meritorious acts of man."
http://unabridged.merriam-webster.com/cgi-bin/Third?book=Encyclopedia&free+will+prob... 3/5/2005

Now let's take **up** how God addresses the needs / desires of a man or women, we are made in His own image in **Genesis 1:27**. So, man should be happy, but it doesn't appear to be that way after the fall and even now. To do this we must go a step farther, in the "**will**" of person and the "**will**" of God the Father for man. At this point, we need to look at the **fall of man,** and how relevant it is to the position of man to God.

The real problem comes down how do you go about fixing those problems in a person's life?

1 Peter 4:12-16 - (10)

V-12 "Beloved, think it not strange concerning the fiery trial which is to try you, as though some strange thing happened unto you:
V-13 But rejoice, inasmuch as ye are partakers of Christ's sufferings; that, when his glory shall be revealed, ye may be glad also with exceeding joy.
V-14 If ye be reproached for the name of Christ, happy *are ye*; for the spirit of glory and of God resteth upon you: on their part he is evil spoken of, but on your part he is glorified.
V-15 But let none of you suffer as a murderer, or *as* a thief, or *as* an evildoer, or as a busybody in other men's matters.

V-16 Yet if *any man suffer* as a Christian, let him not be ashamed; but let him glorify God on this behalf."

The Scriptural view of Self-will exposes our true motives.

At this point we need to look into the **fall of man,** as I have tried to explain the complex nature of man and how man deals in the realms of how do we fix those problems in our life?

Our relationship with another person involves **self** and these attributes of the **will, love,** and then **image,** and a person's **esteem** of one's self is shown by our respect or appreciation for another person based on value and their own **self-worth**. According to Jesus, respect for others is demonstrated by "doing unto others as you would have others do unto you" (**Matthew 7:12; Luke 6:31**). This is known as the "Golden Rule.":

Matthew 25:40-46.

V-40 "And the King shall answer and say unto them, Verily I say unto you, Inasmuch as ye have done *it* unto one of the least of these my brethren, ye have done *it* unto me.

V-41 Then shall he say also unto them on the left hand, Depart from me, ye cursed, into everlasting fire, prepared for the devil and his angles:

V-42 For I was an hungred, and ye gave me no meat: I was thirsty, and ye gave me no drank:

V-43 I was a stranger, and ye took me not in: naked, and ye clothed me not: sick, and in prison, and ye visited me not.

V-44 Then shall they also answer him, saying, Lord, when saw we thee an hungred, or sick, or in prison, and did not minister unto thee?

V-45 Then shall he answer them, saying, Verily I say unto you, Insamuch as ye did *it* not to one of the least of these, ye did *it* not to me.

V-46 And these shall go away into everlasting punishment: but the righteous into life eternal."

A person's worship tells us a lot about a person's love for God, their relationship with God and in their relationships with others. This is pretty strong language coming from Christ, and yet this is one in the same according to Christ's teaching. If one is wrong, then he is wrong both to God and man. You are breaking your fellowship with God when you do the wrong thing toward your spouse, family, and friends, even a stranger. I want to address being out of fellowship with God because of bad a relationship. We will deal with this in our book "SOS NEW BEGINNINGS" on dating, premarital relationships and family. We also deal with drugs and the effects on the family. God loves every one of us, and sees both sides of the situation; there is a problem when a person only sees love to benefits ones **self**. Remember God loves the other person.

Illustration

This was one of my biggest hindrances as a Christian, it caused me a lot pain and heartache. I felt God should punish the other person because they had hurt me, it seemed like nothing was happening to them. There were plenty of bad things happening, I felt God was judging me, in reality my problems were of my undoing I felt I disserved to be punished. According to some interpretations of the Bible I had broken God's laws. I finely came the consolation God would deal with them if I take care of my relationship with God.

That brings us to improving our **love** in our **relationships**, which reflects in our life and attitudes. How we need compare our selfish **"will"** to God love.

We either have selfish will or our choice ott to be to serve Him. When a person seeks God's will and gets their relationships right, we are in line for God's blessings.

CGG Bible Study: Overcoming (Part 4): Self-will

Pages 1-4 [11]

Self-Will **by Martin G. Collins**

Forerunner, "Bible Study," November 2000

"A sixteenth-century doctor, Thomas Fuller, once said, 'Beware of no man more than thyself.' How true is that statement? In our efforts to overcome, we find this statement painfully true. Self-will is part of our **human nature** and always strives to make *self* the center of its own universe. In this selfish manner, our self-will desires to pull God from His throne and deny others justice and mercy to advance its own ambition. This sin is both dangerous and destructive.

A major theme of the Bible shows what God has done to save man from disasters that have overtaken him because of his self-will. In addition, it reveals man's persistent refusal to recognize God's will and it's amazing benefits when followed. Man's own stubbornness is keeping him from lasting peace, health and prosperity! This Bible study will examine this presumptuous obstruction to overcoming.

1. What are some of the harsher characteristics of self-will? **Genesis 49:5-7.**

Comment: "Self-will' occurs only here in the Old Testament. In his curse on Simeon and Levi, Jacob says that in their self-will, they *"digged down a wall'* (KJV), or "hamstrung an ox" (NKJV).

Their vengeful, violent acts against Shechem cause Jacob to pronounce a curse on their anger because it manifested itself in fierceness and cruelty. As a result, the tribes of Simeon and Levi, given no inheritance, are scattered throughout **Israel**.

2. Can ambition be another form of self-will? **Isaiah 14:13-14; Genesis 11:4; II Samuel 15:1-6.**

Comment: How people feel about ambition is plain in the way they say, "I'm a go-getter" in a tone of pride and self-satisfaction. Many people greatly admire this expression of self-will. However, people often frustrate themselves when they try to accomplish and acquire things through their own will. In seeking security and prestige, self-will frequently develops into conformity to a social status, a peer group or an organization. It is slavery to sin.

3. Is presumptuousness a form of self-will? **Deuteronomy 1:34-44; II Peter 2:10; Isaiah 45:9-10.**

Comment: Israel willfully attacked the Amorites after God told them not to go, their presumptuousness brought them bitter defeat. Peter says that all "who walk according to the flesh" are "presumptuous" as well as "self-willed." The Greek word Peter uses literally means "self-pleasing." It denotes the person who, dominated by self-interest and inconsiderate of others, arrogantly asserts his own will. The self-willed person so overvalues any decision he makes that he cannot be dissuaded.

4. Is a self-willed person inclined to listen to advice and act on it? **Isaiah 28:9-12; Proverbs 21:24; John 8:42-47.**

Comment: The person led by self-will commits a very serious sin by refusing to learn God's truth. The people of Ephraim became so proud and self-willed that they could not be taught individually or as a nation. They refused to hear any of God's instruction. One who refuses to listen to what God has to say is not of God.

5. Does God want self-willed men in His ministry? **Titus 1:7; I Timothy 3:2-7.**

Comment: Self-will is insisting stubbornly and arrogantly on one's way, as opposed to following the will of God. Paul states that a minister of God must not allow himself to be self-will must be led by and doing God's will. What kind of minister would a person with false pride and stubbornness make?

6. What is the opposite of self-will? **Matthew 6:10; 26:39; James 4:7-10.**

Comment: Submitting to God's will is the first step in overcoming self-will. This requires obedience and that the law of God be written in our hearts. From this, David writes, we receive delight Psalm 40:8. This process demands that we resist Satan, the father of pride, and develop true humility.

7. What benefits come from doing God's will? **Romans 12:2; John 7:16-18.**

Comment:

Self-will conforms to the world and its beliefs; God's will does not. Doing God's will rather than our own provides understanding of true doctrine and discernment of truth. In the Old Testament, God reveals Himself and His will to pagan man through the agency of a chosen people. In the New Testament, He draws man to Himself in Jesus Christ, who took upon Himself our sins to reconcile us to the Father, becoming the Mediator between man and God. The continual aim of God is to re-establish communion between man and Himself, so that human will converts into His will.

Clearly, we should do, not our will, but God's. God has given us freedom and power, not to do as we want, but to do as He wants—and this is where our security lies. Apart from His will, we are like the undisciplined child—nervous, unstable, and blown about by the winds of whim

we ought to want. In due time, our continuance in doing the will of God will grant us the ultimate benefit: entrance into His glorious Kingdom!"

The Scriptural view of psychology and self-will

It is evident that we have to give up some of the thing we want and let God the Father have His way with us, then we become one with the Father in His will for us on earth. At that point God can bless a person, a Christian needs to smite their will unto the Father. If Christ had to submit His will to God, we as Christian believers have to smite our will unto God? because we really do not know what96 because we really do not know what

Godly Women 4
Laying down our self-will   Pages 1-4 [12]

"Self-will is very well illustrated in **Isaiah 14:12-14**. "How art thou fallen from heaven, O Lucifer, son of the morning? How art thou cut down to the ground, which didst weaken the nations! For thou hast said in thine heart, I will ascend into heaven, I will exalt my throne above the stars of God: I will sit also upon the mount of the congregation, in the sides of the north: I will ascend above the heights of the clouds; I will be like the most High."

It is Satan exercising his own self will. 95% of missionaries return home after their first time out in the field. Why? Because they are unable to work with others in harmony. Our worst enemy is our self. Self-will is exercising our own will apart from God's will. Self-will is doing what I want when I want to do it, and how I want to do it. When we women move out from under our authority we get into trouble.

Self-Will: The #1 big problem.

Self-will is the **"BIG I"** — the root of all problems proceed from unbelief, pride and an evil heart. The writer of Hebrews talks about the Israelites when they couldn't enter into the promised land because of their own evil heart of unbelief. "Take heed, brethren, lest there be in any of you an evil heart of unbelief, in departing from the living God." (**Hebrews 3:12**)

Nehemiah talks about a similar situation. This was after they had already come into the promised land and received all the blessings of God, yet they were proud and refused to obey. **Nehemiah 9:16, 17, 25** and 26 reads: "But they and our fathers dealt proudly, and hardened their necks, and hearkened not to thy commandments, And refused to obey, neither were mindful of thy wonders that thou didst among them; but hardened their necks, and in their rebellion appointed a captain to return to their bondage: but thou art a God ready to pardon, gracious and merciful, slow to anger, and of great kindness, and forsookest them not." How do you like that? They refused to obey! "And they took strong cities, and a fat land, and possessed houses full of all goods, wells digged, vineyards, and oliveyards, and fruit trees in abundance: so they did eat, and were filled, and became fat, and delighted themselves in thy great goodness.

Nevertheless they were disobedient, and rebelled against thee, and cast thy law behind their backs, and slew thy prophets which testified against them to turn them to thee, and they wrought great provocations." The rebellious children of Israel continually did their own thing, turning away from God.

Self-Will is made evident by refusing to take heed to God or His Word

II Kings 17:14 says "Notwithstanding they would not hear, but hardened their necks, like to the neck of their fathers, that did not believe in the LORD their God."

Self-Will is made evident by refusing to walk with God

Psalm 78:10-19 says, "They kept not the covenant of God, and refused to walk in his law; And forgat his works, and his wonders that he had shewed them. Marvellous things did he in the sight of their fathers, in the land of Egypt, in the field of Zoan. He divided the sea, and caused them to pass through; and he made the waters to stand as an heap. In the daytime also he led them with a cloud, and all the night with a light of fire. He clave the rocks in the wilderness, and gave them drink as out of the great depths. He brought streams also out of the rock, and caused waters to run down like rivers. And they sinned yet more against him by provoking the most High in the wilderness. And they tempted God in their heart by asking meat for their lust. Yea, they spake against God; they said, Can God furnish a table in the wilderness?" God wrought miracles among them, and yet they hardened their heart and refused to walk in His ways.

Self-Will is made evident by refusing to heed God's messengers

In **Genesis 19:26** Lot's wife refused to listen to the Angel of the Lord and turned into a pillar of salt as a result. God may also send people as messengers. He may speak to us through people. We need to start to take heed to God's people.

Self-Will is made evident by refusing to hearken to parents

In the Old Testament disobedience to parents was punished severely. If a son (or daughter) refused to listen to their parents, they were to be taken outside of the city gate and stoned. **Deuteronomy 21:18-21** reads, "If a man have a stubborn and rebellious son, which will not obey the voice of his father, or the voice of his mother, and that, when they have chastened him, will not hearken unto them: Then shall his father and his mother lay hold on him, and bring him out unto the elders of his city, and unto the gate of his place; And they shall say unto the elders of his city, This our son is stubborn and rebellious, he will not obey our voice; he is a glutton, and a drunkard. And all the men of his city shall stone him with stones, that he die: so shalt thou put evil away from among you; and all Israel shall hear, and fear." Listen! You may think that is harsh. Thank God we are not under the Law. But if the rebellious son does not obey his parents, what makes you think they will obey God? They will not obey God. We need to start to train our children while they are young to respect authority. If we don't do it then, they will not do it later.

Self-Will is made evident by refusing to receive correction
 Jeremiah 5:3 says,

V-3 "O LORD, are not thine eyes upon the truth? thou hast stricken them, but they have not grieved; thou hast consumed them, but they have refused to receive correction: they have made their faces harder than a rock; they have refused to return."

We want to do our own thing if we simply refuse to take correction or instruction or refuse to repent.

By the same token, we can go to the opposite extreme and project our own way of thinking into our children beliefs. Self projection is manipulating people into **a person's way of thinking.** In other words, it is projecting an opinion on others. In the training of children, let them be themselves within the framework that God has established for them. When we want them to do something, we need to ask ourselves: "Why do I want them to do this? Because I want them? Are you trying to impose your will or away of thinking about them?" We need to make sure that we as parents are not forcing them into something that God is not necessarily desiring of them.

Self-Centeredness

A person that is self-centered lives within his own circle. He is only happy when he's the center of attraction. He is very insecure and defensive. He wants to be worshipped, not corrected.

Self-Pity

People that waddle in self-pity always feel rejected and unappreciated. The feel misunderstood. They want to hang on to their hurts and have no forgiveness for others.

To be selfish or possessive is to be overly concerned about self and neglecting the needs of others.

II Timothy 3:1-5 says,

V-1 "This know also, that in the last days perilous times shall come.

V-2 For men shall be lovers of their own selves, covetous, boasters, proud, blasphemers, disobedient to parents, unthankful, unholy,

V-3 Without natural affection, trucebreakers, false accusers, incontinent, fierce, despisers of those that are good,

V-4 Traitors, heady, highminded, lovers of pleasures more than lovers of God;

V-5 Having a form of godliness, but denying the power thereof: from such turn away."

People will be lovers of self, self-centered, lovers of money and aroused by an inordinate greedy desire for wealth. Paul describes that in the last days people will be proud and arrogant and contemptuous boasters; abusive, blasphemous, scoffers, disobedient to parents, ungrateful, unholy and profane. Isn't that what we are seeing now?

Romans 15:1

V-1 "We then that are strong ought to bear the infirmities of the weak, and not to please ourselves.'

Self Importance or Pride

Self-importance is having an exaggerated opinion of one's own importance. When a person is like that, they are lifted up in a fog.

Romans 12:3

V-3 "For I say, through the grace given unto me, to every man that is among you, not to think of himself more highly than he ought to think; but to think soberly, according as God hath dealt to every man the measure of faith."

Self Righteousness

Self-righteousness is when we think that we are better than others. The Pharisees for example, thought they were better than everyone around them and they did not hesitate to advertise themselves.

II Corinthians 10:12

V-12 "For we dare not make ourselves of the number, or compare ourselves with some that commend themselves: but they measuring themselves by themselves, and comparing themselves among themselves, are not wise."

The self-righteous person begins by comparing, then condemning. Condemning leads to resentment. Resentment comes in and bitterness will take place in the heart. That bitterness will lead to anger, which results in being judgmental and self-righteous and we condemn others for not living up to our expectations.

A self-righteous person is always a perfectionist. **James 1:19-20** says, "Wherefore, my beloved brethren, let every man be swift to hear, slow to speak, slow to wrath: For the wrath of man worketh not the righteousness of God." If self is on the throne, it comes across in everything I say and do. Only God can change my heart. We need to soften our heart toward God and allow Him to change us from the inside out."

http://www.hispraise.com/VOM/godly4.html

This is what Jesus taught the Jews, they understood the Law of Moses, the Jewish man had very little respect for a women or his wife. They thought of themselves as being over the women. In the book of **John**, he wrote of God's love for man, a great book in the Bible for any person to read.

The Apostles wrote "love the world", the great commission "go into all the world and preach the gospel of Christ", Paul being a Roman citizen uses the comparison of "love your wife as yourself" in many of his writings to the Gentiles, so that they could relate to themselves and their wives. As "Christ loved the church and gave himself for it", the ultimate love is God giving His Son for a sacrifice for man. Why is God mindful of man and why? We also know it pleased God to send His Son.

There seems to be some Scriptures could be misleading if a person is going to live by the law, you die by the law, but if you live under grace you are going to die under grace, (Right). Now another is when Jesus taught about the family, and following him in and being disciple that could mean being a Christian:

Luke 14:26 look close at this Scripture and see if I'm right, *"if any man **hate** his father and mother; wife; sister or brother he cannot be my disciple"*.

1 John 4:7-21

V-7 "Beloved, let us love one another: for love is of God; and every one that loveth is born of God, and knoweth God.

V-8 He that loveth not knoweth not God; for God is love.

V-9 In this was manifested the love of God toward us, because that God sent his only begotten Son into the world, that we might live through him.

V-10 Herein is love, not that we loved God, but that he loved us, and sent his Son *to be* the propitiation for our sins.

V-11 Beloved, if God so loved us, we ought also to love one another.

V-12 No man hath seen God at any time. If we love one another, God dwelleth in us, and his love is perfected in us.

V-13 Hereby know we that we dwell in him, and he in us, because he hath given us of his Spirit.

V-14 And we have seen and do testify that the Father sent the Son *to be* the Saviour of the world.

V-15 Whosoever shall confess that Jesus is the Son of God, God dwelleth in him, and he in God.

V-16And we have known and believed the love that God hath to us. God is love; and he that dwelleth in love dwelleth in God, and God in him.

V-17 Herein is our love made perfect, that we may have boldness in the day of judgment: because as he is, so are we in this world.

V- 18 There is no fear in love; but perfect love casteth out fear: because fear hath torment. He that feareth is not made perfect in love.

V- 19 We love him, because he first loved us.

V-20 If a man say, I love God, and hateth his brother, he is a liar: for he that loveth not his brother whom he hath seen, how can he love God whom he hath not seen?

V-21 And this commandment have we from him, That he who loveth God love his brother also."

Matthew 10:37-39 & 42   (11)

V-37 "He that loveth father or mother more than me is not worthy of me: and he that loveth son or daughter more than me is not worthy of me.

V-38 And he that taketh not his cross, and followeth after me, is not worthy of me.

V-39 He that fineth his life shall lose it: and he that loseth his life for my sake shall find it.

V-42 And whosoever shall give to drink unto one of these little ones a cup of cold *water* only in the name of a disciple, very I say unto you, he shall in no wise lose his life."

We have to look at God's love for us to understand His love:

John 15:12-15 (12)

V-12 "This is my commandment, That ye love one another, as I have loved you.

V-13 Greater love hath no man than this, that a man lay down his life for his friends.

V-14 Ye are my friends, if ye do whatsoever I command you.

V-15 Henceforth I call you not servants; for the servants knoweth not what his lord doeth: but I have called you friends; for all things that I have heard of my Father I have made known to you."

This is where some get off track, when a man said I need to say *"fair well, to them which are at home"*

Luke 9:62

V-62 "And Jesus said unto him, No man, having put his hand to the plough and looking back is fit for the kingdom of God."

I John 1: 9

V-9 But under grace all is forgiven if we confess our sins, and he is faithful to for give our sins."

Now let's see if this truth holds true in Christ's life, when Christ was on the cross He said to: *"Not will but Thin be done,"*

Christ said to John the beloved take care of my mother.

John 19:25-27 (13)

V-25 "Now there stood by the cross of Jesus his mother, and his mother's sister, Mary the *wife* of Ce-o-phas, and Mary Mag-daplene.

V-26 When Jesus therefore saw his mother, and the disciple standing by, whom he loved, he saith unto his mother, Women, behold thy son!

V-27 Then saith he to the disciple, Behold thy mother! And from that hour that disciple took her unto his own *home*."

WOW, that is true love, Christ in His dying took time for His mother, how ought we to love one another".

Christ said to His disciples take up my cross and I will make you fishers of men.

Everyone will know that you are his disciples, if you have love one another

John 13:35

In all of this I hope you are beginning to get the picture, the clue is there, **LOVE** your fellow man then you show God's love. A person's love affects their relationship with God and a person's relationships with each other. It is just that simple, how to go about dealing with the **love** question is much harder than saying "I love you", you have to say to yourself "do I really love you" as Christ said to Peter "*do you really love me*," three times and then He said if you do "feed my sheep" in **John 21:15-17**.

This is the next step when it comes to our Christian testimony for Christ and the way we do this is by showing our love for one another.

Now, I hope we are getting somewhere, or are you faking it if you are selfish with your love for yourself, all of us have love needs, the most essential love need is giving love and/or are you filling your heart's desire unselfishly and do you really mean it when you say to someone, I love you. How much is enough when it comes to loving someone? I'm sure, I have given you some ideas, but I know it is all raped up in how we love God and in the fulfillment of a person.

I had an Ant and her favorite saying was "*God love you*" as you were leaving to go home.

The key to life is loving God first, others, and then yourself.

Let's try and clarify this statement, I hope you have gotten the point of loving God with (all your heart, mind, and soul). If you don't love yourself there is something wrong in your life, something has happened in your life usually it has to do with abuses of some kind of (sin or sins) involved in your life. When there is hurt, anger, and bitterness, the love in a person has been damaged very badly, this is where modern psychology may be of help and come into play in the healing process. Here is a Scripture on love:

The Greatest Gift is love
I Corinthians 13:1-13   (14)
V-1 "Though I speak with the tongues of men and of angels, but have not love, I have become sounding brass or a clanging cymbal,
V-2 And though I have *the gift of* prophecy, and understand all mysteries and all knowledge, and though I have all faith, so that I could remove mountains, but have not love, I am nothing.
V-3 And though I bestow all my goods to feed *the poor,* and though I give my body to be burned, but have not love, it profits me nothing.
V-4 Love suffers long *and* is kind; love does not envy; love does not parade itself, is not puffed up;
V-5 does not behave rudely, does not seek its own, is not provoked, thinks no evil; does not rejoice in iniquity,
V-6 but rejoices in the truth;
V-7 bears all things, believes all things, hopes all things, endures all things,
V-8 Love never fails. But whether *there are* prophecies, they will fail; whether *there are* tongues, they will cease; whether *there is* knowledge, it will vanish away.
V-9 For we know in part and we prophesy in par.

V-10 But when that which is perfect has come, then that which is in part will be done away

V-11 When I was a child, I spoke as a child, I understood as a child, I thought as a child; but when I became a man, I put away childish things.

V-12 For now we see in a mirror, dimly, but then face to face. Now I know in part, but then I shall know just as I also am known.

V-13 And now abide faith, hope, love, these three; but the greatest of these *is* love."

We find that people in today's society are much more open about discussing their problems and relationships, in fact all you have to do is watch Dr. Phil and Christian TV. There are several types of programs on relationships these programs do to help build better relationships. There are hundreds books on relationships, this is where this discussion is going? When a person is puffed up this usually leads to a selfish end. I'm not so sure that all this attention is good, especially when it is done to entertain, I know people get emotionally involved because these programs relate to their problems. I do believe in talking about problems in support groups, or in personal counseling.

Definition of Esteem   {10}

Function: *transitive verb*

    1   : **APPRAISE**

    2 a : to view as : **CONSIDER** <*esteem* it a privilege>

      b : THINK, BELIEVE

    3   : to set a high value on

      : regard highly and prize accordingly

        <an *esteemed* guest>

      synonym see REGARD

Definition of Image   {11}

Main Entry: **im•age**

Function: *noun*

Date: 13th century

   1   : a reproduction or imitation of the form of a person
       or thing; *especially*
      : an imitation in solid form

   2 **a** : the optical counterpart of an object produced by
       an optical device (as a lens or mirror)
       or an electronic device

     b : a visual representation of something: as

       : (1) a likeness of an object produced on a
        photographic material

       : (2) a picture produced on an electronic display
       (as a television or computer screen)

   3 **a** : exact likeness : SEMBLANCE
       <God created man in his own *image* –
       Genesis1:27 (Revised Standard Version)>

     b : a person strikingly like another person
       <she is the *image* of her mother>

   4 **a** : a tangible or visible representation
      : INCARNATION <the *image* of filial devotion>

     b : *archaic* an illusory form

   5 **a** : (1) a mental picture or impression of something
       <had a negative body *image* of herself>

      : (2) a mental conception held in common by
       members of a group and symbolic of
       a basic attitude and orientation
       <a disorderly courtroom can seriously tarnish
       a community's *image* -- Herbert Brownell>

b : IDEA, CONCEPT

6   : a vivid or graphic representation or description

7   : FIGURE OF SPEECH

corresponds to a particular subset of the domain
http://unabridged.merriam-webster.com/cgi-
bin/Third?book=Dictionary&imag   3/12/2005

My parents, and older people I know of never discussed their problems openly, I think that was good in some ways. They accepted their problems as a part of life, people are not perfect no matter how bad the other person seems to be. I think this may shed some light on how the loss of love for another.

There are two ways to deal with love in a relationship, one is to ignore and do nothing, there is the person who accepts responsibility for what happens. That is always good approach, at some point there is a need for both to talk about the bad things, especially if it is affecting their love. It may sound like we are going into relationships and how to deal with bad relationships we do that in book "SOS NEW BEGINNINGS".

We want to get back on track and discuss **self** and how to deal with **self**, I think this will help you in your relationships.

Another is why do people stop loving someone or people in general, of course there are many reasons, the personal aspects of **self-esteem** may have bearing. There is a difference in being positive and outgoing compared to thinking their great, or on the other hand someone who feels bad about themselves results in **low-self-esteem**. Most people in America do have **high self-esteem** about themselves compared to third world countries; who have nothing, and barely exist. The social environment may have a lot to do with **self-esteem** and Christians have to deal with the **self-esteem** question from two points of view.

Philippians 2:3

V- 3 "*Let* nothing *be done* through strife or vainglory; but in lowliness of mind let each esteem other better than themselves."

1 Thessalonians 5:13

V-13 "And to esteem them very highly in love for their work's sake. *And* be at peace among yourselves."

A Scriptural view of Esteem

Believers today are being challenged and exhorted to develop a better **self-image**, to exercise more *love*. It is our intent to present both the unscriptural, and the spiritual aspects of this important facet of the Christian life.

Amos 5:14-15;

V-14 "Seek good, and not evil, that ye may live: and so the Lord, the God of hosts, shall be with you, as ye have spoken.

V-15 Hate the evil, and love the good, and establish judgment in the gate: it may be that the Lord God of hosts will be gracious unto the remnant of Joseph."

Matthew 24:12-23

V-12 "And because iniquity shall abound, the love of many shall wax cold."

V-13 But he that shall endure unto the end, the same shall be saved.

V-14 And this gospel of the kingdom shall be preached in all the world for a witness unto all nations; and then shall the end come.

V-15 When ye therefore shall see the abomination of desolation, spoken of by Daniel the prophet, stand in the holy place, (whoso readeth, let him understand:)

V-16 Then let them which be in Judaea flee into the mountains:

V-17 Let him which is on the housetop not come down to take any thing out of his house:

V-18 Neither let him which is in the field return back to take his clothes.

V-19 And woe unto them that are with child, and to them that give suck in those days!

V-20 But pray ye that your flight be not in the winter, neither on the sabbath day:

V-21 For then shall be great tribulation, such as was not since the beginning of the world to this time, no, nor ever shall be.

V-22 And except those days should be shortened, there should no flesh be saved: but for the elect's sake those days shall be shortened.

V-23 Then if any man shall say unto you, Lo, here *is* Christ, or there; believe *it* not.

Self-Concepts

People grow in lots of ways, their age, size, knowledge, or skill, also in their awareness of themselves as a person. This consciousness is called a self-concept. Self means the conscious reflection of one's own identity, as an individual I apart of ones environment. There are a variety of ways to think about ones self. Two of the widely used terms are **self-concept** and **self-esteem**.

Self-Concept is the thinking aspect of **Self-esteem** the emotional generally refers to how a person feels or how they value themselves. **Self-Concept** can also refer to the general idea they have about themselves. **Self-Esteem** can refer to particular values about components of **Self-Concept**. Some authors use these two terms interchangeably. To define **Self-Esteem** as the experience of being capable in meeting life's challenges and being worthy of happiness.

111

People need to develop and maintain their **Self-Concepts** in the process of taking action and then reflective actions, what they have done and what others tell them about what they have done. This is based on one's own expectations and the expectations of themselves and basing their accomplishments according to others.

Self-esteem is an important concept of everyone's life. It is true that we can ignore ourselves, or life will ignore us. What keeps you from enjoying life, doing the things you want to do? Working toward personal goals, given time and energy in exploring your own strengths and weaknesses will help you cope with different circumstances. **Self-Awareness**, will power the need for family support is essential pillars in building high **Self-Concepts** everyone is special, unique, and valuable at the same time and deserves to feel good about ones-self.

II Timothy 3:1-5   (15)

V-1 "This know also, that in the last days perilous times shall come.

V-2 For men shall be loves of their own selves, covetous, boaster, proud, blasphemers, disobedient to parents, unthankful, unholy,

V-3 Without natural affection, trucebreakers, false accusers, incontinent, fierce, despisers of those that are good,

V-4 Traitors, heady, highminded, lovers of pleasures more than lovers of God;

V-5 Having a form of godliness, but denying the power thereof: from such turn away."

1 Corinthians 6:19-20

V-19 "Or do you not know that your body is a temple of the Holy Spirit within you, whom you have from God?

V-20 You are not your own, for you were bought with a price. So glorify God in your body."

1. Options
2. Theory
3. Foundation
4. Application of:
Self-Concepts

Chapter 4

LIFE LINE PRACTICAL AXIOMS & EVALUATIONS

The Life Line = Breaking down of Chart I
1. Life behaviors & patterns = Axioms
2. Life Line Breakdown Axioms
Mental, Emotional, and Physical = Well-being
Stress/Anxiety/ Depression
Nervous Energy
Depression/Bipolar
Adrenalin drives
Self-image & Will-power

Stress Management * Relationships * Personal needs & Desires
* Sexuality
Addictions * Loss of a Love-One * Divorce * Blended Families
& & More
"Where am I going, and where I have *been*"?
Analysis of Out of control:

Hurt	Anger	Bitterness	
Conflicts		**Co-dependencies**	
Controller – **Dominated or**		**Out of Control** **Controlling**	
Depression & Bipolar		Anxieties	
Burnout	Stress & Pressure		Abuse

I would like to answer those two questions:

   1. How many decisions/choices do you make in one day?

   2. How many decisions/choices does a person make

     without thinking about it?

     Think about it for a moment?

     (reactions or impulses)?

1. Personal good decisions is that enough, feeling good about yourself is that enough? We also believe in the rights of a (man & women), their dignity as a person, being a good person is that enough? Being a Christian is that good enough; being positive using a person's talents in a positive way do you expect more out of you than you do from others.

There is no doubt in my mind the importance in our studies is probably one of the most controversial in nature, because there are so many different beliefs and human values, never-the-less.

2. Are you able to cope with your bad decisions in any aspect of your life is there happiness and joy.

Christians have feelings and problems like anyone else. Christian have responsibilities and accountability, with a sense of duty.

There are some that say, "I don't need this study", others will probably just read it, others will want to do something about their life. Some will say "I'm a Christian" God will take care of me. I'll wait until God tells me what to do. *"Who is God and how does man fit in"?*

Our Goal is to Inspire - Encourage - Strengthen = Success

Life is a journey filled with experiences, some (bumps, potholes & even craters).

Let's use our Bible **Study-Guides** we will highlight these Appling Biblical Principles.

I can remember thinking "what's the use" I didn't do anything wrong why do I have to deal with who I am.

The BIG QUSTION is how we deal **life's (bumps, potholes & craters).**

(Illustration) of Life's Hi-way!

I like to think of life as a street, or a busy hi-way / interstate. There are speed zones posted to remind us of how fast to go for our own safety and others. Most of us adjust our speed accordingly to what we think is safe, but there are times when we push or break the speed limit. What usually happens, most of the time (nothing), if an officer is watching or has his radar on we're more than likely going to get a ticket if we speed. Life is a lot like that. We have to watch where were going, **pay-attention** to the signs along the way, if we want to get to our destination on time. There is not only **signs** along the way, but there can be obstacles along the way. We can usually prepare for these eventualities most of the time. (Right), at times they were over whelming obstacles to say the-lest.

Lookout for these **bumps, potholes, & craters**:
- When we come across a **bump** we usually slow down.

When we come to a **pothole** we may have to slow down even more, but we can go ahead or hit the pot hoping nothing will happen.

116

But if it is a big **pothole** we're more than likely going to go around it.

- If it is a **crater** we may have to take or make a detour.

  √ Lookout for **Life's** detour signs along the way. I call them **warning signs** in our studies.

  √ How do we define life in respect to where did we come from?

  √ What does all this mean? Especially, when something goes wrong?

We're going to (**start**) with the heart of the matter/subject: *the heart of a person in relation to (him or herself) and God*? That is clearly stated, the answer/answers become more complex when a person doesn't deal with them.

- The foundation for your life is **faith** in yourselves, others, and yes even God.

- **Hope** brings earthly situations into focus the result is eternal joy and happiness for person's dreams and destiny.

- And **love** is the basis for our emotional **well-being**.

First,

Another has to do with how it is affecting the person by the hurt, anger, damage, and abuse. If a person is unhappy or happy?

We are going try to build on these three fundamentals as we go through this study?

Secondly,

In light of the first elements is being able to pass the test? In the second we're going to address our **attitude, thoughts, motives,** and **feelings**. Then the QUESTION is how (**BIG or small**) they are a person needs to find the answers if possible.

We have to be able to evaluate the sincerity of their **attitude,** reviled in their **thoughts, motives,** and **feelings** in their **actions & reactions in their relationships**; are there any hidden agendas:

1. *what do we see in yourself*? Probably more importantly is?
2. *what do you see in others*? Then what?
3. *how does God see you*?

Thirdly,

Another perplexing QUSTION in this study *"how does a person find the answer"*? Some authorities say read the Bible. Others may say you may need a psychologist to help you. Which puts a person at opposite ends of the spectrum as for as advise or counseling. I believe there is a middle ground, I call it **"Common Ground"** to be truthful with one's self in any situation. Let me say this I don't have all the answers to life's questions? Where does a person start by trying to find the answer/ or answers to the BIGER QUSTIONS first?

Some Examples of motivation & preference

(example) Men are more likely to be job oriented.

(making money/position)

(example) Women are more likely to be family oriented.

(making a home/mothering)

(example) Some are indoor people while others are outdoor people, and these attributes reflect in both or either in a (men or women).

We are going to present three challenging models of proof in the life cycle & growth process.

Demonstration Chart I, Axioms; The Life Line Positive & - Negative responses.

Basic Life Line Skills & Tools.

Demonstration Chart II, (6) Axioms:

Demonstration III Axioms, Information & Profiles.

A Summary & Conclusion

I believe in using all the tools necessary for one's growth and maturity. One of the most basic studies is in the book of Romans, all 16 chapters. We are going to hit some the highlights in the Basic principles in salvation and in the Christian walk.

(Example)

May I continue by saying, I have read the Bible through several times in my lifetime. The difference is in this study, I have spent hours of mediation and deliberation while praying over every thought, I could be of help. I have prayed for every person that reads our studies. I would like for our support and studies to be a help and blessing at the same time, not a hindrance; nor do we want to lead anyone in the wrong direction.

Now as it relates to God creating the Heavens and Earth *and in* **Genesis 1:25***; the last phase says, "God saw that it was good". A key verse as-far-as man is concerned,*

Gen 1:26 *"And God said let us make man in our image, after our likeness: let him have dominion over"---all the living things," the rest of the verse.*

Gen 1:27 *He reemphasis the origin of man "So God created man in his own image in the image of God created he him; male and female created he them."*

Gen 1:27 *He gives them charge, "And God blessed them, and said unto them, Be fruitful, and multiply, and replenish the earth—*

through verse 30. After 6 days He says emphatically at this point **Gen 1:31** *"God saw everything that He had made was good. And the evening and the morning were the sixth day." All is well at this point.*

In Genesis chapter two we see a change in this relationship. An introduction to a third party.

In **Ps 142:4** David said at one point in his life "no man cared for my soul." A good scripture passage relates in principle:

Psalm 8:1-9   (16)

V-1 "O LORD our Lord, how excellent *is* thy name in all the earth! who hast set thy glory above the heavens.

V-2 Out of the mouth of babes and sucklings hast thou ordained strength because of thine enemies, that thou mightest still the enemy and the avenger.

V-3 When I consider thy heavens, the work of thy fingers, the moon and the stars, which thou hast ordained;

V-4 What is man, that thou art mindful of him? and the son of man, that thou visitest him?

V-5 For thou hast made him a little lower than the angels, and hast crowned him with glory and honour.

V-6 Thou madest him to have dominion over the works of thy hands; thou hast put all *things* under his feet:

V-7 All sheep and oxen, yea, and the beasts of the field;

V-8 The fowl of the air, and the fish of the sea, *and whatsoever* passeth through the paths of the seas.

V-9 O LORD our Lord, how excellent *is* thy name in all the earth!"

David said in verses 4 "What is man,"(?) "that thou art mindful of him? And the son of man, that thou visited him?" The relationship between God and man is a vital part of His creation of a (men and women).

Paul was making a profound point here. From the Old Testament, God's Spirit did not dwell in earth, but in heaven. When God gave instructions to Moses to build the tabernacle, He carefully outlined a place for His Spirit to dwell: the Ark of the Covenant. This ark would allow God's presence to dwell with Israel wherever they went. It was an incredible honor, the ark was made of the most expensive, quality materials by the very best craftsmen of the time. When King Solomon built the Temple centuries later, the Ark of the Covenant rested in the Holy of Holies. It was Israel's most precious possession.

So when Paul says our bodies are "temples of the Holy Spirit," he's indicating just how *valuable* our bodies are to God. We have the profound honor, as Christians, to bear the Spirit of God within our very hearts. Because His Spirit dwells in us, we are not our own! This should change both how we view and treat our bodies, also what we use them for.

Real confidence cannot come from something external. Since real confidence is an inner assurance, a boldness based on objective truth, showing off a great body isn't confidence at all. That attitude is completely dependent on something that will not last, a truly confident person needs nothing external to be bold on too.

Our bodies have value in God's eyes. In the beginning, (the men and women) new they were naked and was ashamed of it, because the world was perfect. Stylishly covering our bodies is not a lack of confidence; it shows we are giving our bodies the *same glory and value* that God gives them. Don't cheapen the beauty God gave you by advertising it for the world to see. Remember your value, remember that you are God's temple and give His Spirit an honorable house in which to live.

Chapter 5

HUMAN NATURE ROMANS CHAPTERS 1-9

The second description of sin is disbelief and lack of faith. (Spiritual sins)

Romans Chapters 1-16
The Place and Date of Romans

Based on the material from Acts and the Corinthian epistles, the Book of Romans clearly indicates that it was written from Corinth on Paul's third missionary journey. Paul had never visited Rome; after fulfilling his mission of mercy to Jerusalem, he hoped to go to Rome. At any rate, the date of the book is probably 60 A.D.

The theme of the book centers on the Gospel of Christ (**Rom. 1:16, 17**). Paul is deeply concerned that his readers understand how a sinner may receive righteousness by a righteous God; and how a justified sinner should live daily to the glory of God.

The great theme of the epistle of Paul is to the Romans, rightly stated in:

Romans 1:16-17:

V-16 "*For I am not ashamed of the gospel: for it is the power of God unto salvation to every one that believeth; to the Jew first, and also to the Greek.*

V-17 *For therein is revealed a righteousness of God from faith unto faith: as it is written, But the righteous shall live by faith.*"

The apostle Paul then proceeds to show that all men are in need of justification (**Romans 1:18-3:20**).

Most commentators have said that verses sixteen and seventeen of chapter one are a concise summary of the content of the epistle. C. K. Barrett,

"Goes a step further to say that it is not wrong to see in them a summary of Paul's theology as a whole".

Perhaps we can be very precise here. Perhaps in the text of **Habakkuk 2:4** as it is used in Romans (and elsewhere), we have a pithy expression of the essence of the doctrine of the Word of God— "the just shall live by faith."

Romans has often been described as an exposition of the Old Testament in view of the Gospel of Christ; this is certainly an accurate description in view of the pattern that emerges. The Gospel of Christ tells how sinful people can find access into heaven through the sacrificial atonement of Christ. It is clear that this also was the focus of Israel's sacrificial system. It is little wonder the book draws upon the pattern of those ancient sacrifices.

There were three main types of sacrifices in Israel's worship:

Those that made Expiation or atonement (Sin Offering in **Lev. 4**, Trespass Offering **Lev. 5**, the Whole Burnt Offering in **Lev. 1** as well as the great Day of Atonement in **Lev. 16**), those were for Celebration (Peace Offering in **Lev. 3** as well as other variations, such as the Passover in **Exod. 12**), those that were for Dedication (Meal Offering in **Lev. 2** as well offering the first fruit, first born, paying vows, making other types of dedicatory ritual). Essentially there was forgiveness and acceptance by God through atoning sacrifices, the celebration of being at peace with God in the fellowship or peace offering, the dedication to worship and serve God through the dedication or meal offering.

Christians enjoy Bible study grow in their relationship with God it helps to understand the scriptures. Many consider the book of Romans to be one of the key books in the New Testament, as it outlines the plan of salvation clearly and thoroughly.

We will explain what all this means as we show how Romans relates to human behavior.

Romans chapter 1 declares the Son of God
Romans 1:1-32 (17)
V-1 "Paul, a servant of Jesus Christ, called *to be* an apostle, separated unto the gospel of God,

V-2 (Which he had promised afore by his prophets in the holy scriptures,)

V-3 Concerning his Son Jesus Christ our Lord, which was made of the seed of David according to the flesh;

V-4 And declared *to be* the Son of God with power, according to the spirit of holiness, by the resurrection from the dead:

V-5 By whom we have received grace and apostleship, for obedience to the faith among all nations, for his name:

V-5 Among whom are ye also the called of Jesus Christ:

V-6 To all that be in Rome, beloved of God, called *to be* saints:

V-7 Grace to you and peace from God our Father, and the Lord Jesus Christ.

V-8 First, I thank my God through Jesus Christ for you all, that your faith is spoken of throughout the whole world.

V-9 For God is my witness, whom I serve with my spirit in the gospel of his Son, that without ceasing I make mention of you always in my prayers;

V-10 Making request, if by any means now at length I might have a prosperous journey by the will of God to come unto you.

V-11 For I long to see you, that I may impart unto you some spiritual gift, to the end ye may be established;

V-12 That is, that I may be comforted together with you by the mutual faith both of you and me.

V-13 Now I would not have you ignorant, brethren, that oftentimes I purposed to come unto you, (but was let hitherto,) that I might have some fruit among you also, even as among other Gentiles.

V-14 I am debtor both to the Greeks, and to the Barbarians; both to the wise, and to the unwise.

V-15 So, as much as in me is, I am ready to preach the gospel to you that are at Rome also.

V-16 For I am not ashamed of the gospel of Christ: for it is the power of God unto salvation to every one that believeth; to the Jew first, and also to the Greek.

V-17 For therein is the righteousness of God revealed from faith to faith: as it is written, The just shall live by faith.

V-18 For the wrath of God is revealed from heaven against all ungodliness and unrighteousness of men, who hold the truth in unrighteousness;

V-19 Because that which may be known of God is manifest in them; for God hath shewed *it* unto them.

V-20 For the invisible things of him from the creation of the world are clearly seen, being understood by the things that are made, *even* his eternal power and Godhead; so that they are without excuse:

V-21 Because that, when they knew God, they glorified *him* not as God, neither were thankful; but became vain in their imaginations, and their foolish heart was darkened.

V-22 Professing themselves to be wise, they became fools,

V-23 And changed the glory of the uncorruptible God into an image made like to corruptible man, and to birds, and fourfooted beasts, and creeping things.

V-24 Wherefore God also gave them up to uncleanness through the lusts of their own hearts, to dishonour their own bodies between themselves:

V-25 Who changed the truth of God into a lie, and worshipped and served the creature more than the Creator, who is blessed for ever. Amen.

Description of the Human Nature

V-26 For this cause God gave them up unto vile affections: for even their women did change the natural use into that which is against nature:

V-27 And likewise also the men, leaving the natural use of the woman, burned in their lust one toward another; men with men working that which is unseemly, and receiving in themselves that recompence of their error which was meet.

V-28 And even as they did not like to retain God in *their* knowledge, God gave them over to a reprobate mind, to do those things which are not convenient;

V-29 Being filled with all unrighteousness, fornication, wickedness, covetousness, maliciousness; full of envy, murder, debate, deceit, malignity; whisperers,

V-30 Backbiters, haters of God, despiteful, proud, boasters, inventors of evil things, disobedient to parents,

V-31 Without understanding, covenantbreakers, without natural affection, implacable, unmerciful:

V-32 Who knowing the judgment of God, that they which commit such things are worthy of death, not only do the same, but have pleasure in them that do them."

Paul asks, us to think can a person criticize and judge others when they are doing the same? If a person is doing the same thing then God's judgment will come on you too. Do you think God will judge others for a sin, a person could think they are getting away with a sin thinking God will overlook their sin? We need to respect God's patience and longsuffering? We need to respect God's goodness and know He is patient with all of us? It is because of God's goodness and patience, God is able bring people to repentance and turn them from their sin.

In **Romans 2:1** Paul says,

V-1 *"Therefore you have no excuse, whoever you are, when you judge others; for in passing judgment on another you condemn yourself, because you, the judge, are doing the very same things."*

In the traditional view of judgment, God "will repay according to each one's deeds: to those who by doing good seek for glory and honor, and immortality, he will give eternal life" (**Romans 2:6-7**). If we take this out of context, it suggests that people can be saved on the basis of good works. Paul will soon argue, no one is good enough to earn eternal life through their works. This verse is part of the view that Paul is *critiquing* — he is not endorsing it.

Romans Chapter 2 God is Just in His Judgements
Romans 2:1-29   (18)

V-1 "Therefore thou art inexcusable, O man, whosoever thou art that judgest: for wherein thou judgest another, thou condemnest thyself; for thou that judgest doest the same things.

V-2 But we are sure that the judgment of God is according to truth against them which commit such things.

V-3 And thinkest thou this, O man, that judgest them which do such things, and doest the same, that thou shalt escape the judgment of God?

V-4 Or despisest thou the riches of his goodness and forbearance and longsuffering; not knowing that the goodness of God leadeth thee to repentance?

V-5 But after thy hardness and impenitent heart treasurest up unto thyself wrath against the day of wrath and revelation of the righteous judgment of God;

God's Judgement

V-6 Who will render to every man according to his deeds:

Those who seek His glory

V-7 To them who by patient continuance in well doing seek for glory and honour and immortality, eternal life:

V-8 But unto them that are contentious, and do not obey the truth, but obey unrighteousness, indignation and wrath,

V-9 Tribulation and anguish, upon every soul of man that doeth evil, of the Jew first, and also of the Gentile;

V-10 But glory, honour, and peace, to every man that worketh good, to the Jew first, and also to the Gentile:

V-11 For there is no respect of persons with God.

Sin according to the law, judged by the law demands a penalty

V-12 For as many as have sinned without law shall also perish without law: and as many as have sinned in the law shall be judged by the law;

V-13 (For not the hearers of the law *are* just before God, but the doers of the law shall be justified.

V-14 For when the Gentiles, which have not the law, do by nature the things contained in the law, these, having not the law, are a law unto themselves:

V-15 Which shew the work of the law written in their hearts, their conscience also bearing witness, and *their* thoughts the mean while accusing or else excusing one another;)

V-16 In the day when God shall judge the secrets of men by Jesus Christ according to my gospel.

V-17 Behold, thou art called a Jew, and restest in the law, and makest thy boast of God, V-18 And knowest *his* will, and approvest the things that are more excellent, being instructed out of the law;

Guided by the light of Christ = Verse 19-24

V-19 And art confident that thou thyself art a guide of the blind, a light of them which are in darkness,

The Gentiles do live some have no use for God. The Gentiles by their conscience alone do better than some of the Jews who believed there was the God, but did not believe Christ as a savior.

V-20 An instructor of the foolish, a teacher of babes, which hast the form of knowledge and of the truth in the law.

V- 21 Thou therefore which teachest another, teachest thou not thyself? thou that preachest a man should not steal, dost thou steal?

V-22 Thou that sayest a man should not commit adultery, dost thou commit adultery? thou that abhorrest idols, dost thou commit sacrilege?

V-23 Thou that makest thy boast of the law, through breaking the law dishonourest thou God

V-24 For the name of God is blasphemed among the Gentiles through you, as it is written.

Men is forgiven because of their <u>faith</u> in Jesus

God did not want them being proud and looking down on other people. But that is what happened. The Jews had bad names for people who were Gentiles.

V-25 For circumcision verily profiteth, if thou keep the law: but if thou be a breaker of the law, thy circumcision is made uncircumcision.

V-26 Therefore if the uncircumcision keep the righteousness of the law, shall not his uncircumcision be counted for circumcision?

V-27 And shall not uncircumcision which is by nature, if it fulfil the law, judge thee, who by the letter and circumcision dost transgress the law?

V- 28 For he is not a Jew, which is one outwardly; neither *is that* circumcision, which is outward in the flesh:

V-29 But he *is* a Jew, which is one inwardly; and circumcision *is that* of the heart, in the spirit, *and* not in the letter; whose praise *is* not of men, but of God.

Questions

- What is your attitude toward sinners? Do you tend to condemn them? (verse 1)
- How well do I appreciate God's mercy toward me? (verse 4)
- Does my conscience ever defend me? (verse 15)
- Why is judgment a part of the gospel? (verse 16)

If sin dishonors God in (verse 23), what should our attitude be toward sin?

   1. <u>**Romans 2:6**</u> **Psalm 62:12; Prov. 24:12**
   2. <u>**Romans 2:24**</u> **Isaiah 52:5; Ezek. 36:20, 21**

Romans Chapter 3 God is faithful

What if some do not believe? Will their unbelief make them faithful to God without effect? Certainly not! Indeed, let God be true and every man a liar. As it is written: "*That You may be justified in Your words, and may overcome when You are judged.*"

Notice how many times Paul mentions "faith" in this section (**Romans 3:22, 26, 27, 28, 30**). God is the "*justifier of him that hath faith in Jesus*" (3:26). One can picture the Jewish reaction to this declaration. To them, justification came through being a Jew, the law-of-Moses,-not-through-Jesus-Christ.

Paul anticipates their objection. He asks, "*Do we then make the law of none effect through faith?*" His answer: "*God forbid: nay, we establish the law*" (3:31). That is through the preaching men are justified by faith in Jesus Christ, we are confirming the justification of law. The law of Moses directed men to Jesus Christ. Paul says to the churches of Galatia that "*the law is become a tutor to bring us unto Christ, that we might be justified by faith*" (**Galatians 3:24**).

Paul, himself a Jew, came to this realization. What was his reaction when he learned that man is justified by the grace of God, through faith in Jesus Christ?

We who believe on Christ Jesus, that we might be justified by faith in Christ, and not by the works of the law, "because by the works of the law shall no flesh be justified."

God's righteousness is revealed in the law, the law was full filled by having faith in Jesus Christ for anyone who believes. There isn't any difference between any of us because all of us have sinned and fallen so far short of the glory of God. That's why we must accept His free gift, freely receive it that is the gift of God through faith which could only come through Jesus redeeming blood. God imputed His wrath on Jesus, this is what propitiation means. It involved His suffering, the shedding of His blood, His death and it

131

did satisfy God's judgement. That is why it can only be received by faith. This was how the righteousness of God was displayed in His great patience or forbearing of our sins.

It was just as death passed over the first born of the children in Israel for those who believed God, in Egypt. Now those who believe in Christ have had His deadly wrath pass over them. This passing over, made possible by Christ's work on Calvary, the passing over of our sins and the punishment we deserved. This is why Jesus is both the just and the justifier. (**2 Cor. 5:21**).

The is law given and only when a person <u>humbles</u> themselves, can grace be given, therefore no one could possibly boast about it:

Ephesians 2:8-10

V-8 "For by grace are ye saved through faith; and that not of yourselves: *it is* the gift of God:

V -9 Not of works, lest any man should boast.

V -10 For we are his workmanship, created in Christ Jesus unto good works, which God hath before ordained that we should walk in them."

That doesn't mean that the law is null and void but we live by the law because Jesus Himself said if you really love Me, you will keep or obey My commandments (**John 14:15**). Our love for Him and our faith in Him does mean we should obey Him.

If you want to share the gospel, you must understand Romans Chapter 3 is an important part of the Romans Road to Salvation:

Romans 3:9-12

V-9 "What then? are we better *than they*? No, in no wise: for we have before proved both Jews and Gentiles, that they are all under sin;

V-10 As it is written, There is none righteous, no, not one:

V-11 There is none that understandeth, there is none that seeketh after God.

V-12 They are all gone out of the way, they are together become unprofitable; there is none that doeth good, no, not one."

The law should take away any excuses, when a person finally humbles themselves, before God, tell them that they can only be saved by the free gift of God which is faith in Jesus Christ. There is no other way a person can be saved.

There isn't even one person who is righteous; no one does good all the time! There was no fear of God, much like the unsaved today, then the law exposes our standing before God. It is for this reason the whole world will be held accountable to God unless they accept Christ. Our works cannot justify us. The law's purpose is fulfilled in our lives in the sense that it shows us what sin was and how it was paid for. Paul wrote that *"it was our schoolmaster, bringing us about to the knowledge of sin."* (**Gal 3:24**).

1. **Romans 3:4 Psalm 51:4**
2. **Romans 3:12 Psalms 14:1-3; 53:1-3; Eccles. 7:20**
3. **Romans 3:13 Psalm 5:9**
4. **Romans 3:13 Psalm 140:3**
5. **Romans 3:14 Psalm 10:7**
6. **Romans 3:17 Isaiah 59:7, 8**
7. **Romans 3:18 Psalm 36:1**
8. **Romans 3:22** *through the faithfulness of God*
9. **Romans 3:25** The Greek for *sacrifice an atonement* refers to the atonement cover on the ark of the covenant (**Lev.16:15,16**).

Romans Chapter 4 faith leads to obedience

Romans 4:4 Paul writes:

V-4 "*But to him that worketh not, but believeth on him that justifieth the ungodly, his faith is counted for righteousness. Even as David also describeth the blessedness of the man, unto whom God imputeth righteousness without works, Saying, Blessed are they whose iniquities are forgiven, and whose sins are covered. Blessed is the man to whom the Lord will not-impute-sin.*"

Romans 4:5-8

The phrase "*him that worketh not*" is not describing the disobedient person, or the person who has an inactive faith! This teaching does not exclude all works, it excludes those who depend solely upon their own work; the self-reliant instead of those who trust and obey God. To him who does not rely on himself but on God, "*his faith is counted for righteousness.*"

Note: from here on when we speak of the faith that justifies, IT IS A FAITH THAT PROMPTS OBEDIENCE.

The case of David he was a man who turned to God and did what God said, for a benefit he could not acquire on his own: FORGIVENESS.

In the case of both Abraham and David, what was it that made them righteous before God? Did these men live perfect lives no, to put God in debt to them no? Neither were they made righteous by knowing the word of God, They believed and did the calling of God. This means they were justification by their faith, this is how the gospel works.

1. **Romans 4:8 Psalm 32:1,2**
2. **Romans 4:17 Gen. 17:5**
3. **Romans 4:18 Gen. 15:5**

Romans Chapter 5 The Righteousness of God

The gospel of Jesus Christ promises men the forgiveness of their sins, the certainty of a relationship with God that will last through all eternity. Once we have entered, flowing is our justification.

Romans 5:1-11 (KJV)

[1] Therefore being justified by faith, we have peace with God through our Lord Jesus Christ:

[2] By whom also we have access by faith into this grace wherein we stand, and rejoice in hope of the glory of God.

[3] And not only *so*, but we glory in tribulations also: knowing that tribulation worketh patience;

[4] And patience, experience; and experience, hope:

[5] And hope maketh not ashamed; because the love of God is shed abroad in our hearts by the Holy Ghost which is given unto us.

[6] For when we were yet without strength, in due time Christ died for the ungodly.

[7] For scarcely for a righteous man will one die: yet peradventure for a good man some would even dare to die.

[8] But God commendeth his love toward us, in that, while we were yet sinners, Christ died for us.

[9] Much more then, being now justified by his blood, we shall be saved from wrath through him.

[10] For if, when we were enemies, we were reconciled to God by the death of his Son, much more, being reconciled, we shall be saved by his life.

[11] And not only *so*, but we also joy in God through our Lord Jesus Christ, by whom we have now received the atonement.

What we are saying becomes most evident in a person's response to adversity over the long term. Proven character 5, in turn, produces "**hope**." Seeing that we can endure, and that a person's character has been strengthened in the process of facing life's trials.

As we see God's provisions for the present even in the most difficult circumstances, we become confident that God will surely sustain us to the end. He is the Author, and the Finisher of our faith **(Hebrews 12; James 1:2-4, 12; 1 Peter 4:12-19; 5:9-10; 2 Peter 1:3-11)**.

Although not emphasized here, Paul clearly is teaching that we can gain self-confidence by persevering in tribulation. Rather, we gain confidence in God as we stand amazed at His working in us it should be for every Christian. As our faith endures through tribulations, we become more and more hopeful of that which God will preform. Tribulation produces perseverance, proven character 4, and these produce hope.

As we reflect on God's act of love we are justified, our hope grows. For we see the "timing" of His love, Paul urges us to consider because of God's **"right time,"** when we were **"helpless"** and **"ungodly" (Romans 5:6)**. Christ loved us **"while we were sinners,"** while we were unworthy of His love. It is unlikely any one would be willing to die for a righteous man. Perhaps, one might be willing to die for a **"good"** man, our Lord died for the unrighteous. **"While we were *yet* sinners,"** Christ died for us in (verse 8). Now we begin to comprehend the love of God it was dramatically demonstrated in justification. His love shows up in the believer's heart. This same love assures us we have God's future promises will be fulfilled.

1. **Romans 5:1** Many manuscripts use *let us*
2. **Romans 5:2** *let us*
3. **Romans 5:3** *let us*
4. **Romans 5:4-24**

Romans chapter 6 God's Covenant with Abraham

Paul answered some of the questions people still ask about grace. Does everyone sin is everyone saved? Is everybody going to heaven? What about hell? You mean people do not have to do anything to be saved? Sure, people have to do something to be saved?

Paul declared the effects of faith had on men by using, Abraham as an example. Paul showed that Abraham believed what God had promised, God gave a promise to Abraham and his seed Abraham became what God intended him a son.

Paul repeated what God did in Christ, he did that for all men. All men died in Adam, all men who accept him are justified through Jesus. It is a natural consequence of grace that leads many of the questions listed above.

Paul answered his own question in **Romans 6:1** when he said "God forbid." Grace destroys the power of sin and fulfilled the law. Paul is explaining that God has given everyone an opportunity to be saved, he knew all needed to live above the law. He also knew that grace had nullified the law that a saved person was no longer under the law, but under grace. If the law was nullified, then there was no imputation of sin.

Paul apparently had difficulty explainning how anyone who had come to the knowledge of God would need to understand the need for faith in the grace of God, would man consider continuing to live in sin. To him, this would be a complete anomaly. Men who live by faith and God's grace do not live under the bondage to sin. If they do, it is because they continue to let sin control them.

In **Romans 6:3**, Paul was asking the equivalent question, "Are you ignorant?" Is it possible for a person who does not know, or does not understand God's grace.

What really happens when a person continues in sin? Paul's question carried a sense of action after all he had written and said about the grace of God, and the death of Jesus, people still did not understand he explained it once again.

God bestowed a portion of his spirit upon all flesh, that portion the spirit was *agape*, *love*, and the power to bring it forth in the lives of men.

How are men to acknowledge and be participants in the death of Jesus Christ? Water baptism is a symbol, showing the reality of his death burial and reassertion. Being put under water symbolizes our death together with Jesus. At the same time this goes back to when God acquitted man's redemption, allowing Jesus to take their place. God pronounced Jesus guilty for all and sentenced him to die. God also looked upon all man who were guilty of sin and pronounced man who believe to be righteous through the blood of Christ.

The words **was raised** comes from *egeiro*, meaning to arouse one from sleep. In this case, it means to arouse one from the sleep of death, or sin. Do not forget, Jesus had taken our sins upon himself and he was slain because of those sins. They were not his sins, but our sins. The result was the same sin means "death". All have sinned and fall short of God's righteousness. All died until Jesus Christ provided himself as a sacrifice for sin. Paul said in 6:7 "For he that is dead is freed from sin."

Those who teach that God died did not die for everyone evidently do not understand this scripture. Jesus was a man just as Adam was a man. Sin is a weakness through which death comes, in truth God did not die He eternal. He has no sin, therefore he has no weaknesses, no sin means no death.

Jesus was raised from the dead "*by the glory of the Father.*" The glory of God is manifested by his power. Nowhere is power more evident than when God exercised his power to resurrect Jesus Christ from the dead. This demonstrated the greatness, and the majesty of God.

Romans 6:4, "*even so we also should walk in newness of life,*" Paul drew a parallel between humanity and the resurrection of Jesus Christ. The words **even so**, *outos*, is a comparative equating two things. The equivalence indicated how Jesus was raised from among the dead.

This was the first time Paul used the words "*body of sin,*" in Romans 6:4 which are preceded by the definite article. This indicates that Paul was referring to the entire body of sin. This body of sin is the accumulated sin of all man. Paul had already shown that God dealt with all the sins of man, as a whole, in his judgment of righteousness, brought about by the faithfulness of Jesus Christ. These sins were symptoms of a greater problem, Paul detailed in the first five chapters of Romans is how God dealt with man. Now, Paul was identifying the ultimate source of sins, "*the body of sin.*"

The body **Romans 6:6**

V-6 "Knowing this, that our old man is crucified with *him*, that the body of sin might be destroyed, that henceforth we should not serve sin.,

The Adamic nature. All have experienced God in their own individual body, for this reason the individual bodies of men will be resurrected. Paul taught that the corporate body, as well as the individual body, will be resurrected either to eternal life or in Hell.

The word for **freed from a bondman Romans 6:7** comes from *dedikaiotai*, meaning to justify or render innocent. The indicative shows it is a fact. The passive shows that this is the result of what someone else has done, not something they did themselves. The process has come to a completion, the results continue into the present and future. God has justified through Christ on the cross.

Paul began his individual teaching with the word **"knowing."** **Romans 6:7** was an added thought from **Romans 6:6**. Each one is also to know they have been declared justified from the conglomerate mass of "sin." No person has to live under the bondage of sin any longer; they are **freed** from sinning if they live a pour life in Christ. Everyone has been separated from the power of sin and its domination.

1) If they show they are sorry for their sins,
2) When they asked God to forgive their sins,
3) When they accept Jesus as their personal savior.

Nothing could be further from the truth **Romans 6:7**. The gospel, is the good news that God forgave everyone's sins when Christ died. God does not have to be begged to do something he has already done. Neither can be coerced by anything men might do, the only thing man has to do is believe, accept Christ as their savor.

The word **believe**, *pisteuomen*, according to the grammar in this sentence, could also be translated as **"let us believe."** Because we have died together with Jesus, **Romans 6:8** *"let us believe that we shall also live with him."* Paul used the word believe to indicate that *"we will live together with Jesus"*, at the same time he lives. God has given us access to the Holy Spirit which is a complete life. We shall have when we are born again and then resurrected. We may, if we desire to participate in His Son (Jesus).

Romans 6:9 *"death hath no more dominion over him."* This is an interesting statement. Jesus Christ spent his time on earth knowing death was ruling over him. He was mortal in fact He would die. This was something he had in common with everyone, when he took upon himself **flesh**, *sarx*, with all its evil tendencies. Romans 6:14 again *"death hath no more dominion over you."*

The words **dominion over** comes from *kurieuei*, which comes from the same word as Lord. No longer can death hold its power over man through Jesus Christ. "He has conquered death hell and the grave": He put death in its place. He has pulled its sting. As Paul asked in **I Corinthians 14:55**,

"O death, where is thy sting? O grave, where is thy victory?"

Romans 6:11, Paul used the word **reckon**, *logizesthe*, meaning to take the strands of thought which he had been telling them, weave them together, and came up with the conclusion, *"to be dead indeed unto sin."* Although we are still in the flesh, we are no longer under the domination of sin, so we are dead to sin. The power and domination of sin through the fear of death is gone, or at least it should be.

Hebrews 2:14-15

"Forasmuch then as the children are partakers of flesh and blood, he also himself likewise took part of the same; that through death he might destroy him that had the power of death, that is, the devil; And deliver them who through fear of death were all their lifetime subject to bondage."

Also, the son is to be honored, only God is to be worshiped. The son is to be obeyed as Lord because of God's commands are those who believe, and are in complete compliance with the desires of God.

In verse 6:12, **"therefore"** points back to our death, then our resurrection, and then to life together with Christ. We have a new life now, we should believe it, thereby activating our good works. Faith always energizes action. Faith without works is dead (**James 2:20**). Because of all the things God has done for us in Jesus, Paul advised that we not let sin reign in our bodies.

We cannot say that God failed to give us the means to overcome sin in our lives. God did this for the conglomerate body of man, excluding no one. Others either ignore it, disbelieve it, therefore continue under the dominion of sin. All believers are under the grace of God, only believers can utilize the power God when we get victory in our life here on earth.

Romans 6:12 *"Let not sin – reign your body, that ye should obey it in the lusts thereof."* The "it" refers to the sin spoken of previously. No one has to be under the domination of sin unless they summit to it in their mortal body or unless they so desire. At least, they can hate what they do and confess it to God that it is a sin. Confessing means agreeing with God that it is sin. Failure to confess them is why so many people struggle with recurring sins in their lives.

I John 1:9

"If we confess our sins, he is faithful and just to forgive us our sins, and to cleanse us from all unrighteousness." John is speaking to the believer.

When we confess our sins, God is willing to forgive us, He is acting like our natural father, He not only forgives our sins, but also cleanses us. Confession becomes a stepping stone to cleansing. Agreeing with God about the reality of our sins is a necessary step to overcoming those sins, they will no longer have dominion over us. By failing to call sins by name we remain under their dominion.

The present tense shows this to be a continual action upon the part of the believer. Paul had already covered some of the individual sins which result from this attitude of yielding in the early chapters of Romans.

142

God, through the sacrifice of Jesus Christ, has broken the power of this body of sin by placing men under grace. God has destroyed the power of this body to sin, or as the scriptures say (**John 16:11**) *"the prince of this world is (has been) judged"*
"but yield yourselves unto God,"

Not only did Paul tell people to yield themselves to God, even their innermost self, but also their "members." By this he meant the various parts of the body. The members are to be yielded as instruments for God to use. God works out the righteousness in our lives. He will do the same with who yield their members unto Him.

Paul told people he **wanted them to "know" certain things, for the purpose of increasing their faith. In Romans 10:17**, he says, *"faith cometh by hearing, and hearing by the word of God."*

Paul said the reason we sin we need to yield to the lord who is over you because you *"are not under law."* Attempting to keep the law to gain salvation is futile. By doing so, one may think they are **"saved**," but they are not. However, salvation has already been accomplished in God who did this through Jesus Christ.

In **Ephesians 1:13**,

V-13 *"In whom ye also trusted, after that ye heard the word of truth, the gospel of your salvation: in whom also after that ye believed, ye were sealed with that holy Spirit of promise."*

If we do not acknowledge sin, we wind up serving sin in **Romans 6:16**. Confessing, or acknowledging, sin is very similar concept it has to do with our obedience to righteousness. When we acknowledge our sin, God does not judge that sin, but continues to forgive us. In other words, when we confess or acknowledge our sins, the Holy Spirit God for gives us and He will continue to keep us on track if we produce good works.

The rest of this chapter is devoted to the subject of yielding or not yielding, and the inevitable results of following our choices. Paul also showed the relationship of yielding and obedience, which is often taught out of context and leads many back into the bondage of the law.

Galatians 5:1, Paul said,

V-1 *"Stand fast therefore in the liberty wherewith Christ hath made us free, and be not entangled again with the yoke of bondage."*

Paul's message was simple: every person has a choice, whether to be a slave to sin or a slave to righteousness. Ironically, people become a slave to sin by simply never opting to serve righteousness. If we serve Him we will receive blessings. **Romans 8:28** says,

"And we know that all things work together for good to them that love God, to them who are the called according to his purpose."

Rome was a center of the worship of false gods the people were under the domination of sin when Paul first approached them. He referred to their former condition with the words **Romans 6:20** *"that ye were the servants of sin."*

Why did Paul refer to their condition in the past tense? What changed? They knew, yielded, and then obeyed something other than the body of sin which had once dominated their lives. They turned themselves over to God as *douloi*, slaves; a living sacrifice.

Because we have been set free, we are responsible to God. To present our bodies and members to God. He appealed to their good sense to choose correctly. They must choose not to continue to be free. Jesus taught the same thing in:

Matthew 6:33, when he said,

V-33 *"Seek ye first the kingdom of God, and his righteousness; and all these things shall be added unto you."*

Both **holiness** and **sanctification** come from the same word, *hagiasmon*. Why the translators were not consistent in their application remains a mystery. Translating it sometimes as **sanctification**, and other times as **holiness**, leads to a common misunderstanding that somehow there is a difference between the two terms when they are used, in fact, they are the same attribute one God the other term of man's relationship to God.

Romans 6:21, Paul was continuing his thought about the need for knowing, **reckoning**, and **yielding** our members into **subjection** and **obedience**. Here, he asked a rhetorical question: "*What fruit had ye then?*" In other words, what did you bring forth by your efforts before you presented, or yielded, yourselves to God?

"**Everlasting**," or "**Eternal**", life primarily conveys a sense of length of time. When we believe, or accept God's good news as truth, a different quality is added to our lives. This quality affects our lives both now and in the hereafter. The quality added to our lives is what makes us want to serve God. It removes the selfishness from our lives and replaces it with concern for others.

The wages of sin was paid by Christ's death to sin, separation He went into outer darkness. Ever Lasting Life is not earned, it comes as a free gift from God. What is the evidence of this gift? The pouring out of Holy Spirit upon all flesh. Every person, having been set free from the bondage of sin by the death of Christ, has also been endoud with the Holy Spirit according to Paul, which empowers a person to serve God. The Holy Spirit will empower a person who yields to Him, willing will receive God's blessings. That is what Paul meant by the term "eternal life."
Notice: Paul used the word "**eternal**" quite sparingly, only five times in Romans.

Paul wrote about what he wanted people to "**know**." Then, he asked people to "**reckon**" certain things to be true. In the light of these things they now know, and those things they reckon to be true, he urged, even commanded, them to yield themselves to God. Yielding to God is the only way in which God can work and mold a person's life into the likeness of Jesus Christ.

We are never our own masters. We are either servants of sin or servants of God, but never our own. Therefore, when God set us free from the body of sin, he enslaved us to himself.

1. **Romans 6:6** *be rendered powerless*
2. **Romans 6:23** *through*

Romans chapter 7 Wretched man
1. **Romans 7:5** In contexts like this, the Greek word for *flesh* (*sarx*) refers to the sinful state of man, often presented as a power in opposition to the Spirit.
2. **Romans 7:7 Exodus 20:17; Deut. 5:21**
3. **Romans 7:18** *my flesh*
4. **Romans 7:25** *in the flesh*

"**Wretched man**" means "**miserable man**." See the same word "**wretched**" in
Revelation 3:15-17
V-15 "I know thy works, that thou art neither cold nor hot: I would thou wert cold or hot.
V-16 So then because thou art lukewarm, and neither cold nor hot, I will spue thee out of my mouth.
V-17 Because thou sayest, I am rich, and increased with goods, and have need of nothing; and knowest not that thou art wretched, and miserable, and poor, and blind, and naked:"

Every believer needs to come to the place where they recognizes their own weakness. We need to see our needs, even as believers.

146

When man is a captive a slave to sin they let sin control them. A person should want to do what is right, when sin has control to the point they have no power over sin or know what is good they usually end up doing the things they hate!

"Who shall deliver me?" In this cry for a Deliverer, notice what a person says: WHAT SHALL I DO? or HOW SHALL I DELIVER MYSELF? This person has come to the end of them self. Dependence on SELF means they render themselves utterly powerless and helpless without hope.

Finally, a person cries out for deliverance, how can they do this outside of them self. The law cannot help because the law cannot make a person holy. The law cannot sanctify when things go wrong. This is when a person should cry out to the LORD GOD, not the law. The law is fulfilled IN US (as we shall see in **Rom. 8:4**) by the power of the Holy Spirit whose fruit is LOVE which is the fulfilling of the law (**Gal. 5:22**; **Rom. 13:8-10**).

"The body ends in a psychical death"
Romans 6:6 *"the body was born sin"*; **Romans 7:23** *"the law of sin is **in our members**"*. Our bodies are yet unredeemed (**Rom. 8:23**). The body is the headquarters for the sin nature and the members of the body are the instruments of sin (compare **Rom. 6:13**).

The Lord Jesus Christ is the great Deliverer (**Rom. 11:26** compare **2 Cor. 1:10**). The word **"thank"** means, Thank God! I believe that Jesus Christ is my Deliverer from sin. I believe that I am no longer a slave to sin's. I believe that I'm no longer a prisoner of sin, I'm a prisoner of Jesus Christ. My help does not come from within my SELF, because Christ is my SAVIOUR and hope! Victory comes through knowing and believing in a living God.

There are two great lessons for every person to learn.

"Now thanks be unto God, which always causeth us to triumph in Christ" (**2 Cor. 2:14**).

The **first** lesson pertains to salvation;

The **second** lesson pertains to living the Christian life:

Lesson #1 -- I CANNOT SAVE MYSELF (I need a Deliverer, One who can save me). See **Titus 3:5; Ephesians 2:8-9; Jeremiah 13:23**.

A person must come to that point in their life when they recognize that I am a sinner, I am hopeless and helpless (**Rom. 5:6** *"without strength"*). The Lord must do and the Holy Spirit indwells. A person needs to stop trying and start trusting God does the saving.

Lesson #2 –

I CANNOT LIVE THE CHRISTIAN LIFE WITHOUT CHRIST

(I need a Deliverer, One who can save and keep me from the power of sin.

I trusted Christ for my salvation now I am saved. I love Christ, and want to please Him, serve Him, do His will, and walk in His presents. At first things seem to be going very well, later I begin to have problems. I couldn't understand why this happened? At times it seemed I was losing more than winning. It seemed there are more failures than victories. **The Romans 7** helped me see my struggles were real. Finally, I come to the point where I realized "I CAN'T!" "I cannot live my life this way!" (**Romans7:18**)

I don't have what it takes to live the Christian life! I can't do it! This is exactly what God wanted me to discover! Just as I needed God for salvation, I need God for sanctification (to live and set my life apart and live a holy life). It's God's life now:

Galatians 2:20-21

V-20 "I am crucified with Christ: nevertheless I live; yet not I, but Christ liveth in me: and the life which I now live in the flesh I live by the faith of the Son of God, who loved me, and gave himself for me.

V-21 I do not frustrate the grace of God: for if righteousness *come* by the law, then Christ is dead in vain."

it's God's GRACE; it's God's WORKING it's God's power.

Philippians 3:9-12

V-9 "And be found in him, not having mine own righteousness, which is of the law, but that which is through the faith of Christ, the righteousness which is of God by faith:

V-10 That I may know him, and the power of his resurrection, and the fellowship of his sufferings, being made conformable unto his death;

V-11 If by any means I might attain unto the resurrection of the dead.

V-12 Not as though I had already attained, either were already perfect: but I follow after, if that I may apprehend that for which also I am apprehended of Christ Jesus."

According to **Romans Chapter 7**, Christians are not to leave **Romans Chapter 7** before they get into **Romans Chapter 8**, they need to understand as Christians we are not to stay in **Romans Chapter 7** throughout our Christian experience. These verses simply describe the conflict of the two natures in the child of God. Thus they would say **Romans 7:14-25** describes the normal,

Romans 7:14-25

V-14 "For we know that the law is spiritual: but I am carnal, sold under sin.

V-15 For that which I do I allow not: for what I would, that do I not; but what I hate, that do I.

V-16 If then I do that which I would not, I consent unto the law that *it is* good.

V-17 Now then it is no more I that do it, but sin that dwelleth in me.

V-18 For I know that in me (that is, in my flesh,) dwelleth no good thing: for to will is present with me; but *how* to perform that which is good I find not.

V-19 For the good that I would I do not: but the evil which I would not, that I do.

V-20 Now if I do that I would not, it is no more I that do it, but sin that dwelleth in me.

V-21 I find then a law, that, when I would do good, evil is present with me.

V-22 For I delight in the law of God after the inward man:

V-23 But I see another law in my members, warring against the law of my mind, and bringing me into captivity to the law of sin which is in my members.

V-24 O wretched man that I am! who shall deliver me from the body of this death?

V-25 I thank God through Jesus Christ our Lord. So then with the mind I myself serve the law of God; but with the flesh the law of sin."

God-intended for everyone to be saved and yelled their body's to him. "*There is no present deliverance from the carnal nature with out the power of the Holy Spirit*" it's God's VICTORY.

We must learn to accept the truth for it to change our lives. It is true that the believer will have a conflict between the two natures also the body. The sin nature will never be eradicated and uprooted.

150

There are certain things about this passage in **Romans Chapter 7** which is true in each believer. The more we mature in the faith the more we should be conscious of our own sinfulness (**Romans 7:24**). The more we grow in the Lord the more we will know of our own sinful nature. We need to perform that which is good in the site of God. *"Without Christ we can do nothing"* (**John 15:5**), this is true. Thus we agree with the Word of God we should always remember knowing our sinfulness, helplessness and our need for Deliverance who is Christ Jesus.

On the other hand, we must disagree for the following reasons. **Romans Chapter 7** describes a person who is contrary to God's will (**Rom. 7:19**). This may become the common experience for some Christians. This would run contrary to all of the Scriptures which teach that the believer is responsible not only to the will of God, but also to do it (**Phil. 2:13; James 1:22**).

Christian's intends to live for God. If we let Satan in we will have failures, defeat, and be frustrated if he controls a person's life. It is not God's desire that we fail to do good we need to desire God's presence we should not let evil have any control of any part of our life. **Romans Chapter 7** brings us to the point where we cry out, "I CAN'T", **Romans Chapter 8** gives the answer, "GOD CAN!"

Romans 7:24 (*"who shall deliver us"*) indicates that there is a present "deliverance" from the carnal nature by the power of the Holy Spirit. Christians will not be delivered *"from this body of death"* until the future coming of Christ. This teaching shows us no present deliverance from the power of sin certainly runs contrary to many passages of Scripture. Indeed, Paul himself in verses later writes, *"For the law of the Spirit of life in Christ Jesus hath made me free (past tense!) From the law of sin and death"* (**Rom. 8:2**). That such a deliverance is now, Paul says it has already been accomplished! Believers need to claim it by faith!

It is true that our final redemption of the body is yet in the future (as we will see in **Rom. 8:23**). That we live in unredeemed bodies that are subject to sin and death. We need to make a distinction between deliverance from the PENALTY OF SIN (God has delivered us from penalty of sin), from the POWER OF SIN (God is delivering us from sin by faith in the finished work of Christ (**Romans Chapter 6**) deliverance from the very PRESENCE OF SIN (God shall do this when we've brought our bodies under subject to Christ).

The God-intended for Christian's to live their life free from the evil in this world and failing to do the good in (**Romans 7:19**). God-intended Christian to live life free from captivity and the bondage of sin (**Rom. 7:23**). Christ came to set us free (**John 8:31-36**)! It is not God's desire that we should live in defeat and failure, frustration without end. No, God-intended Christians in: **Colossians 1:10-12; 1 John 3:18, 22; Ephesians 4:1-3; Philippians 4:1-9; 1 Corinthians 15:10; Galatians 2:20; 5:22-23**.

As we go through **Romans Chapters 7 and 8**. We need to understand **Romans Chapters 1 thou 6** because it deals with the sin question. There is a lot of support **information after Romans Chapter 7** and between **Romans Chapter 8.** I think it's important to understand **Romans Chapter 7** as Paul explains the law. It is odd we just used **Matthew 22:23-33,** what Christ said about divorce. **Rom 7:1-13** In **Romans 7:1** introduces the law & (**Romans 7:2-3**) law of divorce.

V-4 *we* "become dead to the law by the body of Christ;
    that ye should be married to another,
    even to him who is raised from the dead.
    that we should bring forth fruit unto God."

V-5a "in the flesh, the motion of sins,
    which were by the law,
V-5b did work in our members to bring"
    forth – (*what the law meant*)
    "forth fruit unto death".
V-6a "But now we are delivered from the law
    that being dead
    wherein we were held;
V-6b that we should serve in newness of spirit,
    and not *in* the oldness of the letter.
V-7a "delivered from the law,"
V-7b that being dead wherein we were held;
    that we should serve in newness of spirit,
    and not *in* the oldness of the letter."
V-8a "What shall we say then? Is the law sin?"
    If it had not been for the law, Paul says I would not have
        "known lust, "known sin" & (*the law had said,*)
        Thou shalt not covet."
V-8b "For without the law sin *was* dead."
V-9-11 *I can't say it any better,*
V-9a "For I was alive without the law once:"
    (*look and see what Paul is saying* V 9b)
V-9b "but when the commandment came, sin revived,
    and I died."
V-10 "And the commandment, which *was ordained* to life,
    I found *to be* unto death."
    The law (commandment) brought death.

V-11 "For sin, taking occasion by the commandment, deceived me
and by it slew *me.*"

We are going to talk about the good/bad/(sin) in the law and man in verses 12-13.

V-12 "Wherefore the law is holy,

and the commandment holy

and just, and good."

V-13 "Was then that which is good

made death unto me?

God forbid.

But sin, that it might appear sin,

Working death in me

By that which is good;

That sin by the commandment

Might become exceeding sinful."

Rom. 7:14-25 describes the nature and intent of the law and the relationship of sin.

V-14 "For we know that the law is spiritual: but I am carnal, sold under sin.

John – *(we are born into sin)*

V-15a *is the key verse says,*

V-15b "For that which I do I allow not:

for what I would, that I do not;

but what I hate, that do I."

Paul makes reference to hating the Christians before he was saved. Now that he is a Christian,

now he loves the Christians. He is still a Jew at heart and loves the Jews.

V-16a *He gives another comparison*

he lived by the Old Testament law as a Jew.

V 16b "If then I do that which I would not,

I consent unto the law that it is good."

154

So now he brings up the sin question and answers it in

V-17 "Now then it is no more I that do it,

> but sin that dwelleth in me.

V-18a *he describes the flesh,*

V-18b "For I know that in me

> (*that is, in my flesh,*)
>
> dwelleth no good thing;
>
> but *how* to perform that
>
> which is good I find not."

V-19 "For the good that I do not:

> but the evil which I would not,
>
> that I do."

V-20a *he goes through the whole analogy again.*

V 20b "but sin that dwelleth in me."

V 21   "I find then a law, that,

> when I would do good,
>
> evil is present with me."

It is hard not to have bad feeling about people that persecute us and do evil things, even to the point of abuse.

V-22a *says it very well*

V-22b "For I delight in the law of God after the inward man:"

V-23   "But I see another law in my members,

> warring against the law of my mind,
>
> and bringing me into captivity to the law of sin which is in
>
> my members."

 V-24 "O wretched man that I am!

> who shall deliver me from the body of this death?"

V-25 "I thank God through Jesus Christ our Lord.

> So then with the mind I myself serve the law of God;
>
> but with the flesh the law of sin."

The law reminds us daily as to who we are in the flesh.

I find 9 laws in (verses 14-25):
1. The law of the Spiritual & Carnality (14 – 15).
2. The Old Testament Law is good (16 & 17).
3. The law of the flesh (18 - 20).
4. The law of good and evil (21).
5. The law of God, after the inward man (22).
6. The law in my members (23a).
7. The law of my mind (23b).
8. The mind I myself serve the law of God (25a).
9. The law of the flesh and sin (25b).

*After reading **Romans chapter 7** we know of the conflict of man is to do "good & deal with the bad" but we still don't have a clear-cut definition Sin.*

Rom. 14:22, 23, we deal with **faith!**

V 22 "Hast thou faith?

     have *it* to thyself before God.

     Happy *is* he that condemneth not himself

     in that which he alloweth.

V-23 "And he that doubteth is damned if he eat,

     because *he eateth* not of faith:

     for **whatsoever *is* not of faith is sin**."

If you believe it to be wrong, you can be sure it is a sin. If disbelief or lake of faith, so the opposite must be true. Even if you are not confident is this disobedience by the law of God? The heart/mind/conscious are governed by God's grace or the law of the society.

Let me pose another question? *Who is God and what does He think of sin*? That He would be *mindful of man*? There are two ways to take care of the sin question confess it and forgive.

Ps. 103:1-22, is the second part **forget your trespasses and sin/sins**, God does.

V-11 "For as the heaven is high above the earth,

   so great is his mercy toward them that fear him."

V-12 "As far as the east is from the west,

   so far hath he removed our transgressions from us."

I like the next verse 13, God takes pity on the children that fear him.

V-17 "But the mercy of the Lord *is* from everlasting to everlasting upon them that fear Him, And his rightousness unto children's children;

V-18 "To such as keep his covenant, and to those that remember his commandments - (*laws*) to do them."

Romans chapter 8 is one of the great chapters in Romans
Romans 8:28

V-28 "And we know that all things work together for good to them that love God, to them who are the called according to *his* purpose."

Key is love, God (Christians) who are called with a purpose. (Unbelievers cannot clam this scripture).

I don't care how bad you've been or how bad you think your sins are they are not too bad for God to forgive. The big problem is forgiving yourself then others. This study in **Romans** is about helping us understand how to deal sin, the sins before salvation and after we become a Christian. In The Old Testament David wrote most of his Psalms with a broken heart over two grievous sins murder & adultery.

Romans Chapter 8 gives us what it is like after salvation if we take advantage of living for God.

The breakdown of **Romans 8**.

1. <u>**Romans 8:2**</u> The Greek is singular; some manuscripts *me*
2. <u>**Romans 8:3**</u> In contexts like this, the Greek word for *flesh* (*sarx*) refers to the sinful state of human beings, often presented as a power in opposition to the Spirit; also in verses 4-1
3. <u>**Romans 8:3**</u> *flesh, for sin*
4. <u>**Romans 8:10**</u> *you, your body is dead because of sin, yet your spirit is alive*
5. <u>**Romans 8:11**</u> Some manuscripts *bodies through*
6. <u>**Romans 8:15**</u> The Greek word for *adoption to sonship* is a term referring to the full legal standing of an adopted male heir in Roman culture; verse 23.
7. <u>**Romans 8:15**</u> Aramaic for *father*
8. <u>**Romans 8:21**</u> *subjected it in hope.*
9. <u>**Romans 8:28**</u> *that all things work together for good to those who love God, who*; or *that in all things God works together with those who love him to bring about what is good—with those who*
10. <u>**Romans 8:36 Psalm 44:22**</u>
11. <u>**Romans 8:38**</u> *nor heavenly rulers*

Romans **chapter 8** is one of the greatest chapters in the Bible. It is jammed with wonderful teachings the key hinges on our faith. I believe this **chapter 8** gives us some of the most important teachings we can make in developing an enduring Faith. One that will carry us and sustain us through our trials and tribulations.

God wants each of us to walk in the freedom provided us in salvation through Jesus Christ. In **chapter 8** we learn that there is NO Condemnation in Jesus Christ, if our thinking and actions are in line with the Word. We are justified in our lives by what Jesus has done for us. We are instructed to live by the Spirit. He also explains what it means to be a child of God which can lead us into understanding of who are the "**Sons of God!**"

Paul also explains that we have been set free by the Holy Spirit. Set free of what? We will see how the Lord has given us all the tools to be set free as we learn from God's Word. Some of society's problems are emotional and mental problems. Many conditions like Anxiety disorder, many forms of Depression and all sorts of Bondage that a person can suffer from can be validated and cured through the power of prayer, the Word and the Holy Spirit.

Bondage like fear, anger, guilt, shame and resentments can all be handled by the way we worship God. Alcoholism, drugs, and addictions can be conquered by the proper application support groups, prayer and God's word.

One of the responsibilities of the Christian is to walk and the need to constantly keep their mind on Christ. If one loses sight of these truths given to us, Christ died for our sins, we are justified by His blood, we have the fellowship with God the Father and His Son Jesus Christ. He has prepared us a home in heaven. We need to resist sin and temptation, by keeping the light of Christ shining in our lives and heart. All of us deal with temptations and lusts. In order to remain secure and to keep fighting the good fight of faith. We must constantly encourage one another. Remember the greater gift is Christ and the glory for us in heaven.

To that end **Romans 8** is perhaps the greatest encouragement let us now examine our lives and gain the encouragement.

Romans 8 is a discussion of the contrasts between those who live by the flesh and those who live by the Spirit. Those who live by the Spirit are after the things of the Spirit, having put away the desires of the flesh the death contained therein, and live anew in Christ. Those who live according to the flesh, however, do not live for God, in fact against God, they live in constant friction and are at enmity against God their end is only condemnation. Those who live by the Spirit have the Spirit within them and will live for God.

Paul continues with his discussion of the glory of Heaven that is to come and the momentary suffering that we live in now.

Romans 8:17-19

V-17 "And if children, then heirs; heirs of God, and joint-heirs with Christ; if so be that we suffer with *him*, that we may be also glorified together.

V-18 For I reckon that the sufferings of this present time *are* not worthy *to be compared* with the glory which shall be revealed in us.

V-19 For the earnest expectation of the creature waiteth for the manifestation of the sons of God."

In these verses we find ourselves worn down by constant temptation and suffering, for no matter how hard it may be, it will not compare to the glory that awaits. Let's look at the glory of a woman her child has caused her to forget the pain she suffered. So shall we forget our sufferings, when we reach Heaven, we will account them as nothing compared to the glory of Heaven.

Romans 8:20-25

V-20 "For the creature was made subject to vanity, not willingly, but by reason of him who hath subjected *the same* in hope,

V-21 Because the creature itself also shall be delivered from the bondage of corruption into the glorious liberty of the children of God.

V-22 For we know that the whole creation groaneth and travaileth in pain together until now.

V-23 And not only *they*, but ourselves also, which have the firstfruits of the Spirit, even we ourselves groan within ourselves, waiting for the adoption, *to wit*, the redemption of our body.

V-24 For we are saved by hope: but hope that is seen is not hope: for what a man seeth, why doth he yet hope for?

V-25 But if we hope for that we see not, *then* do we with patience wait for *it*."

2 Peter 3:8-18   (19)

V-8 "But, beloved, be not ignorant of this one thing, that one day *is* with the Lord as a thousand years, and a thousand years as one day.

V-9 The Lord is not slack concerning his promise, as some men count slackness; but is longsuffering to us-ward, not willing that any should perish, but that all should come to repentance.

V-10 But the day of the Lord will come as a thief in the night; in the which the heavens shall pass away with a great noise, and the elements shall melt with fervent heat, the earth also and the works that are therein shall be burned up.

V-11 *Seeing* then *that* all these things shall be dissolved, what manner *of persons* ought ye to be in *all* holy conversation and godliness,

V-12 Looking for and hasting unto the coming of the day of God, wherein the heavens being on fire shall be dissolved, and the elements shall melt with fervent heat?

V-13 Nevertheless we, according to his promise, look for new heavens and a new earth, wherein dwelleth righteousness.

V-14 Wherefore, beloved, seeing that ye look for such things, be diligent that ye may be found of him in peace, without spot, and blameless.

V-15 And account *that* the longsuffering of our Lord *is* salvation; even as our beloved brother Paul also according to the wisdom given unto him hath written unto you;

V-16 As also in all *his* epistles, speaking in them of these things; in which are some things hard to be understood, which they that are unlearned and unstable wrest, as *they do* also the other scriptures, unto their own destruction.

V-17 Ye therefore, beloved, seeing ye know *these things* before, beware lest ye also, being led away with the error of the wicked, fall from your own stedfastness.

V-18 But grow in grace, and *in* the knowledge of our Lord and Saviour Jesus Christ. To him *be* glory both now and for ever. Amen."

The entire creation waits with fervent desire to be purged from the stain of sin and death which has marked and scarred the creation since the expulsion from the Garden. We as Christians, who are the *"first fruits of the Spirit,"* also groan for the same redemption from sin and death which we find in Christ Jesus and will come to pass on the last day:

Acts 17:31-34   (20)

V-31 "Because he hath appointed a day, in the which he will judge the world in righteousness by *that* man whom he hath ordained; *whereof* he hath given assurance unto all *men*, in that he hath raised him from the dead.

V-32 And when they heard of the resurrection of the dead, some mocked: and others said, We will hear thee again of this *matter*.

V-33 So Paul departed from among them.

V-34 Howbeit certain men clave unto him, and believed: among the which *was* Dionysius the Areopagite, and a woman named Damaris, and others with them."

We constantly hope in **Romans 8:24-25** hope for what is in **1 Corinthians 13** does for love and what **Hebrews 11:1** does for faith: provide the proper definition. Our hope is in our belief which we have not seen, but constantly desire to realize. This hope will only be fulfilled when we stand in the presence of Christ; at this moment our faith will be vindicated and love will triumph at last.

Romans 8:29-34

V-29 "For whom he did foreknow, he also did predestinate *to be* conformed to the image of his Son, that he might be the firstborn among many brethren.

V-30 Moreover whom he did predestinate, them he also called: and whom he called, them he also justified: and whom he justified, them he also glorified.

V-31 What shall we then say to these things? If God *be* for us, who *can be* against us?

V-32 He that spared not his own Son, but delivered him up for us all, how shall he not with him also freely give us all things?

V-34 Who shall lay any thing to the charge of God's elect? *It is* God that justifieth."

Paul's conclusions in verse 31. The fact that there is no condemnation for those who are in Christ Jesus, we are considered sons of God and co-heirs with Christ. Our present sufferings will reach the glorious presence God the Father and His Son Jesus Christ.

Can the sword separate us from Christ? Famine? There is no power that can break through the mighty hand of God, no amount of force can change the grace manifested in us through His sacrifice and resurrection. We overcome through Christ nothing can separate us from the love of Christ. We will conquer life,-death,-and-hell.

This wonderful security is in our salvation, therefore, cannot exist for the one who never obeys Christ or the one who ceases to obey Him. The lost sinner unless they accept Christ and turn to God. No temptation can separate you from the love of Christ; no immorality and ungodliness surrounding us has that power. You alone in your spirit make the decision to accept the love of Christ.

Hebrews 4:1-12   (21)

V-1 "Let us therefore fear, lest, a promise being left *us* of entering into his rest, any of you should seem to come short of it.

V-2 For unto us was the gospel preached, as well as unto them: but the word preached did not profit them, not being mixed with faith in them that heard *it*.

V-3 For we which have believed do enter into rest, as he said, As I have sworn in my wrath, if they shall enter into my rest: although the works were finished from the foundation of the world.

V-4 For he spake in a certain place of the seventh *day* on this wise, And God did rest the seventh day from all his works.

V-5 And in this *place* again, If they shall enter into my rest.

V-6 Seeing therefore it remaineth that some must enter therein, and they to whom it was first preached entered not in because of unbelief:

V-7 Again, he limiteth a certain day, saying in David, To day, after so long a time; as it is said, To day if ye will hear his voice, harden not your hearts.

V-8 For if Jesus had given them rest, then would he not afterward have spoken of another day.

V-9 There remaineth therefore a rest to the people of God.

V-10 For he that is entered into his rest, he also hath ceased from his own works, as God *did* from his.

V-11 Let us labour therefore to enter into that rest, lest any man fall after the same example of unbelief.

V-12 For the word of God *is* quick, and powerful, and sharper than any twoedged sword, piercing even to the dividing asunder of soul and spirit, and of the joints and marrow, and *is* a discerner of the thoughts and intents of the heart.

Chapter 6

GOD'S PROMES IN ROMANS CHAPTERS 9-16

Romans chapter 9 God's Faithfulness
1. **Romans 9:3** *relatives*
2. **Romans 9:7 Genesis 21:12**
3. **Romans 9:9 Genesis 18:10, 14**
4. **Romans 9:12 Genesis 25:23**
5. **Romans 9:13 Malachi 1:2, 3**
6. **Romans 9:15 Exodus 33:19**
7. **Romans 9:17 Exodus 9:16**
8. **Romans 9:25 Hosea 2:23**
9. **Romans 9:26 Hosea 1:10**
10. **Romans 9:27 Isaiah 10:22, 23**
11. **Romans 9:28** Text reads *For the Lord will finish the work and cut it short upon the earth.*
12. **Romans 9:29** Literally, in Hebrew, *Hosts*
13. **Romans 9:29 Isaiah 1:9**
14. **Romans 9:31** Text omits *of righteousness.*
15. **Romans 9:32** Text reads *by works.*
16. **Romans 9:33 Isaiah 8:14; 28:16**

The interpretation of **Romans Chapter 9** assumes that Paul is concerned with the individual's salvation in this chapter. In fact, this is not the issue Paul is addressing it is whether it's "*the word of God had failed*" (**Rom 9:6**). That is, had God's promise to be the God of the Jews and to have them as his covenant people been rescinded?

The question was a burning one for Paul, for to many Jews this shocking conclusion seemed to follow what Paul was preaching. Most Jews of the day understood God's covenant was going to be set aside because the Jews crucified Christ would God's faithfulness toward the Jews would depened on two things: their nationality and their obedience to the law.

If what Paul was preaching was true, if salvation was available to anyone, including the Gentiles, simply on the basis of their faith, then their obedience did the law count for anything:

Galatians 5:8-26   (22)

V-8 "This persuasion *cometh* not of him that calleth you.

V-9 A little leaven leaveneth the whole lump.

V-10 I have confidence in you through the Lord, that ye will be none otherwise minded: but he that troubleth you shall bear his judgment, whosoever he be.

V-11 And I, brethren, if I yet preach circumcision, why do I yet suffer persecution? then is the offence of the cross ceased.

V-12 I would they were even cut off which trouble you.

V-13 For, brethren, ye have been called unto liberty; only *use* not liberty for an occasion to the flesh, but by love serve one another.

V-14 For all the law is fulfilled in one word, *even* in this; Thou shalt love thy neighbour as thyself.

V-15 But if ye bite and devour one another, take heed that ye be not consumed one of another.

V-16 *This* I say then, Walk in the Spirit, and ye shall not fulfil the lust of the flesh.

V-17 For the flesh lusteth against the Spirit, and the Spirit against the flesh: and these are contrary the one to the other: so that ye cannot do the things that ye would.

V-18 But if ye be led of the Spirit, ye are not under the law.

V-19 Now the works of the flesh are manifest, which are *these*; Adultery, fornication, uncleanness, lasciviousness,

V-20 Idolatry, witchcraft, hatred, variance, emulations, wrath, strife, seditions, heresies,

V-21 Envyings, murders, drunkenness, revellings, and such like: of the which I tell you before, as I have also told *you* in time past, that they which do such things shall not inherit the kingdom of God.

V-22 But the fruit of the Spirit is love, joy, peace, longsuffering, gentleness, goodness, faith,

V-23 Meekness, temperance: against such there is no law.

V-24 And they that are Christ's have crucified the flesh with the affections and lusts.

V-25 If we live in the Spirit, let us also walk in the Spirit.

V-26 Let us not be desirous of vain glory, provoking one another, envying one another.

It seemed that the Jews identity and calling had been undermined. Because they strove for righteousness based on the external observation of the law (works) instead of faith, they were now being hardened as evidenced by the fact that so few believed in Jesus (**Rom 9:31, 32**). This meant if Paul's Gospel was true, the very ones whom God made the covenant promises to *were now being hardened!* Hence it looked like "*the word of God had failed.*"

This is the question Paul is addressing in **Romans Chapter 9** (as well as in **chapters 10** and **11**). It's a question of God's fidelity to Israel as a nation and the basis God makes them a covenant partner. *It has nothing whatsoever to do with how God giving gospel to individuals for their salvation.* We are misguided if we try to use this passage to answer this question.

In offering these examples, Paul was defending God's right to choose whoever wants to follow Him and by any means he chooses. Paul is arguing, it shouldn't be shocking to Jews if God chooses to enter into a covenant with Gentiles on the basis of their faith.

At the same time, it is important to remember that in using Isaac and Jacob to illustrate God's prerogative. His concern was to show God's sovereignty is related the nation of Israel.

Definition sovereignty   {12}

1. *1a* : superlative in quality
    b : of the most exalted kind : <u>supreme</u> *sovereign virtuec*
        : having generalized curative powers *a sovereign remedyd*
        : of an unqualified nature : <u>unmitigated</u> *sovereign contempte*
        : having undisputed ascendancy : <u>paramount</u>
2. *2a* : possessed of supreme power *a sovereign rulerb*
        : unlimited in extent : <u>absolutec</u> : enjoying autonomy
        : <u>independent</u> *sovereign states*
3.   : relating to, characteristic of, or befitting a supreme ruler
        : <u>royal</u> *a sovereign right*

Merriam Webster.com   3/25/2017

To underscore God's sovereignty, Paul emphasized how God brought about a chosen people, through Isaac and Jacob, whose mission was to serve God and the world by being a nation and priests for religious ceremonies, (**Isa 61:6**) a *"light to all the nations"* (**Isa 42:6; 49:6; 60:3**). They were to be the means by which all the nations of the world would be blessed by hearing about the one true God (**Gen 12:2-3; 18:18; 22:18; Isa 2:2-4; 55:5; 61:9-11; 66:19-20; Jer 3:17; Rom 4:12-18**). God chose the profits of Israel to prophecy of a coming a savior.

This is extremely significant. Paul explains everything he's been talking about throughout **Romans Chapter 9** *by appealing to the morally responsible choices of the Israelites and Gentiles.* The one thing God has always looked for in people is their faith.

The Jews did not "strive" to fellow God by faith, **(10:3)**. They rather chose to trust in their own works. The Gentiles, however, simply believed that God would justify them by faith.

This theme recurs throughout **Chapters 9** through **11**. Paul says, the Jews *"were broken off because of their unbelief..."* (**Romans 11:20**) they hardened their hearts (**Rom. 11:7, 25**) while the Gentiles sought God by faith, they have been "grafted in" (**Romans 11:23**).

We see that God's process of hardening some and having mercy on others is *not arbitrary*: God expresses *"severity toward those who have fallen* [the nation of Israel] His kindness toward us as [**believers**] provided we continue in his kindness" (**Romans 11:22**).

God has mercy on people who believe in Christ and hardens people *in response to* their belief or unbelief. God is willing both to harden and have mercy on those who believe, God cannot change.

If Gentiles become arrogant and cease walking by faith, they will be "cut off." If the Jews who are now hardened will not *"persist in their unbelief,"* God will *"graft them in again"* (**Rom. 11:22-23**).

To the Jews who trusted in their national identity and/or external obedience to the law, this hardening seemed arbitrary. Paul chides them by asking, *"Who indeed are you to argue with God?"* What is molded say to the one who molds it, *"Why have you made me like this?"* (**Rom. 9:20**). Paul makes it abundantly clear throughout **Romans Chapters 9-11**, the hardening was in fact not arbitrary. It was perfectly consistent with God's nature the criteria of faith in God has always been true. He gives mercy *in response to faith* and he hardens *in response to unbelief.* It's not the other way around. People who don't have faith in the true God *as a result of* God having mercy on them, and people who do not believe *as a result of* God hardening their heart even today.

Yet, the Jews who remained convinced that their national identity and/or good works were the basis of God giving mercy, it is the same today God arbitrarily hardens the heart and arbitrarily extending mercy to those who believe.

In **Jeremiah 18** the Lord showed Jeremiah a potter who was working on a vessel that didn't turn out right. The potter formed a different kind of pot out of it (**Jere 18:1-4**). In the same way, the Lord said, since he is the potter and Israel is the clay his plans for Israel to with their willingness to repent (**Jere. 18:4-11**). The Lord announces he's going to judge a nation, he is willing to change his mind if the nation repents. Conversely, whenever God announces that he's going to bless a nation, he will change his mind if that nation turns away from him. In other words, the point of the potter-clay analogy is not God's unilateral control, *God's willingness and right to change his mind in response to the changing their hearts.*

This passage fits perfectly with the point Paul is making in **Romans Chapter 9**. While some individual Jews had accepted Jesus as their savior, the nation as a whole has rejected Jesus, thus rejected God's purpose for them (**Luke 7:30**). God had previously blessed Israel, the Jews were finding themselves in the same position Pharaoh did against Israel. He had hardened his heart toward God, God responded by hardening him further in order to raise to raise up the Jews to rebel and leave Egypt. In (**Romans 9:17**) Paul is arguing, God was now hardening the Jews because of their unbelief. He was going to use their rebellion to show he had always hoped for their obedience: namely, bring the non-Jewish (**Romans 11:11-12**).

Romans chapter 10 the Old Testament supports the New Testament Romans 10:1-4

1. **Romans 10:5 Lev. 18:5**
2. **Romans 10:6 Deut. 30:12**
3. **Romans 10:7 Deut. 30:13**
4. **Romans 10:8 Deut. 30:14**
5. **Romans 10:11 Isaiah 28:16** (see Septuagint)
6. **Romans 10:13 Joel 2:32**
7. **Romans 10:15 Isaiah 52:7**
8. **Romans 10:16 Isaiah 53:1**
9. **Romans 10:18 Psalm 19:4**
10. **Romans 10:19 Deut. 32:21**
11. **Romans 10:20 Isaiah 65:1**
12. **Romans 10:21 Isaiah 65:2**

Again in **Romans Chapter 10**, Paul uses the Old Testament for support. (There are more quotes per verse in **chapters 9-11** than anywhere else in the New Testament.)

In **Romans 10:5**, he quotes **Leviticus 18:5**: *"For Moses writes about the righteousness that is by the law:*

"The one who does these things will live by them." The old covenant included faith, but it emphasized obedience. Since no one could do everything the law required, it could never be a means of righteousness. The new covenant, however, is based on Christ, so it succeeds where the old covenant could not.

"But the righteousness that is by faith says: Do not say in your heart, *"Who will ascend into heaven?"* (that is, to bring Christ down) or *"Who will descend into the abyss?"* (*that is, to bring Christ up from the dead*)" (**Romans 10:6-7**, quoting parts of **Deuteronomy 30:4, 12-13**).

In **Deuteronomy 30**, Moses told the Israelites that God did not choose them because they were righteous, they should have known God would reveal himself to sinners, including Gentiles. Moses told the Israelites the commandments are revealed. God's word Paul applied this principle to Christ and the gospel the word of God.

What does it say in **Romans Chapter 8**, then he quotes **Deuteronomy 30:14**: *"The word is near you, in your mouth and in your heart."* **Deuteronomy 30:14** goes on to say *"so you may obey it,"* but Paul does not quote that, for he is applying the principle to the gospel, not the law. He says instead, *"…that is, the word of faith that we preach."* The message about righteousness through faith is near you, it is not hard to find if you believe in faith.

Paul in contrast shows how accessible true righteousness is: *"If you confess with your mouth that Jesus is Lord and believe in your heart that God raised him from the dead, you will be saved"* (**Romans 10:9**). Paul is not giving a new formula for salvation requires spoken words showing how the words come from the *mouth* and *heart*. It is Christ (not the law) in a person's heart and mind.

"For with the heart one believes and thus has righteousness and with the mouth one confesses and thus he salvation" (**Romans 10:10**). Paul puts faith and confession as parallel ideas, not distinctly different, and he puts righteousness and salvation in equivalent terms. The law required obedience, the gospel requires acceptance.

"For the scripture says," Paul notes in **Romans 10:11**, *"Everyone who believes in him will not be put to shame."*

This is quoted from **Isaiah 28:16**, which says that God will lay a cornerstone in Zion for a sure foundation, and people who have faith in this cornerstone will not be found short on the day of judgment. Paul quoted in **Romans 9:33**; here he just repeats the part about believing in Christ as the key to salvation

Paul repeats the theme: *"For there is no distinction between the Jew and the Greek, for the same Lord is Lord of all, who richly blesses all who call on him. For everyone who calls on the name of the Lord will be saved"* (**Romans 10:12-13**, quoting **Joel 2:32**).

Salvation comes by calling on the Lord, looking to him for salvation. In Joel, the Lord was Yahweh, Paul uses Christ, showing that he accepted Jesus as God.

Salvation comes by accepting Jesus Christ as Lord. The problem is the Jews are rejecting the message. He highlights this in: **Romans 10:14**: *"How are they to call on one they have not believed in?"*

They have to call on the Lord to be saved, but if people think he is a crucified criminal instead of the savior, they won't call on him.

"And how are they to believe in one they have not heard of? And how are they to hear without someone preaching to them? And how are they to preach unless they are sent?" (**Romans 10:14-15**). Salvation comes in response to the preaching. But the problem can't be solved by sending more preachers, most of the Jews still haven't believed. There disbelief is a consequence for the Jews.

As it is written, *"How timely is the arrival of those who proclaim the good news"* (**Romans 10:15**). This is quoted from **Isaiah 52:7**, which uses the common New Testament verb for preaching the gospel. In Isaiah's day, the good news was the prophecy the people being restored to their land in 1948.

Paul says in verse 16: *"But not all have obeyed the good news, for* **Isaiah 53:1** *"Lord, who has believed our report?"* The people didn't accept the message then, it is an old problem, found throughout the history of Israel. Isaiah says that the message has to be believed, it's a matter of faith, one of Paul's favorite topics. Paul says in **Romans 10:17**: *"Consequently faith comes from what is heard, and what is heard comes through the preached word of*

174

Christ." Paul seems to be completing the evangelistic message in **Romans 10:15**. People need to hear the message before they can believe it.

However, it's not enough just to hear the words in **Romans 10:18**, Paul asks: "*But I ask, have they not heard? Yes, they have: Their voice has gone out to all the earth, and their words to the ends of the world.*" This is quoted from **Psalm 19:4**, which says "*the heavens declare the glory of God.*" If the whole world has heard the message, the Jews have also heard.

Paul writes in **Romans 10:19**, "*didn't Israel understand?*" First Moses says in advance that he would:

Deuteronomy 32:21, "*I will make you jealous by those who are not a nation; with a senseless nation I will provoke you to anger.*" Israel failed, God told them work with those believe. This verse revealed what God was doing in Paul's ministry: He wanted the salvation of Gentiles to make Israel jealous, so the Jews would then accept the gospel. That is what Paul worked so hard to achieve.

Isaiah is even bold enough to say, "*I was found by those who did not seek me; I became well known to those who did not ask for me*" (verse 20, quoting **Isaiah 65:1**). Isaiah is talking about wayward Israelites, Paul applies it here to Gentiles. If God can reveal himself to disinherited Jews, he can do it to anyone. God turned away from the zealous, he blesses people who didn't even know to ask.

Paul concludes the chapter by saying, But about Israel he says, "*All day long I held out my hands to this disobedient and stubborn people!*" (verse 21, quoting **Isaiah 65:2**). God did not want the Jewish people to go astray, but they would not listen. Israel had an opportunity for salvation, but most have refused it.

Romans Chapter 11

1. **Romans 11:3** **1 Kings 19:10,14**
2. **Romans 11:4** **1 Kings 19:18**
3. **Romans 11:8** **Deut. 29:4; Isaiah 29:10**
4. **Romans 11:10** **Psalm 69:22,23**
5. **Romans 11:26** *and so*
6. **Romans 11:27** *will be*
7. **Romans 11:27** **Isaiah 59:20, 21; 27:9; Jer. 31:33, 34**
8. **Romans 11:31** Some manuscripts do not have *now.*
9. **Romans 11:33** *riches and the wisdom and the*
10. **Romans 11:34** **Isaiah 40:13**
11. **Romans 11:35** **Job 41:11**

Romans Chapter 11 *"Only a remnant of Israel will be saved,"* Paul argues as he uses several Hebrew Bible texts to prove his point. He proves that God would call Jews and non-Jews on the basis of their conviction in Jesus Christ. Now this brings us to. We have learned how and why the Jews were abandoned as a nation, for their disbelief. The logical question to follow is raised by Paul,
"I ask, then, did The God reject His People?"

Romans 11:1

V-1 *"No, never! For I am an Israelite! From the seed of Abraham, the tribe of Benjamin! The God did not reject His People whom He knew first."*

Judging from what we have read, Paul must mean rejected absolutely as though no Jew could attain unto God's righteousness and salvation. He explains why this is not the case:

Romans 11:1-11   (23)

V-1 "I say then, Hath God cast away his people? God forbid. For I also am an Israelite, of the seed of Abraham, *of* the tribe of Benjamin.

V-2 God hath not cast away his people which he foreknew. Wot ye not what the scripture saith of Elias? how he maketh intercession to God against Israel, saying,

V-3 Lord, they have killed thy prophets, and digged down thine altars; and I am left alone, and they seek my life.

V-4 But what saith the answer of God unto him? I have reserved to myself seven thousand men, who have not bowed the knee to *the image of* Baal.

V-5 Even so then at this present time also there is a remnant according to the election of grace.

V-6 And if by grace, then *is it* no more of works: otherwise grace is no more grace. But if *it be* of works, then is it no more grace: otherwise work is no more work.

V-7 What then? Israel hath not obtained that which he seeketh for; but the election hath obtained it, and the rest were blinded

V-8 (According as it is written, God hath given them the spirit of slumber, eyes that they should not see, and ears that they should not hear;) unto this day.

V-9 And David saith, Let their table be made a snare, and a trap, and a stumblingblock, and a recompence unto them:

V-10 Let their eyes be darkened, that they may not see, and bow down their back alway.

V-11 I say then, Have they stumbled that they should fall? God forbid: but *rather* through their fall salvation *is come* unto the Gentiles, for to provoke them to jealousy.

V-12 Now if the fall of them *be* the riches of the world, and the diminishing of them the riches of the Gentiles; how much more their fulness?

Paul points to himself as an example God did not make a blanket rejection of the Jews. He then proceeds in **Romans 11"2-4** to draw a parallel with Elijah and the 7,000 from among the millions of

Israel who had served Baal. He then writes: **Romans 11:5** *"So, then, also, at the present time a remnant [of Israel] has come to be by [God's] choosing and unmerited favor."* This "**remnant**" composed of Jews, by believing in Jesus Christ, became a part of "**Israel**" composed of "**true Jews**."

Paul writes in **Galatians 3:29** and **Galatians 6:15** about "Israel" composed of Jews and Greeks. Peter also writes in like manner using language similar to Paul's: *"But you [non-Jews].*

1 Peter 2:9 *are 'a chosen race, a royal priesthood, a holy nation, a people for special possession, that you should declare abroad the excellencies' of the one that called you out of darkness into his wonderful light. For you [non-Jews] were once not a people, but are now God's people; you were those who had not been shown mercy, but are now those who have been shown mercy."*.

In **Matthew 22** replies Jesus again spoke to [the Jews] with illustrations, saying: *"The kingdom of heaven has become like a man, a king that made a marriage feast for his son Jesus."*

He sent forth his servants to invite people to the marriage feast, but they were unwilling to come. Again he sent forth other servants, saying, 'Tell those invited: *"Look! I have prepared my dinner, and all things are ready. Come to the marriage feast."* They gave excuses, one to his own field, another to his commercial business; asking his servants. Then he said to his servants, '*The marriage feast indeed is ready, invited the worthy. Therefore go to the roads leading out of the city, invited them to the marriage feast."* According to those servants in the room for the wedding ceremonies was filled with poor and needy coming to the wedding!

Matthew 22:1-33 (24)

V-1 "And Jesus answered and spake unto them again by parables, and said,

V-2 The kingdom of heaven is like unto a certain king, which made a marriage for his son,

V-3 And sent forth his servants to call them that were bidden to the wedding: and they would not come.

V-4 Again, he sent forth other servants, saying, Tell them which are bidden, Behold, I have prepared my dinner: my oxen and *my* fatlings *are* killed, and all things *are* ready: come unto the marriage.

V-5 But they made light of *it*, and went their ways, one to his farm, another to his merchandise:

V-6 And the remnant took his servants, and entreated *them* spitefully, and slew *them*.

V-7 But when the king heard *thereof*, he was wroth: and he sent forth his armies, and destroyed those murderers, and burned up their city.

V-8 Then saith he to his servants, The wedding is ready, but they which were bidden were not worthy.

V-9 Go ye therefore into the highways, and as many as ye shall find, bid to the marriage.

V-10 So those servants went out into the highways, and gathered together all as many as they found, both bad and good: and the wedding was furnished with guests.

V-11 And when the king came in to see the guests, he saw there a man which had not on a wedding garment:

V-12 And he saith unto him, Friend, how camest thou in hither not having a wedding garment? And he was speechless.

V-13 Then said the king to the servants, Bind him hand and foot, and take him away, and cast *him* into outer darkness; there shall be weeping and gnashing of teeth.

V-14 For many are called, but few *are* chosen.

V-15 Then went the Pharisees, and took counsel how they might entangle him in *his* talk.

V-16 And they sent out unto him their disciples with the Herodians, saying, Master, we know that thou art true, and teachest the way of God in truth, neither carest thou for any *man*: for thou regardest not the person of men.

V-17 Tell us therefore, What thinkest thou? Is it lawful to give tribute unto Caesar, or not?

V-18 But Jesus perceived their wickedness, and said, Why tempt ye me, *ye* hypocrites?

V-19 Shew me the tribute money. And they brought unto him a penny.

V-20 And he saith unto them, Whose *is* this image and superscription?

V-21 They say unto him, Caesar's. Then saith he unto them, Render therefore unto Caesar the things which are Caesar's; and unto God the things that are God's.

V-22 When they had heard *these words*, they marvelled, and left him, and went their way.

V-23 The same day came to him the Sadducees, which say that there is no resurrection, and asked him,

V-24 Saying, Master, Moses said, If a man die, having no children, his brother shall marry his wife, and raise up seed unto his brother.

Opinions vary on the meaning some see the future conversion of the Israel nation to Christ. It is clear the Saints *"will sit on thrones judging the twelve tribes of Israel"* on the Day of Judgment. **Matthew 19:28 (Luke 22:30).** Everyone will be judged on that Day. **Roman 2:12-16**; compare **Matthew 12:33-37, 39-42; Matthew 16:27 = Mark 8:38.**

Matthew 12:22-45   (25)

V-22 "Then was brought unto him one possessed with a devil, blind, and dumb: and he healed him, insomuch that the blind and dumb both spake and saw.

V-23 And all the people were amazed, and said, Is not this the son of David?

V-24 But when the Pharisees heard *it*, they said, This *fellow* doth not cast out devils, but by Beelzebub the prince of the devils.

V-25 And Jesus knew their thoughts, and said unto them, Every kingdom divided against itself is brought to desolation; and every city or house divided against itself shall not stand:

V-26 And if Satan cast out Satan, he is divided against himself; how shall then his kingdom stand?

V-27 And if I by Beelzebub cast out devils, by whom do your children cast *them* out? therefore they shall be your judges.

V-28 But if I cast out devils by the Spirit of God, then the kingdom of God is come unto you.

V-29 Or else how can one enter into a strong man's house, and spoil his goods, except he first bind the strong man? and then he will spoil his house.

V-30 He that is not with me is against me; and he that gathereth not with me scattereth abroad.

V-31 Wherefore I say unto you, All manner of sin and blasphemy shall be forgiven unto men: but the blasphemy *against* the *Holy* Ghost shall not be forgiven unto men.

V-32 And whosoever speaketh a word against the Son of man, it shall be forgiven him: but whosoever speaketh against the Holy Ghost, it shall not be forgiven him, neither in this world, neither in the *world* to come.

V-33 Either make the tree good, and his fruit good; or else make the tree corrupt, and his fruit corrupt: for the tree is known by *his* fruit.

V-34 O generation of vipers, how can ye, being evil, speak good things? for out of the abundance of the heart the mouth speaketh.

V-35 A good man out of the good treasure of the heart bringeth forth good things: and an evil man out of the evil treasure bringeth forth evil things.

V-36 But I say unto you, That every idle word that men shall speak, they shall give account thereof in the day of judgment.

V-37 For by thy words thou shalt be justified, and by thy words thou shalt be condemned.

V-38 Then certain of the scribes and of the Pharisees answered, saying, Master, we would see a sign from thee.

V-39 But he answered and said unto them, An evil and adulterous generation seeketh after a sign; and there shall no sign be given to it, but the sign of the prophet Jonas:

V-40 For as Jonas was three days and three nights in the whale's belly; so shall the Son of man be three days and three nights in the heart of the earth.

V-41 The men of Nineveh shall rise in judgment with this generation, and shall condemn it: because they repented at the preaching of Jonas; and, behold, a greater than Jonas *is* here.

V-42 The queen of the south shall rise up in the judgment with this generation, and shall condemn it: for she came from the uttermost parts of the earth to hear the wisdom of Solomon; and, behold, a greater than Solomon *is* here.

V-43 When the unclean spirit is gone out of a man, he walketh through dry places, seeking rest, and findeth none.

V-44 Then he saith, I will return into my house from whence I came out; and when he is come, he findeth *it* empty, swept, and garnished.

V-45 Then goeth he, and taketh with himself seven other spirits more wicked than himself, and they enter in and dwell there: and the last *state* of that man is worse than the first. Even so shall it be also unto this wicked generation."

After Judgment Day the compliment of righteous will be a force for good on the New Earth. **2 Peter 3:13** and **Isaiah 65:17**. The Thousand Year reign of the Messiah. **Isaiah 65:17-24; 66:22, 23**.

This "fullness" is further explained by Paul to involve the resurrection of the Jews from the dead:

Romans 11:13-32   (26)

V-13 "For I speak to you Gentiles, inasmuch as I am the apostle of the Gentiles, I magnify mine office:

V-14 If by any means I may provoke to emulation *them which are* my flesh, and might save some of them.

V-15 For if the casting away of them *be* the reconciling of the world, what *shall* the receiving *of them be*, but life from the dead?

V-16 For if the firstfruit *be* holy, the lump *is* also *holy*: and if the root *be* holy, so *are* the branches.

V-17 And if some of the branches be broken off, and thou, being a wild olive tree, wert graffed in among them, and with them partakest of the root and fatness of the olive tree;

V-18 Boast not against the branches. But if thou boast, thou bearest not the root, but the root thee.

V-19 Thou wilt say then, The branches were broken off, that I might be graffed in.

V-20 Well; because of unbelief they were broken off, and thou standest by faith. Be not highminded, but fear:

V-21 For if God spared not the natural branches, *take heed* lest he also spare not thee.

V-22 Behold therefore the goodness and severity of God: on them which fell, severity; but toward thee, goodness, if thou continue in *his* goodness: otherwise thou also shalt be cut off.

V-23 And they also, if they abide not still in unbelief, shall be graffed in: for God is able to graff them in again.

V-24 For if thou wert cut out of the olive tree which is wild by nature, and wert graffed contrary to nature into a good olive tree: how much more shall these, which be the natural *branches*, be graffed into their own olive tree?

V-25 For I would not, brethren, that ye should be ignorant of this mystery, lest ye should be wise in your own conceits; that blindness in part is happened to Israel, until the fulness of the Gentiles be come in.

V-26 And so all Israel shall be saved: as it is written, There shall come out of Sion the Deliverer, and shall turn away ungodliness from Jacob:

V-27 For this *is* my covenant unto them, when I shall take away their sins.

V-28 As concerning the gospel, *they are* enemies for your sakes: but as touching the election, *they are* beloved for the fathers' sakes.

V-29 For the gifts and calling of God *are* without repentance.

V-30 For as ye in times past have not believed God, yet have now obtained mercy through their unbelief:

V-31 Even so have these also now not believed, that through your mercy they also may obtain mercy.

V-32 For God hath concluded them all in unbelief, that he might have mercy upon all."

"However, I tell you in as much as I really am, then, an apostle to the Gentiles, I glorify my ministry if somehow I might provoke my own flesh to jealousy and might save some from among Israel for the casting away of Israel means reconciliation of the world. What will their reception mean if not life from the dead? Now, if the first fruits are the whole harvest; if the Root is holy, so also the branches."

Paul seems to make it clear that Israel as a whole was "*cast away*" but the entire body of all Israel would be raised from the dead and restored to God, or received by God. Over these "*tribes of Israel*" the Church of Christ will reign. So their "reception" or "restoration" would involve the resurrection. *"What will their reception mean if not life from the dead"* is also rendered: Jesus taught the Jews of his generation would be resurrected on Judgment Day, the example of Sodom, the Queen of Sheba, and citizens of Nineveh difficult to endure.

Matthew 11:24; Matthew 12:33-36, 41, Paul teaches a resurrection of both the righteous and unrighteous on the Day of Judgment. **Acts 17:31; Acts 24:15** this is likely the "*reception*" Paul has in mind, the resurrection of the righteous among all who have ever lived and those who live during Messiah's reign here on earth. **Revelation 20:12-14.** Not all Hebrews or Jews will gain everlasting life **Matthew 23:33**.

In **Romans 11:25-32** (27)

Paul writes you, brothers that you be not ignorant of this mystery, so that you do not become wise in your own eyes. Israel will be saved, just as it has been written, *"A Deliverer will come from Zion. He will cast out any irreverence from Jacob. And this is my covenant to them when I take away their sins."* **Isaiah 59:20, 21** regarding the Gospel of Christ are enemies to your benefit, regarding the choosing of

Israel beloved because of their forefathers. God will not change His mind regarding the gift of His Son. Now you have received mercy because of His obedience of God's mercy, that now they may also receive mercy. For The God has shut them out all together because of their disobedience, so that He may show mercy to all that believe in His Son.

God who has purposed from the beginning His "*riches*" **Romans 2:4** and **Romans 9:23. (Psalm 139:6) On "wisdom" see 1 Corinthians 1:22, 30; 2:7; see notes on Ep. 1:8, Ep.1:17, Ep. 3:10.** On "knowledge" see **2 Corinthians 4:6; 10:5; Colossians 2:2, 3.** *"Unsearchable are His judgments."* The word "*judgment*" is right at the center of Paul's theme throughout Romans. See **Romans 2:2, 3, 5,16; Romans 3:3:4, 6, 7, 8; Romans 3:8; Romans 5:16; Romans 13:2; Romans 14:10. (Psalm 36:6),**

Paul quotes **Isaiah 40:13**, *"Who ever knew the LORD'S mind?"* The Greek for "mind" is a noun in this quote of **Isaiah 40:13** which draws on the Greek *Septuagint*.

For the Hebrew Text uses RHUACH, also rendered "spirit." Paul does the same at **1 Corinthians 2:16**. This proves that the "spirit of God" is the "mind of God." In Hebrew, and likely in the oldest Greek copies of the *Septuagint*, the Tetragram of YHWH occurs in **Isaiah 40:13**. Speaking of Yehowah, Paul affirms, *"Everything originated from Him and because of Him."* all things we find it originates from God Yehowah, the center of their being. This includes His Son who originated from his Father. (**Proverbs 8:22; John 1:18; 1 Corinthians 8:6**)

Romans Chapter 12
1. **Romans 12:6** *the*
2. **Romans 12:8** *to provide for others*
3. **Romans 12:16** *willing to do menial work*
4. **Romans 12:19** **Deut. 32:35**
5. **Romans 12:20** **Prov. 25:21, 22**

In the first eleven chapters we have studied the doctrines and the *"mystery"* concerning the three earth ages, the relationship between God and His children. We studied the plan of God concerning the free will. It may seem difficult, the Word, God will reveal to each the depth of understand that it is intended for them to understand, and to some He has a choice to believe or stay in his unbelieve.

Romans 12:1-2

V-1 "I beseech you therefore, brethren, by the mercies of God, that ye present your bodies a living sacrifice, holy, acceptable unto God, *which is* your reasonable service.

V-2 And be not conformed to this world: but be ye transformed by the renewing of your mind, that ye may prove what *is* that good, and acceptable, and perfect, will of God."

We have Paul's teaching on doctrine and the men of the Old Testament, and now we enter into the study of practical living for man. In verses one and two Paul presents his instruction in regards to God, and then from the third verse, continuing through **Romans 15:7.** Paul is giving us the guidelines for practical living that we ought to apply to our own lives, as part of the body of Christ. Now in **Romans 12** we have Paul's teaching of the ages, and now we enter into the study of practical living for man. In verses one and two Paul presented this instruction with regards to God, and then from the third verse, and continuing through **Romans 15:7** Paul is giving us the guidelines for practical living that we ought to apply to our own lives, as part of the body of Christ.

Paul is saying, I appeal to you fellow Christians, by all the mercies that God has extended to each of us in His grace; that we commit our lives to God as a living sacrifice. A dead sacrifice as far as this earth is concerned, how about that a *"living sacrifice"* is how we live our lives each day of our lives. It is shown in the words we say the kindness that we show one another. Those words and acts become our living sacrifice unto the Lord. To be holy and acceptable unto God can only come by our individual study of His Word, knowing exactly what is acceptable to Him. In the next three chapters Paul will instruct us as to what is holy and acceptable to Him in our reasonable service to Him.

The *"living sacrifice"* includes our testimony that is expect of us in our relationship to the Father. We accept those challenges by our own free will, we have accepted Jesus Christ then we come into the family of God. Paul is telling us that as a family member, the family expects each of us to represent the family, especially the Head of that family, our Heavenly Father. We are to set the example, where people see our lives by our conversation.

Romans 12:2 *"This world"* doesn't mean the ground that we walk on, but in the Greek word *"world"* is *"aion"*, the world society, the way the world does things. We are not to conform to the pattern, or fashion that is set by the world standards for our lives, because the one that sets those standards is the prince of peace, Christ.

We are not to conform to those things that the world considers a way of doing things, of bribery, stealing, lying, you can probably run the list as long as I can, but those things are of Satan. When you become a new creature in Christ, not only your soul and spirit become changed, but you are to transform by changing of our mind that is what is teaching. That means the way that you think says a lot

188

about what you are going to do, the standards you set for yourselves. Upon repentance of your sins and your belief in Jesus Christ, even your goals change. All those things are important. Now the things that are important to us are the things that are important to our heavenly Father.

When the *"transforming"* takes place within your mind and in your spirit, for God does the transforming there. It becomes your *"duty"* to change your mind, this is done by seeking the knowledge of God. You can only renew your mind when the knowledge of God's Word is your study guide, you fill your mind with help of the Holy Spirit.

Then you become a *"sacrifice"* for God, as a sacrifice, it is not for your pleasure that the sacrifice is made, let's get real, Christianity is not a religion, it is a reality in the way we live our lives. You can't help people if you are not filled with the Holy Spirit. The point we are making you just don't conform to what the world is doing, but transformed by the example by the renewing of you're mind.

You don't have to say a word, by your example you can be a wealth of information to those around you, as the struggles you're dealing with. It is while in their presence you plant the seeds of truth, the Holy Spirit can work and transform your thoughts and build your mind. If they think you are a nut and off your rocker, why would they ever listen to anything you have to say. Then your life can seen as credible, God will use you to plant the seed, when you give your life to Him.

God has given everyone certain gifts, the measure of those gifts are yours to give to God, depending on the faith you have in using those gifts. When we receive a gift to perform a certain task for the Lord, you are responsible for the way you develop and use that gift.

If God places that gift in you, you shouldn't take any credit for that gift from God, give Him all the glory that comes from those gift's use them to honor of our Lord and Savior.

The wise person takes these gifts and gives himself to the glory of God. When a person does what they are supposed to do with their gifts, souls are reached. That type of thinking God can use. We see it everywhere in many ministers, they elevate themselves to a point where the ministry gets the glory, and God becomes a matter of fact. Even to the point of filling their daily conversation with personally platitudes. You know the type; God told me to do this, like park my car over there, when in fact even common sense would give you the common sense to do what is right. God doesn't like it when people attribute something to Him when He just didn't say it.

When you have a gift use it for God, then you know He will receive all the credit. Whether that gift is teaching, singing, sports, fishing, helping the sick, praying, or whatever it is, that gift is placed within you for the sole purpose of glorifying God, and not you. When a person takes the credit, and becomes high-minded.

Wisdom is creditable, knowledge, ability and any wealth that you may have is God's and you are the servant of those gifts that God has given you. It is our heavenly Father that makes it all click, workable, and believable. Each person in the body of Christ does not have the same function.

Paul uses the analogy of a body, because we can easily see that each member of the body has a specific function to make the body function, in a way that is how God uses us. You don't walk on your head, you think with your head and walk on your feet. Your heart pumps blood, while the blood carries the oxygen. Your hands pick up things and your nose breaths the air. You get the picture: the body of Christ is the same way, every part is necessary, and the body suffers when any part of the body is hurting. When something gets into your eye, the whole body stops until the eye is able to function, when one of you step on a nail, the whole body is under attack. This is how it ought to be within the body of Christ, when we are in the will of God.

"Prophecy" is teaching what God has spoken. Prophecy can be trusted because it is based upon God Word. In the prime root of the word *"prophecy"* it is the teaching. *"Exhorteth"* means that you have the gift of speaking, to make God's Word clear and understandable in the mind of the listener.

When you give, just don't make a big deal out of it. The joyful giver is what makes the Word of God flow. We are to give God's Word to accomplish the task that is set before us for them. It becomes a pleasure to give, because the center of the giving is not the gift of money, but the satisfaction that comes from the end results brought in the spreading of the gospel.

"Showing mercy, with a cheerful heart", to those that are gifted with the ability to heal the sick and down trodden, the gift to lift them up, by being in presence of the Holy Spirit. That is a gift from God, when you have the ability to make those around you feel good, just by your being there.

Remember when God gives a gift to you, it is without repentance, He will not take it back from you. However, when you misuse that gift, He will take the Holy Spirit a way, we need to stay corrected To the Holy Spirit. God has his ways to get you back to the reality we need Christ. That is why there are many different gifts for each person. All members of the flock do not have the same ability, when you realize your gift you can share it with others, get busy and find it. Don't sit back and do nothing, take the lead. When you apply your gifts. God will bless you.

You will be able to share it in good times as well as the bad; not only in this world, but in the ages to come for those services you rendered in this present age. <u>You cannot out give God.</u>

That is the time to bring it to the Lord in prayer, ask for the Father's help in this matter. Say it to yourself and He can read your mind. Our Heavenly Father knows the intent of your heart and mind. <u>When you are *"rejoicing in hope"*, it documents your faith</u>, for your *"hope"* is that which is not seen, and it tells others that you are a believer, you can rejoice in hope. You are rejoicing in the belief that the thing hoped for, has already come to pass.

Romans 12:3-12 (28)

V-3 "For I say, through the grace given unto me, to every man that is among you, not to think *of himself* more highly than he ought to think; but to think soberly, according as God hath dealt to every man the measure of faith.

V-4 For as we have many members in one body, and all members have not the same office:

V-5 So we, *being* many, are one body in Christ, and every one members one of another.

V-6 Having then gifts differing according to the grace that is given to us, whether prophecy, *let us prophesy* according to the proportion of faith;

V-7 Or ministry, *let us wait* on *our* ministering: or he that teacheth, on teaching;

V-8 Or he that exhorteth, on exhortation: he that giveth, *let him do it* with simplicity; he that ruleth, with diligence; he that sheweth mercy, with cheerfulness.

V-9 *Let* love be without dissimulation. Abhor that which is evil; cleave to that which is good.

V-10 *Be* kindly affectioned one to another with brotherly love; in honour preferring one another; V-11 Not slothful in business; fervent in spirit; serving the Lord;
V-12 Rejoicing in hope; patient in tribulation; continuing instant in prayer;

This is addressed only to them that are persecuted for their witness in living their life as a Christian. When you correct a fellow brother in Christ, He slaps you, it doesn't hurt you to say **"bless you brother."** You don't know what convictions and persecutions that person has gone through, and your act of turning the other cheek is given in service to the Lord. This is what turning the other cheek is all about. Say you planted a seed concerning what God wants you to do according to Word. What a person took it in the wrong way and hit you. Say you're doing the work of the Lord, and God will bless you for it. Don't curse, it may be best to just turn and walk away.

"Be not wise in your own conceits", is in reference to trying to carry on a conversation with someone that thinks that they know it all. When we communicate with others in the Lord, we are to be open minded, consider their views so we can understand what they are saying and what to pray for.

To be of the same mind one toward another is like a choir, each member having the same mind of the song, yet each using their voices what God has given them adds to the song. Though they are singing different notes for harmony, and in tune with each another, it makes beautiful harmony the same is true in the Lord. Each of us has different part in God's work. Our love for Christ puts us in harmony in the Word of God. The teachings of God's Word brings maturity into the body of Christ, it strengthens our faith in God as different members of the body. Don't let the little things divide us and cause problems to the body of Christ.

Paul is telling us not to trade evil for evil when someone takes advantage of us in some way, don't return evil with evil they given you, learn to forgive. It also means, don't go back and give the person a second crack at you either that is wrong. Be smarter then the serpent, learn his ways so that you will not be caught in his trap of evil doing. <u>You will never lose in the long run when you strive to present things honorable in the sight of men and God.</u>

It is a misconception when people think Christians should be a mat for everybody to walk on. Notice: what Paul says; **"If it be possible, as much as lieth in you,"** that means **"as much as physically you can take."** **"Live peaceable with all men"**, is directed not only to the body of Christ, be a good neighbors when possible, when it is possible make peace with them. When this doesn't work, we should not treat them as an enemy but set ourselves apart from them. Just don't go around them, and have nothing to do with them. Both of you may claim that in the Lord, this is what was Paul's teaching in:

II Thessalonians 3:6

V-6 *"Now we command you, brethren, in the name of the Lord Jesus Christ, <u>that ye withdraw yourselves from every brother that walketh disorderly, and not after the tradition which he received of us</u>."*

II Thessalonians 3:7

V-7 *"For yourselves know how ye ought to follow us: for we behaved not ourselves disorderly among you;"*

This quotation, *"Vengeance is Mine; I will repay saith the Lord,"* comes from the song of Moses, in **Deuteronomy 32.** The song that the overcomers sing on the day when Jesus Christ defeats the Antichrist, before he is changed and cast into the bottomless pit.

Deuteronomy 32:41

V-41 *"If I whet My glittering sword, And Mine hand take hold on judgment; I will render vengeance to Mine enemies, and will reward them that hate Me."* Then in verse 43;

Deuteronomy 32:43

V-43 *"Rejoice, O ye nations, with His people: <u>For He will avenge the blood of His servants, And will render vengeance to His adversaries, And will be merciful unto His land, and to His people</u>."* *"If he thirst, give him drink."* What is God saying *"the living water"* that quenches all thirst in the end times? <u>The "Living water" is the Word of God.</u> Even the heathen in a desert will never refuse to give a drink of water to strangers. It is their custom. It doesn't take preaching to turn your enemy to God, it takes actions by Christians, and you setting the example of God's Word in your live.

Proverbs 25:21, 22 *"Heaping coals of fire upon his head"* comes from the reference to the shame that will come upon that person.

Proverbs 25:21, 22

V-21 *"If thine enemy be hungry, give him bread to eat; And if he be thirsty, give him water to drink"*

V-22 *"For thou shalt heap coals of fire upon his head, And the Lord shall reward thee."*

<u>We are talking about different kinds of spirits, not actions here. Be not overcome by an evil spirit, but overcome the evil spirit, with the Holy Spirit.</u> The spirits of this world will tempt us, but with the Holy Spirit of God within us, we have an advantage because in Christ we are given the power and authority over all evil spirits including Satan, the devil.

When we have the Spirit of God in us, we are guided by His Spirit. Even when Satan's evil spirits tempt us, we have the power to order them away, but do we? Many times Christians find pleasure in entertaining the thoughts of demonic power, sad to say they are playing games with Satan, they need to order them out of their lives. Friend that is the start of real trouble, for anyone who gives place to them in their mind.

Paul is telling us that when these evil spirits come, we should order them out with the authority of Christ in His power we have dominion over them, in the power of the Holy Spirit.

Romans 12:13-21   (29)

V-13 "Distributing to the necessity of saints; given to hospitality.

V-14 Bless them which persecute you: bless, and curse not.

V-15 Rejoice with them that do rejoice, and weep with them that weep.

V-16 *Be* of the same mind one toward another. Mind not high things, but condescend to men of low estate. Be not wise in your own conceits.

V-17 Recompense to no man evil for evil. Provide things honest in the sight of all men.

V-18 If it be possible, as much as lieth in you, live peaceably with all men.

V-19 Dearly beloved, avenge not yourselves, but *rather* give place unto wrath: for it is written, Vengeance *is* mine; I will repay, saith the Lord.

V-20 Therefore if thine enemy hunger, feed him; if he thirst, give him drink: for in so doing thou shalt heap coals of fire on his head.

V-21 Be not overcome of evil, but overcome evil with good.

V-22 Distributing to the necessity of saints; given to hospitality.

V-23 Bless them which persecute you: bless, and curse not.

Romans chapter 13 the power in the Holy Spirit
1. **Romans 13:9** Exodus 20:13-15,17;
   Deut. 5:17-19,21
2. **Romans 13:9** Lev. 19:18
3. **Romans 13:14** In contexts like this, the Greek word
   for *flesh* (*sarx*) refers to the sinful state of man, often
   presented as a power in opposition to the Spirit.

When Paul wrote this, he was planning to visit Jerusalem, where there were many political tensions. Jewish Zealots were taking up weapons to fight against Rome. There were also political difficulties in Rome: Jews had been involved in so many disturbances that Claudius had forced them to leave (**Acts 18:2**). After Claudius died, many Jews returned, but the tensions were still there.

Paul knows his advice will not be accepted automatically, he supports it with sound principles. The authorities that exist have been established by God. Consequently, whoever rebels against the authority is rebelling against what God has instituted.

Caesar demands to be called "*Lord and God*", Christians should refuses at risk of their lives. There is a big difference between refusing to obey one law, a rebellion that claims Caesar should not rule. It is not wrong to resist specific injustices, it is wrong to work against government itself. Those who rebel against God's authority "*will bring judgment on themselves.*", it has been established by God in (**Dan. 4:17**)

John 19:10, 11

"Then saith Pilate unto him, Speakest thou not unto me? knowest thou not that I have power to crucify thee, and have power to release thee?

"Jesus answered, Thou couldest have no power *at all* against me,

197

except it were given thee from above: therefore he that delivered me unto thee hath the greater sin. It is not our place to try to overthrow the government."

Romans 13:3 *"Do you want to be free from fear of the one in authority? Then do what is right and you will be commended"*.

If you are a law-abiding citizen, you should have no reason to fear the government. (However, governments sometimes go awry and persecute Christians. **Revelation 13**, using imagery from **Daniel**, depicts civil government as a terrifying *"beast."*)

Paul then makes the astonishing statement: *"For the one in authority is God's servant for your good"* (**Romans 13:4**). When Paul wrote **Romans**, Nero was the emperor. He turned evil, and tradition says Paul was executed under his reign. The fact that rulers often sin, even serving Satan at times.

"Therefore, it is necessary to submit to the authorities, not only because of possible punishment also as a matter of conscience" (**Romans 13:5**). We should obey civil laws not only because the government might punish us, because God wants us to be law-abiding people (**1 Peter 2:12-14**).

Paul's own experience with the government is an example of a balanced approach. When he was on trial for his life in Judea, he was respectful, he did not passively submit to whatever the rulers wanted. Rather, he used his rights as a Roman citizen to prevent a flogging (**Acts 22:25**) to prevent being sent back to Jerusalem.

After saying that we should pay whatever we owe, Paul shifts the subject back to love in the Word: *"Let no debt remain outstanding, except the continuing debt to love one another (…)"* (**Romans 13:8; 12:9-10**). We need to love one another; it is an eternal obligation.

Why? Because *"whoever loves others has fulfilled the law."*

The logic implies that "the law" "The commandments" is the primary goal, love is a stepping-stone toward that goal. To be accurate, love is the goal, the law provides guidance about how we are to love.

"*Love does no harm to a neighbor*," but love must go further than simply avoiding harm it should actively seek to be a *good* neighbor.

He concludes, "*Therefore love is the fulfillment of the law*" (**Romans 13:10**). If we love others, we have fulfilled the purpose of the law and have gone further than what it requires. If we love our neighbor. Even if the government is evil, we should respond to evil by doing good, not by taking matters into our own hands.

Paul then gives the alternative: "*Rather, clothe yourselves with the Lord Jesus Christ, and do not think about how to gratify the desires of the flesh*" (**Romans 13:14**). Drunkenness and immorality comes from the sinful nature; so does jealousy and dissension. People who give their allegiance to Jesus Christ, we clothe ourselves with him, cooperation and mutual esteem will replace selfishness.

Romans 13:1-14   (30)

V-1 "Let every soul be subject unto the higher powers. For there is no power but of God: the powers that be are ordained of God.

V-2 Whosoever therefore resisteth the power, resisteth the ordinance of God: they that resist shall receive to themselves damnation.

V-3 For rulers are not a terror to good works, but to the evil. Wilt thou then not be afraid of the power? do that which is good, and thou shalt have praise of the same:

V-4 For he is the minister of God to thee for good. But if thou do that which is evil, be afraid; for he beareth not the sword in vain: for he is the minister of God, a revenger to *execute* wrath upon him that doeth evil.

V-5 Wherefore *ye* must needs be subject, not only for wrath, but also for conscience sake.

V-6 For this cause pay ye tribute also: for they are God's ministers, attending continually upon this very thing.

V-7 Render therefore to all their dues: tribute to whom tribute *is due*; custom to whom custom; fear to whom fear; honour to whom honour.

V-8 Owe no man any thing, but to love one another: for he that loveth another hath fulfilled the law.

V-9 For this, Thou shalt not commit adultery, Thou shalt not kill, Thou shalt not steal, Thou shalt not bear false witness, Thou shalt not covet; and if *there be* any other commandment, it is briefly comprehended in this saying, namely, Thou shalt love thy neighbour as thyself.

V-10 Love worketh no ill to his neighbour: therefore love *is* the fulfilling of the law.

V-11 And that, knowing the time, that now *it is* high time to awake out of sleep: for now *is* our salvation nearer than when we believed.

V-12 The night is far spent, the day is at hand: let us therefore cast off the works of darkness, and let us put on the armour of light.

V-13 Let us walk honestly, as in the day; not in rioting and drunkenness, not in chambering and wantonness, not in strife and envying.

V-14 But put ye on the Lord Jesus Christ, and make not provision for the flesh, to *fulfil* the lusts *thereof*."

Romans Chapter 14 believer has their own mind

1. **Romans 14:10** The Greek word for *brother or sister* (*adelphos*) refers to a believer, (man or woman), as part of God's family; also in **Romans 14:13, 15, and 21**.

2. **Romans 14:11** Isaiah 45:23

3. **Romans 14:23** Some manuscripts place Romans 16:25-27 here; others after 15:33.

A man consulted a doctor. *"I've been misbehaving, Doc, and my conscience is troubling me,"* he complained.

"And you want something that will strengthen your willpower?" asked the doctor.

"Well, no," said the fellow. *"I was thinking of something that would weaken my conscience."*

In **Romans Chapter 14** Paul is dealing with matters of the Christian's conscience and personal convictions, especially as they relate to the relationships of the strong and the weak convictions'. Paul's prescription in this chapter is far from those who were sought by the person just mentioned. He does not praise the overly sensitive conscience, nor does he condemn it. He accepts Christians where they are in their faith and pleads with us to do the same.

The favorite indoor sport of Christians is trying to change each other Paul says we should not endeavor to change one another to suit our preferences, but instead we should change our conduct so as not to offend the weaker brother.

Romans 14:1-12 deal with our responsibility to respect the convictions of one another. **Romans 14:13-23** instructs us to refrain from exercising our own liberties when they will harm another.

It is important to our understanding of **Romans Chapter 14** to be absolutely clear as to the issue at hand.

The issues Paul speaks is the matter of personal convictions. Individual Christians will often differ over matters of conscience and of liberties. The differences which Paul speaks of are not over absolutes or fundamental doctrines of the faith.

Paul mentions the matter of eating meat or only vegetables (**Romans 14:2**), of observing certain holy days (**Romans 14:5**), about drinking wine (**Romans 14:21**).

While two Christians may disagree over whether or not a Christian should drink wine or eat only vegetables, no Christian should dispute the fact that lying, stealing, and immorality are sin. These are biblical and moral absolutes. No two Christians should differ over the virgin birth or the deity of Christ, the physical resurrection of our Lord or the substitutionary atonement. These are doctrinal certainties.

When we understand that Paul is speaking in regard to individual liberties, Christian rights, and personal convictions, then it is easy to see the differences in our attitude as compared with **Galatians Chapter 5** and **Colossians Chapter 2**. There were those who taught that it was impossible to be saved apart from the keeping of the Law. *"And some men came down from Judea and began teaching the brethren," "Unless you are circumcised according to the custom of Moses, you cannot be saved"* (**Acts 15:1**).

I'm going to say some Christians is not just the one who believes something which in fact is a Christian liberty is prohibited, but he is one who is inclined to go ahead and follow the example of the strong in spite of his scruples. The weak Christian, then, is not just the one who heartily condemns drinking wine, In my estimation, those who preach on the evils of wine are not weaker.

That is precisely what Paul is trying to get his point across to us in verse 4: *"Who are you to judge the servant of another? To his own master he stands or falls, and stand he will, for the Lord is able to make him stand"* If we are judging our brothers, we are taking upon ourselves the prerogatives of God, He takes it out of hands.

He who observes it for the Lord, he who eats, does so for the Lord, for he gives thanks to God; *we die for the Lord; therefore whether we live or die, we are the Lord's* (**Romans 14:6, 8**). Here is Paul's argument the Christian has no business trying to conform his brother to his own personal convictions, since convictions are private, since God has accepted him as he is, since every servant is accountable only to his own master.

Paul's instruction to us is found in verse 13, where he writes, *"Therefore let us not judge one another any more, but rather determine this—not to put an obstacle or a stumbling block in a brother's way"* (**Romans 14:13**).

The basis for Paul's exhortation in **Romans 14:13-23** is that neither the exercise of Christian liberties nor the abstinence from them is intrinsically good or evil. The rightness or wrongness of these liberties is determined by our attitude toward them: *"I know and am convinced in the Lord Jesus that nothing is unclean in itself; but to him who thinks anything to be unclean to him it is unclean"* (**Romans Chapter 14**)

If we sincerely believe eating ice cream is sinful for the Christian, it is wrong, not because God said so, but because we suppose so. Paul, in **1 Corinthians 9:22** says, "I h*ave become all things to all men."* *"For if because of food your brother is hurt, you are no longer walking according to love. Do not destroy with your food him for whom Christ died"* (Romans 14:15). We are not to be preoccupied with our Christian liberties, but rather with love. Love never causes a brother to stumble, but seeks to strengthen the weak.

(V-21, 22). Paul's admonition for the strong is expressed in verses 21 and 22: "*It is good not to eat meat or to drink wine, or to do anything by which your brother stumbles. The faith which you have, have as your own conviction before God. Happy is he who does not condemn himself in what he approves.*" The strong Christian should never practice matters of Christian liberty (such as eating meat or drinking wine) thereby cause another, weaker brother to follow in his footsteps and fall into sin. The weaker brother who drinks wine, not because he is convinced it is his liberty, in doubt only because another Christian is doing so, is thereby sinning against his conscience and God.

It is not wrong to enjoy a good meal, but it is wrong to destroy our physical bodies by over-eating. It is not wrong to drink (for an alcoholic, for whom this would inevitably lead to sin), it is wrong to get drunk. It may not be wrong to enjoy a good smoke, it is wrong to endanger a person's life because it can cause cancer, to allow our bodies to become the slave of food, drink, nicotine, or aspirin, or whatever. What may not be wrong categorically may be wrong on the basis of one or more clear Biblical principles.

Some would endeavor to use the word "**grieve**" or "**hurt**" to support their contention that if any brother is offended (upset) by our liberties, we should give it up. The word hurt here cannot have such a meaning: "*Hence a weak believer 'is grieved'* when he has violated his religious convictions is afflicted with the vexation of his conscience which is the consequent sense of quilt involves. It is this tragic result for the weak believer that the strong believer must take into account. When the exercise of his liberty emboldens the weak to violate his conscience, then, out of deference to the religious interests of the weak, the exercise of what are intrinsically his rights.

Romans 14:1-23   (31)

V-1 "Him that is weak in the faith receive ye, *but* not to doubtful disputations.

V-2 For one believeth that he may eat all things: another, who is weak, eateth herbs.

V-3 Let not him that eateth despise him that eateth not; and let not him which eateth not judge him that eateth: for God hath received him.

V-4 Who art thou that judgest another man's servant? to his own master he standeth or falleth. Yea, he shall be holden up: for God is able to make him stand.

V-5 One man esteemeth one day above another: another esteemeth every day *alike*. Let every man be fully persuaded in his own mind.

V-6 He that regardeth the day, regardeth *it* unto the Lord; and he that regardeth not the day, to the Lord he doth not regard *it*. He that eateth, eateth to the Lord, for he giveth God thanks; and he that eateth not, to the Lord he eateth not, and giveth God thanks.

V-7 For none of us liveth to himself, and no man dieth to himself.

V-8 For whether we live, we live unto the Lord; and whether we die, we die unto the Lord: whether we live therefore, or die, we are the Lord's.

V-9 For to this end Christ both died, and rose, and revived, that he might be Lord both of the dead and living.

V-10 But why dost thou judge thy brother? or why dost thou set at nought thy brother? for we shall all stand before the judgment seat of Christ.

V-11 For it is written, *As* I live, saith the Lord, every knee shall bow to me, and every tongue shall confess to God.

V-12 So then every one of us shall give account of himself to God.

V-13 Let us not therefore judge one another any more: but judge this rather, that no man put a stumblingblock or an occasion to fall in *his* brother's way.

V-14 I know, and am persuaded by the Lord Jesus, that *there is* nothing unclean of itself: but to him that esteemeth any thing to be unclean, to him *it is* unclean.

V-15 But if thy brother be grieved with *thy* meat, now walkest thou not charitably. Destroy not him with thy meat, for whom Christ died.

V-16 Let not then your good be evil spoken of:

V-17 For the kingdom of God is not meat and drink; but righteousness, and peace, and joy in the Holy Ghost.

V-18 For he that in these things serveth Christ *is* acceptable to God, and approved of men.

V-19 Let us therefore follow after the things which make for peace, and things wherewith one may edify another.

V-20 For meat destroy not the work of God. All things indeed *are* pure; but *it is* evil for that man who eateth with offence.

V-21 *It is* good neither to eat flesh, nor to drink wine, nor *any thing* whereby thy brother stumbleth, or is offended, or is made weak.

V-22 Hast thou faith? have *it* to thyself before God. Happy *is* he that condemneth not himself in that thing which he alloweth.

V-23 And he that doubteth is damned if he eat, <u>because *he eateth* not of faith: for whatsoever *is* not of faith is sin</u>."

Romans chapter 15
1. **Romans 15:3 Psalm 69:9**
2. **Romans 15:8** Greek *circumcision*
3. **Romans 15:9 2 Samuel 22:50; Psalm 18:49**
4. **Romans 15:10 Deut. 32:43**
5. **Romans 15:11 Psalm 117:1**
6. **Romans 15:12 Isaiah 11:10**
7. **Romans 15:21 Isaiah 52:15**

Paul gives a powerful reason why we should receive one another. This is the example of our Savior in his earthly ministry, He never pleased Himself. As evidence of this a verse from *Psalm 69 "The reproaches of those who reproached You fell on Me"* (**Romans 15:9**). Instead of pleasing Himself, Christ bore our reproaches!

Think for a moment about how differently the life of Christ would have looked had He only pleased Himself. He wouldn't have gone to the cross, that's for sure. He would not have said in the Garden of Gethsemane, *"Nevertheless, not My will, but Yours be done"* (**Luke 22:42**). Christ didn't please Himself?

Paul's desire for unity, that is the occasion for his call for mutual acceptance, is a desire for God's glory. He desires unity in the church in order that the church (made up of both Jews and Gentiles) lift up their voices as one *"glorify the God and Father of our Lord Jesus Christ"*! Paul wants the Romans to see what is at stake in their petty disputes. It is nothing less than the worship of the one true and living God! Likewise, this is what is at stake over our own petty disagreements! Paul's conclusion is verse seven: *"Therefore receive one another, just as Christ also received us, to the glory of God."*

In (**Romans 15:13-18**) Paul urges the believers in Rome to receive one another based on the Exposition of the Scriptures. His point is to show from the Old Testament Scriptures (which was all they had at this point) that both Jews and Gentiles are included in God's purpose of redemption. He shows this by declaring that Jesus Christ came in order to fulfill the promises made to the Patriarchs in order that the Gentiles might glorify God for His mercy. The promise which Christ's coming has fulfilled is the promise first made to Abraham in **Genesis 12:3** which states *"In you shall all the nations of the earth be blessed."* The first promise to Father Abraham (the father of the Jewish people) was that God would bless all nations through him! In other words, God's purpose has always included both Jews and Gentiles! As Paul explains in **Galatians 3:8**,

Paul uses a series of four quotations from the Old Testament to demonstrate God's saving purpose has always included both Jews and Gentiles. Paul intentionally uses verses from all three of the major divisions of (the Law, the Prophets, and the Writings).

- The first quotation is from **Psalm 18:49**. Notice the emphasis on worship!

"For this reason I will confess to You among the Gentiles, And sing to Your name."

- The second quotation is from **Deuteronomy 32:43**. *"Rejoice, O Gentiles, with His people!"*
- The third quotation is from **Psalm 117:1**. *"Praise the LORD, all you Gentiles! Laud Him, all you peoples!"*
- The fourth and final quotation is from **Isaiah 11:10**. *"There shall be a root of Jesse; And He who shall rise to reign over the Gentiles, In Him the Gentiles shall hope."*
- Aren't you glad that we are a part of something bigger than ourselves! We're a part of God's eternal plan of redemption. God purposed from all eternity to make us one body in Christ. Why, then, do we get hung up over petty disagreements? Note Paul's concluding prayer in verse 13:

- Now may the God of hope fill you with all joy and peace in believing, that you may abound in hope by the power of the Holy Spirit.

In **Romans 15:14-33** we are called to glorify Christ in all that we do! Paul fervently urges the in Roman Christians (and us, too) that when we worship (as a life style as opposed to just a gathering for a service) and are obedient to Christ, we must also demonstrate His love in how we relate to others. Paul seeks missionary support for his journeys because of the urgent need of the world to hear the Gospel. He desires prayers and respect. We must give the same to one another.

Paul reassures the Roman church of his intentions. He does not want to create division or doubt, but merely states how the Christian life is to be practical and outgoing, not sedentary and inclusive (**Col. 3:16**). Paul continues in his theme of our debt to the lost, his vision to evangelism. Since God saved us, we are in turn obligated to work in Christ's behalf, to be His agent, powered by the Holy Spirit to proclaim the Gospel message.

The Trinity (**Romans 15:17-20**); God the Father in verses 17-18); God the Son (verses-17-20); God the Spirit (verses-16, 19).

"Signs and wonders" refers to the miracles produced by the Holy Spirit through the apostles, especially Paul, as a testimony to God's power and glory (**Ex. 7:3; Duet. 4:34; 6:22; 7:19; Isa. 8:18; Dan. 6:27; book of Acts**).

The Bible gives no indication that the Signs and Wonders have stopped! When we do see them, we are to be discerning and seek reasons before we jump to conclusions. If we will not get ourselves in trouble by falling prey to manipulators using tricks to distract us away from God's truth.

Remember the purpose of Signs and Wonders was to glorify Christ, not put on a show! When the manifestations, placing the focus on the delivery of the message!

Paul was seeking support for his trip to Spain, one of the main reasons for his letter. It is fascinating to speculate if Paul ever went to Spain or died right after his house arrest in Rome. The fact is, we just do not know (**Acts 28**). Most scholars assume that Paul was released after the house arrest in Rome then was martyred, he never made it to Spain. However, Spanish legend says he did ("*Paul's Situation*") Romans. As Paul preached to the Jews to accept the Gentiles, now he turns the table to expound them to help their fellow troubled Christians who are Jewish (**Rom. 11:17; 1 Cor. 9:3-14; Gal. 6:6**)! Paul seeks their support in prayer, and perhaps money, in three areas that he will be safe to travel to Judea to bear the Gospel, that the Jerusalem church accept their gifts, that he can visit them personally in Rome.

"The God of Peace" (**2 Cor. 13:11; Phil. 4:9; 1 Thess. 5:23; 2 Thess. 3:16**) Even in Paul's struggles and hardships, he refers to God as comfort! If we just live our lives with the attitude of how things affect "*me*".

Christ died that this very relationship might be established, namely, that "*whether we live or die, we are the Lord's.*" (14:8) His death, with His resurrection, enables Him to have ALL AUTHORITY over the living, in heaven and on earth (**Matt. 28:18**).

Through His death, we became His! He died to redeem us that He might be our lord. Because of His resurrection, He exercises His authority. (*Lord* - Ownership; "*to own completely, in the sense of both owning and controlling.*".) (**14:14, 20b; cf. 1 Cor. 8:4, 8; 10:25-29Phil. 2:1-3**)

Romans 15:1-33   (32)

V-1 "We then that are strong ought to bear the infirmities of the weak, and not to please ourselves.

V-2 Let every one of us please *his* neighbour for *his* good to edification.

V-3 For even Christ pleased not himself; but, as it is written, The reproaches of them that reproached thee fell on me.

V-4 For whatsoever things were written aforetime were written for our learning, that we through patience and comfort of the scriptures might have hope.

V-5 Now the God of patience and consolation grant you to be likeminded one toward another according to Christ Jesus:

V-6 That ye may with one mind *and* one mouth glorify God, even the Father of our Lord Jesus Christ.

V-7 Wherefore receive ye one another, as Christ also received us to the glory of God.

V-8 Now I say that Jesus Christ was a minister of the circumcision for the truth of God, to confirm the promises *made* unto the fathers:

V-9 And that the Gentiles might glorify God for *his* mercy; as it is written, For this cause I will confess to thee among the Gentiles, and sing unto thy name.

V-10 And again he saith, Rejoice, ye Gentiles, with his people.

V-11 And again, Praise the Lord, all ye Gentiles; and laud him, all ye people.

V-12 And again, Esaias saith, There shall be a root of Jesse, and he that shall rise to reign over the Gentiles; in him shall the Gentiles trust.

V-13 Now the God of hope fill you with all joy and peace in believing, that ye may abound in hope, through the power of the Holy Ghost.

V-14 And I myself also am persuaded of you, my brethren, that ye also are full of goodness, filled with all knowledge, able also to admonish one another.

V-15 Nevertheless, brethren, I have written the more boldly unto you in some sort, as putting you in mind, because of the grace that is given to me of God,

V-16 That I should be the minister of Jesus Christ to the Gentiles, ministering the gospel of God, that the offering up of the Gentiles might be acceptable, being sanctified by the Holy Ghost.

V-17 I have therefore whereof I may glory through Jesus Christ in those things which pertain to God.

V-18 For I will not dare to speak of any of those things which Christ hath not wrought by me, to make the Gentiles obedient, by word and deed,

V-19 Through mighty signs and wonders, by the power of the Spirit of God; so that from Jerusalem, and round about unto Illyricum, I have fully preached the gospel of Christ.

V-20 Yea, so have I strived to preach the gospel, not where Christ was named, lest I should build upon another man's foundation:

V-21 But as it is written, To whom he was not spoken of, they shall see: and they that have not heard shall understand.

V-22 For which cause also I have been much hindered from coming to you.

V-23 But now having no more place in these parts, and having a great desire these many years to come unto you;

V-24 Whensoever I take my journey into Spain, I will come to you: for I trust to see you in my journey, and to be brought on my way thitherward by you, if first I be somewhat filled with your *company*.

V-25 But now I go unto Jerusalem to minister unto the saints.

V-26 For it hath pleased them of Macedonia and Achaia to make a certain contribution for the poor saints which are at Jerusalem.

V-27 It hath pleased them verily; and their debtors they are. For if the Gentiles have been made partakers of their spiritual things, their duty is also to minister unto them in carnal things.

V-28 When therefore I have performed this, and have sealed to them this fruit, I will come by you into Spain.

V-29 And I am sure that, when I come unto you, I shall come in the fulness of the blessing of the gospel of Christ.

V-30 Now I beseech you, brethren, for the Lord Jesus Christ's sake, and for the love of the Spirit, that ye strive together with me in *your* prayers to God for me;

V-31 That I may be delivered from them that do not believe in Judaea; and that my service which *I have* for Jerusalem may be accepted of the saints;

V-32 That I may come unto you with joy by the will of God, and may with you be refreshed.

V-33 Now the God of peace *be* with you all. Amen."

Romans chapter 16 conclusion

We have finally reached the last chapter in our study in Romans. Some of you are old enough to remember when we started! I want to say the 16 chapter tells us a lot about why Paul wrote the book of **Romans** about the turmoil in the Church of Rome. I think, they see nothing but a list of names long since died. But in many ways this is one of the most exciting chapters in Romans, as I think you will see.

But here in **Romans 16** gives us a lot of the people in Rome a list of names men and women who never knew that they were going to be famous. Give them honor for some of the first to accept the gospel of Christ.

In these verses there are 33 names mentioned. Nine of these people were with Paul eight men and one woman.

There are 24 names mentioned in Rome, 17 men and 7 women. There are two households mentioned, two unnamed women the mother of Rufus and the sister of Nereus as well as some unnamed brethren. There is quite a list of people the apostle knew personally in Rome, though he himself had not yet visited that city. These people he had known somewhere else. We tend to think of those ancient days as a time of limited travel. It took weeks to reach cities that we now reach in less than an hour by plane. Nevertheless, these people got around, here is a record of that fact.

You cannot read **Chapter 16 of Romans** without being impressed by the number of women Paul mentions many more than in any other literature of that day. Women occupy a prominent place in these letters of the New Testament. Evidently, they handled very important tasks within the church, according to the gifts they had. There is a strong suggestion Phoebe was a teacher or an evangelist, a laborer for the gospel with Paul. We do not know much more about her, but her name has been preserved forever because of this mention. Paul now turns to greet those he knew in Rome, he begins with a very well-known husband and wife team, **Romans 16:3-4**:

Greet Priscilla and Aquila, my fellow workers in Christ Jesus. They risked their lives for me. Not only I but all the churches of the Gentiles are grateful to them. Greet also the church that meets at their house. (**Romans 16:3-5**)

Epaenetus was never forgotten, for he was the first one to believe the gospel when Paul came to the province of Asia, of which Ephesus was the capital. You never forget that first one you lead to Christ. No matter how many others follow, you never forget the firstfruits. We do not know what Epaenetus was doing in Rome, but

214

he was cherished because he was the first to exercise faith in Asia. They were associated with him is Mary, whom Paul calls "Mary the toiler." She is one of the group of unknown women in the Gospels who had the gift of helps. She could not teach, preach or evangelize, she could have worked, and she did. Paul is very careful to remember these women and men who had the gift of helps. Then he mentions some relatives and friends, **Romans 16:7-10**.

Andronicus and Junias were relatives of Paul, since he says they were "*in Christ before me,*" this takes us back to the very first days of the church, back to the ministry of Stephen in Jerusalem. What it must have meant to the young Saul of Tarsus, who was breathing forth threatening's and slaughter against the Christians two of his own kinsmen had become Christians! Undoubtedly the prayers of Andronicus and Junias affected the apostle. It is hard to tell whether this is a husband and wife team, or two brothers. It all depends on the name "Junias." If it is "*Junias*" with an "s," as we have it here, it is a male; if it is "*Junia,*" the KJV has it female. They were Jews, relatives of Paul, who had become Christians.

Ampliatus in an interesting name. In the cemetery at Domitilla, found among the catacombs in Rome, there is a highly decorated tomb with the single name "*Ampliatus,*" written on it. A single name like this implies that the man was a slave, but as the tomb is rather ornate, it indicates that he was a Christian, highly respected by the leaders in Rome. Paul mentions here, he most likely is this man, though a slave, had a great ministry among the brethren in Rome.

Urbanus and Stachys we know no more about than what Paul mentions here. Somewhere, Urbanus joined Paul's team, and also "*his dear friend Stachys,*", we know. I have always been fascinated by this man Apelles, whom Paul says has been "*tested and approved in Christ.*" (I wish that is what I would merit on my tombstone.

Would that be a great inscription, Tested and approved in Christ"?) This man will forever be known as one who endured a testing of his faith who stood against the pressure.

The most famous Narcissus we know in Roman history was a former slave who became the personal secretary of the Emperor Claudius. He gained much wealth, because he was in charge of the correspondence of the emperor. (His palm had to be greased before a letter got through to the emperor.) When Claudius was murdered, Nero took over, he also took over the household of Narcissus.

We know nothing about Paul's dear friend Persis, other than that she too had worked with him somewhere, perhaps traveling in his company of evangelists. In Verse 13 we have Rufus, chosen in the Lord, and his mother, who had been a mother to the apostle too. There seems to be little doubt that Rufus, along with his brother Alexander, mentioned in the Gospel of Mark, were the sons of Simon of Cyrene.

His two sons, Alexander and Rufus, became outstanding men in the Christian community. There is an Alexander who comes to the rescue of Paul in the city of Ephesus, at the time of the outcry there. There is a Rufus here in Rome, who is well known, Paul sends his greetings to him, and reminds him also that Rufus' mother had been his mother too, at some time. This again takes us back to the earliest days of the gospel ministry when perhaps young Saul of Tarsus, coming to Jerusalem to sit at the feet of Gamaliel, the great Jewish teacher, had probably stayed in the home of Simon of Cyrene and his two sons, Alexander and Rufus. Later they became Christians, and Paul cherished them as friends he had known even before his own Christian days. We cannot be certain of all those details, but much is suggested by this.

Philippiansologus means "*a lover of the word,*" this was probably a nickname given to him, just as Barnabas was called "the son of consolation," even though that was not his name. Here was a man who loved the Word of God, and gathered with him these men and women - Julia, Nereus and his sister.

There is a very helpful passage here on what to do about problems within the church: Here is a group of people who are professing Christians, but, who, to judge by the apostle's language, are not truly believers. The danger, as Paul outlines it, is that they create factions within a church, little dissident groups that gather about and emphasize one particular point of doctrine or teaching, to the exclusion of everything else. That is always a problem within the church when people think one particular thing is most important. We have people today who emphasize tongues, or prophecy, or some phase of teaching that they think is the mark of a true believer, to the exclusion of everything else. Paul warns about this.

The second thing they do is introduce practices or ceremonies that Paul calls "obstacles to faith," certain rituals or practices that these groups insist are the marks of true Christianity. They build a sense of superiority. They say, "If you have this mark, then you really are a Christian." Their motives, Paul says, are not to serve Christ, even though they say they do. These factions are really out to advance themselves, to get a following, to gain prestige. You can tell by the way they act that is what they want. Their methods are to come on with smooth and plausible talk. They always use scriptural language. They always appear to be the most dedicated and devoted of believers. Have you noticed how many of the cults today are trying to go back to the Scriptures, arguing from them a groundwork for their faith?

When you obey this, God will work. The God of peace, who will preserve the peace of the church, will also crush Satan under your feet." Something will happen to open the eyes of people to the unscriptural position of these groups, and they will lose their following. The peace will be preserved without a lot of warfare and dissension. In Verses 21-23 we have the greetings of those who are with Paul in Corinth:

Timothy, my fellow worker, sends his greetings to you, as do Lucius, Jason and Sosipater, my relatives.I, Tertius, who wrote down this letter, greet you in the Lord. Gaius, whose hospitality the whole church here enjoy, sends you his greetings. Erastus, who is the city's director of public works, our brother Quartus send you his greetings. (**Romans 16:21-24**)

That brings us to the final paragraph when, as was his custom, Paul takes his pen and writes the last words himself. Up to this point he has been dictating this letter to a man who identifies himself in Verse 22: "*I, Tertius, who wrote down this letter, greet you in the Lord.*" Evidently, the apostle said something to him, such as, "*Tertius, you've written this whole thing and you must have writer's cramps by now. Just write another line and send your own greetings.*" The name indicates that he, too, was a slave, because his name means "***Third.***" In slave families they did not bother to think up names; they just numbered the children, First, Second, Third, Fourth, Fifth, etc. Here are Third and Fourth of a family of slaves. (His brother, Quartus, Fourth, is mentioned in Verse 23.) They are educated slaves who have become Christians. They can read and write, and are part of this group in Corinth.

You can picture them gathered in the home of Gaius, this gracious, genial, generous host of the city, mentioned in Paul's first letter to the Corinthians. Gaius opened his house to the entire

Christian community, Paul, sitting there with his friends. Tertius is writing down the letter, the others are gathered around listening to Paul as he dictates, and profiting much from the writing of these great truths. With Paul, of course, is his dear son in the faith, Timothy, whom we know so well from the two letters addressed to him. Paul spoke of him his beloved son in the faith, who had stayed with him and remained faithful to the end. The very last letter Paul wrote from his prison cell in Rome was to Timothy. Paul also mentions Lucius, Jason, and Sosipater, his relatives.

Here in **Romans 16** are six members of Paul's family, who are now Christians. Some were Christians before him, Paul influenced them toward Christ.. Lucius appears to be the same one who comes from Cyrene, mentioned in **Chapter 13 of Acts** as one of the teachers in the city of Antioch. Jason was evidently Paul's host when the apostle went to the city of Thessalonica, in Macedonia. Paul stayed in Jason's home when a riot broke out in the city. Sosipater may be the man from Beroea, mentioned in Acts 20 as "*Sopater.*" Paul met him in Macedonia may have accompanied him to Jerusalem with the offering to the churches there.

Four things ring clearly throughout their lives:

One, they were not their own. "*You are not your own; you are bought with a price,*" (**1 Corinthians 6:19-20**). They believed that. They did not have a right to direct their lives any longer. God had sent them into the world, God would take them through it.

Second, they believed that life is a battle, a battle to the death. It is not a picnic. They were engaged in warfare that never ended until they left this life, they kept the faith and fought a good fight.

Third, they believed that there is need for rest and leisure at times, but only to restore them to go back into the battle. They never

219

envisaged retiring and enjoying themselves for the remaining years of their lives. They only envisaged getting adequate rest in order to come back and fight through to the end.

Fourthly, they understood that the gifts of the Holy Spirit among them opened up a ministry for every single believer. No Christian was without a ministry. Some of these dear people had only the gift of help (although I should not say "only" the gift of help, for that is a great gift.) They could not teach or preach but they could help, they did, right to the end.

You can learn a lot about people by what they tell you about what they do and like. When I am first getting to know someone, I like to ask them about their work and family. This helps me measure their levels of stress, satisfaction, and overall health. This can be particularly enlightening when I'm talking with a small business owner. When I ask small business owners questions about their business, it can be nearly impossible to shut them up. Even if they are introverted they can ramble on about their lives or the state of their business. Why is this so? Most people have great quantities of time, money, energy invested in their work and lives. This results in them caring a great deal about their life. So when I talk with such people, I will often let them know things about my life.

You can learn a lot about people by what they tell you about their life. When I am first getting to know someone, I like to ask them about their family. This helps me measure their levels of stress, satisfaction, and overall health. This can be particularly enlightening when I'm talking about sports and things they like to do their spare time. When I ask questions about their friends, it can be nearly impossible to shut them up. Especially have great quantities of time, money, and energy invested in their work.

When comes women they love to talk about their family and children. So when I talk with such people, I will often ask the question, "How are things going in their life?"

This is a question I pose with a twist maybe do they go to church. I'm not referring to how you make a living; I'm asking about how they feel God. Whether you know it or not, you're responsible to conduct according to God's Word. In fact, you are called to be a witness for God. But your business may not be what you think it is. You've heard it said, "It's none of your business!" Well, in **Rom 16,** we see: *God's work IS your business*. Paul states that you are to be about the people business, the protection, and the praise of God.

Paul clearly expressed in (**Titus 3:10**). After observing those who cause dissensions and hindrances, it is critical to confront the offender. If the person repents we are to try and win our brother or sister. But often erring members can be hardhearted. Nonetheless, we must not shrink back from our responsibility to help them.

Gifts of the Spirit - What Are They?

Gifts of the Spirit are special abilities provided by the Holy Spirit to Christians for the purpose of building up the body of Christ. The list of spiritual gifts in **1 Corinthians 12:8-10** includes wisdom, knowledge, faith, healing, miracles, prophecy, discerning of spirits, speaking in tongues, and interpretation of tongues. Similar lists in **Ephesians 4:7-13** and **Romans 12:3-8**. The gifts of the Spirit are simply God enabling believers to do what He has called us to do. **2 Peter 1:3** says, "*His divine power has given us everything we need for life and godliness through our knowledge of him who called us by his own glory and goodness*." The gifts of the Holy Spirit are part of the "everything we need" to fulfill His purposes for our lives.

Gifts of the Spirit

There is some controversy as to the precise nature of each of the gifts of the Spirit, here is a list of spiritual gifts and their basic definitions.

- The gift of wisdom seems to be the ability to make decisions and give guidance that is according to God's will.
- The gift of knowledge is the ability to have an in-depth understanding of a spiritual issue or situation.
- The gift of faith is being able to trust God and encourage others to trust God, no matter the circumstances.
- The gift of healing is the miraculous ability to use God's healing power to restore a person who is sick, injured, or suffering.
- The gift of miracles is being able to perform signs and wonders that give authenticity to God's Word and the Gospel message.
- The gift of prophecy is being able to proclaim a message from God.
- The gift of discerning spirits is the ability to determine whether or not a message, person, or event is truly from God.
- The gift of tongues is the ability to speak in a foreign language that you do not have knowledge of, in order to communicate with someone who speaks that language.
- The gift of interpreting tongues is the ability to translate the tongues speaking and communicate it back to others in your own language.
- The gift of administration is being able to keep things organized and in accordance with God's principles.
- The gift of helps is always having the desire and ability to help others, to do whatever it takes to get a task accomplished.

Gifts of the Spirit - Which One(s) Do I Have?

The Holy Spirit distributes the gifts of the Spirit as He sees fit (**1 Corinthians 12:7-11**). God does not want us to be ignorant of how He wants us to serve Him. However, it is very easy for us to get gift(s) then serve God in that area of ministry. God calls us to be obedient and serve Him. He will equip us with the gifts of the Spirit. We need to accomplish the task or tasks He has called us to. Yes, God calls some to be teachers and gives them the gift of teaching that does not excuse the person from serving God in other ways as well. Is it beneficial to know what spiritual gift(s) God has given a person? Of course, it is. Is it wrong to focus so much on spiritual gifts that we miss other opportunities to serve God?-Yes!

There is no magic formula or spiritual gift test that can tell you what gifts of the Spirit a person possess. What we need to focus on is serving God. Do you see a need in your church? Do what you can to meet it. Is there a position in a ministry that is vacant? Pray as to whether God would have you fill it. If we seek God's will and obey His leading, He will always equip us with whatever gifts of the Spirit we need. Spiritual gift tests can be of some value in determining what areas God has especially gifts a person has. As always, though, place far more emphasis on God's Word and submitting to the Lord's leading than you do on the results of a spiritual gift test.

Gifts of the Spirit - What Are the Gifts Used For?

The Apostle Paul indicated that the gifts of the Spirit are equally valid, but not equally valuable. Their value is determined by the worth a person gift of the spirit should be used in the church. In dealing with this matter, he used the analogy of the human body.

All members of the body have functions, Paul declared some are more important than others (**1 Corinthians 12:12-26**). The service of each Christian should be in proportion to the gifts which he or she possesses (**1 Corinthians 12-14**). All believers, as members of the body of Christ, must be serving together in order for the body to be fully-functional. That is why a church needs pastors, teachers, helpers, servants, administrators, those with great faith, etc. All of the gifts of the Holy Spirit working together are needed to produce the full potential of the church. Since the gifts of the Spirit are gifts of grace, their use must be controlled by the rule of love - the greatest of all the gifts of the Spirit (**1 Corinthians 13**).

Jesus said we are to forgive others in (**Matthew 18:21-22**). To fully understand what Jesus was saying, we must look at the context of the whole chapter, for Jesus was speaking not only about forgiving one another but about Christian character, both in and out of the church. The admonition to forgive our brother seventy times seven follows Jesus' discourse on discipline in the church (**Matthew 18:15-20**), in which He lays down the rules for restoring a-brother.

That are these gifts of the Spirit? How can you know that a person has particular gifts of the Spirit? Can others give us an indication of what our gift is? What does the believer do with these gifts in the church? Are some gifts more important than others? Are the gifts of healing still being accessed today by believers? Is the gift of miracles still existent in the church today?

Each and every believer has been given by the indwelling of the Spirit of God, gifts of the Spirit (**Acts 2:38**). In **Acts chapter 8** and in 1 **Corinthians Chapters 12-14** we see external gifts of the Holy Spirit. They were not gifts that they have been developed by human capacities, therefore the believer has absolutely no right to brag on these gifts. If we exalt in our gifts, we are taking credit for something that we have not earned ourselves. It is like taking credit for a gift you receive on your birthday. It is just that; a gift that was not yours given to your freely it is given apart from any inherent capabilities that you have. It is not like changing the old hymn from How Great Thou Art to How Great I Am.

No believer can say that they have no gift of the Spirit from God. God has given all believers gifts; some have several everyone has these gifts. These gifts of the Spirit are given not for the believer for the Body of Christ. These gifts are intended for the church, to strengthen them, to feed people, to exhort, to encourage, and to have strengthen the Body of Christ empowered to do the work of Christ. These gifts are always to exalt Christ, to witness of God's power, to build up the Body, and to work to enlarge the Body of Christ by sharing the gospel of Jesus Christ with the lost. There are several biblical tools and surveys that believers can use to discover their own gifts of the Spirit. These are helpful applications to allow the Christian to see what their gifts are and therefore how they can best help the church. No believer in Christ has any gift of the Spirit.

Isaiah 11:2-3 speaks of seven different spirits or gifts: "*And the Spirit of the Lord will rest on him—the Spirit of wisdom and understanding, the Spirit of counsel and might, the Spirit of knowledge and the fear of the Lord. He will delight in obeying-the-Lord*".

He will not judge by appearance nor make a decision based on hearsay (called discernment). These are important gifts some of them are similar but different from the gifts of the Spirit. Paul talks about in the New Testament in **I Corinthians chapter twelve**. There are nine gifts of the Spirit in **I Corinthians chapter twelve**:

1) Word of Wisdom
2) Word of Knowledge
3) Faith
4) Gifts of Healing
5) Working of Miracles
6) Prophecy
7) Discerning of Spirits
8) Divers (or different) kinds of Tongues
9) Interpretation of (different) Tongues

Peter, wishing to appear especially forgiving and benevolent, asked Jesus if forgiveness was to be offered seven times. The Jewish rabbis at the time taught that forgiving someone more than three times was unnecessary, citing **Amos 1:3-13** where God forgave Israel's enemies three times, then punished them. By offering forgiveness more than double that of the Old Testament. When Jesus responded that forgiveness should be offered four hundred and ninety times, far beyond that which Peter was proposing.

By saying we are to forgive those who sin against us seventy times seven, Jesus was not limiting forgiveness to 490 times, a number that is, for all practical purposes, beyond counting. Christians with forgiving hearts not only do not limit the number of times they forgive; they continue to forgive with as much grace the thousandth   time   as   they   do   the   first   time.

Jesus' parable of the unforgiving servant follows directly after His "seventy times seven" speech, driving home the point we are not forgiven the sin against a Holy Spirit, how much more should we be eager to forgive those who sin against us,. Paul parallels this example in **Ephesians 4:32** where he admonishes us to forgive one another *"even as God for Christ's sake has forgiven you."* Clearly, forgiveness is not to be meted out in a limited fashion.

For when we realize that God is a God of order and purpose we can then better understand who He is and why. You don't have to look very hard to see how orderly God is. Just look at how ants working together, watch ducks flying in formation, or simply look at the structure of a leaf on a tree you'll see that God is indeed a God of order and purpose. If you take an even deeper look at creation from a scientific standpoint you'll really begin to realize this.

The period of time I'm referring to here was the 70 YEAR CAPTIVITY OF JUDAH AND JERUSALEM beginning with Nebuchadnezzar King of Babylon in 496 B.C. ending in 426 B.C. during the reign of Cyrus king of Persia (**Jer. 25:11** and **Dan 9:2**)

So not only do we see from this that 490 years is a part of God's law concerning time, but 70 years is as well. Again, God does nothing by chance, everything He does has a specific purpose.

70 x 7 = 490

Now it's important to point is the "number 490" actually written in the Bible. 490 is either written as SEVENTY TIMES SEVEN or SEVENTY SEVENS. The reason is so that we can recognize God's natural divisions of time. You see all basic increments of Biblical time are ordered by the number SEVEN.

All departments of nature are marked all over with mathematics. In this realm practically everything is in SEVENS. Notice next time the shape of frost when it crystallizes on the window. Notice the small snow flakes. It is wonderful how God formed everything in a pattern of SEVENS.

It would be well for the reader to always remember that SEVEN means COMPLETENESS or SPIRITUAL PERFECTION. When ever you come to a SEVEN.

SEVEN is found 735 times in the Bible. SEVENFOLD is mentioned 6 times and SEVENTH is found 119 times.

Romans 16:1-27 (33)

V-1 "I commend unto you Phebe our sister, which is a servant of the church which is at Cenchrea:

V-2 That ye receive her in the Lord, as becometh saints, and that ye assist her in whatsoever business she hath need of you: for she hath been a succourer of many, and of myself also.

V-3 Greet Priscilla and Aquila my helpers in Christ Jesus:

V-4 Who have for my life laid down their own necks: unto whom not only I give thanks, but also all the churches of the Gentiles.

V-5 Likewise *greet* the church that is in their house. Salute my wellbeloved Epaenetus, who is the firstfruits of Achaia unto Christ.

V-6 Greet Mary, who bestowed much labour on us.

V-7 Salute Andronicus and Junia, my kinsmen, and my fellowprisoners, who are of note among the apostles, who also were in Christ before me.

V-8 Greet Amplias my beloved in the Lord.

V-9 Salute Urbane, our helper in Christ, and Stachys my beloved.

V-10 Salute Apelles approved in Christ. Salute them which are of Aristobulus' *household*.

V-11 Salute Herodion my kinsman. Greet them that be of the *household* of Narcissus, which are in the Lord.

V-12 Salute Tryphena and Tryphosa, who labour in the Lord. Salute the beloved Persis, which laboured much in the Lord.

V-13 Salute Rufus chosen in the Lord, and his mother and mine.

V-14 Salute Asyncritus, Phlegon, Hermas, Patrobas, Hermes, and the brethren which are with them.

V-15 Salute Philologus, and Julia, Nereus, and his sister, and Olympas, and all the saints which are with them.

V-16 Salute one another with an holy kiss. The churches of Christ salute you.

V-17 Now I beseech you, brethren, mark them which cause divisions and offences contrary to the doctrine which ye have learned; and avoid them.

V-18 For they that are such serve not our Lord Jesus Christ, but their own belly; and by good words and fair speeches deceive the hearts of the simple.

V-19 For your obedience is come abroad unto all *men*. I am glad therefore on your behalf: but I would have you wise unto that which is good, and simple concerning evil.

V-20 And the God of peace shall bruise Satan under your feet shortly. The grace of our Lord Jesus Christ *be* with you. Amen.

V-21 Timotheus my workfellow, and Lucius, and Jason, and Sosipater, my kinsmen, salute you.

V-22 I Tertius, who wrote *this* epistle, salute you in the Lord.

V-23 Gaius mine host, and of the whole church, saluteth you. Erastus the chamberlain of the city saluteth you, and Quartus a brother.

V-24 The grace of our Lord Jesus Christ *be* with you all. Amen.

V-25 Now to him that is of power to stablish you according to my gospel, and the preaching of Jesus Christ, according to the revelation of the mystery, which was kept secret since the world began,

V-26 But now is made manifest, and by the scriptures of the prophets, according to the commandment of the everlasting God, made known to all nations for the obedience of faith:

V-27 To God only wise, *be* glory through Jesus Christ for ever. Amen."

Chapter 7
HUMAN NATURE AND EMOTIONS

So you see there are a lot of aspects to other FACTORS rather than sin we may have raised more questions, than answers right now, as we go through this part of the study.

I'm going to ask you some personal questions.

One, do you have peace in your life?

Two, are you happy with the decisions/choices you have made in your life?

Three, may I ask you another question can life be better or is it just ok?

Fourth, what would you say to those questions?

Think it over before you answer, can I, or am I in charge of my life, do I have balance and control? Most of us do very well with certain aspects of life and fail at others, there can be a point where some areas are out of control and balance.

I have asked four questions and ask about how you're handling the different areas and influences, be honest with yourself and me. I'm not talking about divorcing someone, or starting all over again. I'm not talking about erasing your past that is a part of you. A person tends to make the same mistakes they usually follow a pattern, the way to identify them they will show-up over and over again. **(human nature at work)**!

Would you like to make some changes or improvements in your life? I know I was not happy with the way things were going at one time as I presented a profile of my life. I didn't want any changes because I was happy being unhappy, and thought that was the way life should be. I liked being unhappy and negative about myself. I hope I haven't offended anyone by saying that. Now let's look at our (**Human Nature**) and a (**Self Evaluation**). A person's emotional make-up, most reactions come from (our feelings). Another are the influences in our (relationships), genetics, and how they affect a person's life and emotions.

How does a person live up to Christian standards and moral values? How do you deal with your relationships, circumstances, and problems? Sometimes Christians think we're exempt from certain things, or think God will judge us, and He does. I like this phrase *"what is in a name?"* **Prov. 22:1** says *"a GOOD name"*.

When Moses was leading the children of Israel out of the land of Egypt they sinned by breaking the commanement which made of stone God's pronounced the judgment on the generation that broke the (stone) "The 10 Commandments" they would not enter "the promised land":

Exodus 34:1-9   (34)

V-1 "And the LORD said unto Moses, Hew thee two tables of stone like unto the first: and I will write upon *these* tables the words that were in the first tables, which thou brakest.

V-2 And be ready in the morning, and come up in the morning unto mount Sinai, and present thyself there to me in the top of the mount.

V-3 And no man shall come up with thee, neither let any man be seen throughout all the mount; neither let the flocks nor herds feed before that mount.

V-4 And he hewed two tables of stone like unto the first; and Moses rose up early in the morning, and went up unto mount Sinai, as the LORD had commanded him, and took in his hand the two tables of stone.

V-5 And the LORD descended in the cloud, and stood with him there, and proclaimed the name of the LORD.

V-6 And the LORD passed by before him, and proclaimed, The LORD, The LORD God, merciful and gracious, longsuffering, and abundant in goodness and truth,

V-7 Keeping mercy for thousands, forgiving iniquity and transgression and sin, and that will by no means clear *the guilty*; visiting the iniquity of the fathers upon the children, and upon the children's children, unto the third and to the fourth *generation*.

V-8 And Moses made haste, and bowed his head toward the earth, and worshipped.

V-9 And he said, If now I have found grace in thy sight, O Lord, let my Lord, I pray thee, go among us; for it *is* a stiffnecked people; and pardon our iniquity and our sin, and take us for thine inheritance."

I believe in principle verse 7, visiting the iniquity of the fathers and mothers upon the children and grandchildren, upon the children's children, unto the third and to the fourth *generation*." We know genetics go as far back as three generations or more because of DNA testing. We can trace behaviors back three generations in the tests we perform on children and young people. This is very evident in **abuse** and **addiction** testing we do. Check with us at Support Outreach Services if you like this test?

Now let's take a closer look at the problem and check to see if there is **abuse** in situation and then the **hurt & pain involved**. When someone **abuses** or **hurts** a person. A (**human reaction**) maybe to get even or be spiteful, or even worse vengeance - wrath, anger - revenge. That is (**human nature**) at work at its worst.

Those natural reactions influence our safety devices the brain registers the violation done, in that way a person's feelings have been altered to some degree, or even worse left them with hurt, anger, and bitterness to deal with. That can be some of the reasons why a person makes bad decisions/choices and even hurt people others in return. Because they have been hurt, whether they want to admit it or not, sometimes people hurt people subconsciously (even if we're a Christian) or not.

To intentionally **abuse** or **hurt** someone is a completely different story. That must be dealt with. If we don't God will at some point in their life. Judging the heart should start at home, within one's self. That is why we have no room to judge others. *"Judge not, that ye be not judged."* (verse 1) of **Matt. 7:1-6**; in (verses 2-5) gives a spiritual application to judging.

Matthew 7:1-6   (35)

V-1 "Judge not, that ye be not judged.

V-2 For with what judgment ye judge, ye shall be judged: and with what measure ye mete, it shall be measured to you again.

V-3 And why beholdest thou the mote that is in thy brother's eye, but considerest not the beam that is in thine own eye?

V-4 Or how wilt thou say to thy brother, Let me pull out the mote out of thine eye; and, behold, a beam *is* in thine own eye?

V-5 Thou hypocrite, first cast out the beam out of thine own eye; and then shalt thou see clearly to cast out the mote out of thy brother's eye.

V-6 Give not that which is holy unto the dogs, neither cast ye your pearls before swine, lest they trample them under their feet, and turn again and rend you."

Look at yourself and see what judgments you do fall back on you. *"Whatever you sow ye shall also reap"*. Look at:

"For God there is no respect of persons with God" "Dearly beloved, avenge not yourselves, but rather give place unto wrath: for it is written Vengeance is mine; I will repay, saith the Lord." We all need to work on these principles (daily).

There is another influence that is in our lives. Some influences have to do with "the flesh", we need to be aware *"the Devil, - (Satan)"*.

I Peter 5:8,

V-8 "Be sober, be vigilant; because your adversary the devil as a "roaring lion, walking about, seeking whom he may devour":

I choose to believe we have to deal all those strong influences in our lives.

We have discussed some of these influences, the cause and effects of abuses that causes hurt, bitterness for the purpose of setting up this study on (**human nature**), these influences could go back as far as childhood even parents behaviors are pasted to their children. I don't feel we should not go any farther without at least discussing this (**human emotions**). Also, as we look at the fleshly desires, our needs and despairs, in the way a person expresses their love.

Definition of Foundation: {13}

(Webster Colligate Dictionary), "ground; foundation, that which supports and assertion of the good and bad in a person, an action, or series of actions, or reasoning".

Paul is describing the conflict, struggle, and the warfare from within.

Demonstration Chart I, Axiom; + Positive + 5 is best down to +1; there are NO, 0's

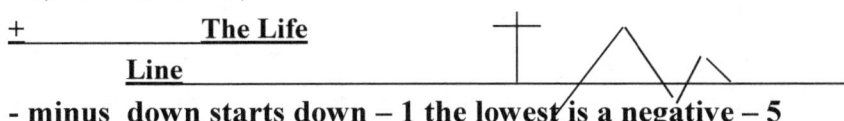

+	The Life	
	Line	

- minus down starts down – 1 the lowest is a negative – 5

SOS Life Enhancement - Evaluations

We want to see how "**The Life Line**" fits into "**Demonstration Chart I, Axiom**:

We have just introduced the second aspect of our Services!

Our newsletter is called **SOS Life Line**. Also, in our lifeline there are many different stages and events that happen to a person. (Illustration),

We see a cross $+$ in our **Life Line** that is an illustration of our Christian experience. This we call salvation it is a definite experience with Christ. This should be one of the major events in your life, becoming a Christian is very important because it affects the decisions/choices you make throughout life. "*Who is God and how does man fit in*"?

Now we want to expose you to the "**Two Natures**" in action. (The good & bad, the positive & negative.). We hope to show you how the "**Two Natures**" **are at work in a person's life** and **their reacts** affect the situations and are at work in every situation. Now, how does this relate to God is even more important? I hope the rest of our study will help with other aspects of your life.

I want to examine the **"Two Natures" even farther. Man** is not all good, nor all bad. That is why we incorporated the scale above.

The negative side of the situation is how bad it is and to what point does it become sin? Are there big sins and little sins? Are all sins the same in the site of God?

To me the best example in any situation is the amount of **love or lack of love shown**, Compare this to God's **love** for each person and their **love** for the world, *"God so loved the world, that He gave his only begotten Son,"* **John 3:16**. He sent his Son into the world so *"that whosoever believeth in him should not perish, but have everlasting life."* Is the second half of **John 3:16** which represents **the cross on "The Life Line". Now let's look at some practical applications.**

In the Life Line we use the term Breaking Down in Chart I, Practical Axioms & Skills.
SOS Life Enhancement, Information & Study guide! Our goal is to *Help People, Help Themselves*
Personal-Attention & Care, Who is that person in your mirror? (Book)
Now we're actually going to apply some of these principles to (human nature).

Demonstration Chart I, Axiom:
+ 1 - 5 is 1. good, 2. better, 3. best, 4. very best 5. perfection
          The Life Line Skills & Practical
Axioms

- 1 - 5 1. blow average, 2. poor 3. bad, 4. very bad, 5. abusive

I want you to see how "The Life Line" fits into **"Demonstration Chart I, Axiom**:

Input & Output There is one thing for sure, what you put into your life is what is going to come out of your life. Another thing about a person's life that is just as certain, their conduct and (character) may be reflective of their back ground. May I ask this question again? *Who are you*, and who is in control of your life, if you're not sure, *who is*? Let's make no mistake about one thing you are responsible for your conduct and actions as a Christian or non-Christian. You may want help, God put us on earth to help each when were in trouble, you're accountable for your actions, every word, and the deeds done in this mortal body.

They affect a person's family, friends, and relationships, etc. I emphases at this point every person, even individual families have to deal with problems. No one or family is exempt from problems, no matter how rich or poor, good or bad at some point and time. Every life is intertwined with your relationships, family, your vocation, etc. God deals with us in respect to your relationships. He cares is true; He loves each of us, Wow!

(The Life Cycle) has our Age + Stage enters the picture as we look at our life, family, and situation!

At each **Age + Stage** there are **Identity Problems = Problems and Even Crises.**

Cycle 1. Growth Stage: Conception and Childhood to about age 1 to 14 = growth

Cycle 2. Exploratory Stage: About age 15 to about age 25 = rebellious stage.

Cycle 3. Establishment Stage: About age 26 to about age 45 = family life.

Cycle 4. Maintenance Stage: About age 46 to about age 65 = health & prosperity.

Cycle 5. Stage of Decline: About age 66 to about age 72 = retirement time.

Cycle 6. The Golden years: About age 73 and up = ending & eternity.

Age + stage is another influence that affects a person's life and family always influenced by their age. Add in the **stress** of a family and life, a person lives under stress every day, in knowing that their everyday decisions/choices may have an effect on them and their **family**. Then a person has the big or major decisions/choices to face from time to time.

The first thing is your **birth** that brings you into a wonderful experience called life. The first few years are very much controlled by your patents. Then your **childhood** is a wonderful time, as time goes along you start to declare your independence, as you get older. Which creates some conflict in some cases, but on the other-hand it can create some major crises too.

The **Growth Stage** is under mom and dad's guidance and help. In some cases this is not a happy time for a child because of their parents or other influences. Sometimes, in a child's life they feel unhappy and helpless, especially when they have been hurt and abused. Sometimes adults take advantage of a child's growth process and parents use them to their advantage. To this degree they will influence their success or failure, other influences will determine a person's life's patterns, hidden agendas, **Walls, Barriers, Prejudices, Blind-spots, Closed-doors, & Skeletons.**

Exploratory Stage, the teens and young adult years are the most exciting times in your lives. Going to school, dating, falling

238

probably in and out of love. One of the problems is everything is happening so fast. There are the physical and emotional changes.

There is another thing about being young they think they can do anything and their knowledge has no boundaries. With all of that knowledge life still can be confusing, even to the point that some even think about suicide.

The teen and young adult years are so important because each decision/choices affects your destiny. This is when your relationship with your parents is so important. In some cases a person doesn't see things like their parents or don't do the right thing. They may want to be popular, peer pressure, they want to do what they want to do, rather than do what is best for their lives. If a person has had a bad relationship with their parents or others, I hope our program will be a help to you. As a teen it is the best time to set the right kind of values and principals in your life. Another thing about being a teen their life is relative free to choose and make the decisions/choices in their life. Be careful this is when the devil can do his worst damage.

Another, young adults make major a decision such as who they are going to marry? Then a person has what is called the **Establishment Stage** having children come along and job/vocation; then comes the **Maintenance Stage,** your grandchildren. Then if you live long enough **Stage of Decline**. **The Golden years** retirement and usually some health problems. Each of these stages in your life can bring about a new set of problems to deal with. This is a brief look at the **Ages + Stages** in your life.

Every One, each set of circumstances brings about a new set of problems to deal with. Now, that I have introduced these aspects into your life, then what? I think this is a step in the right direction, but each **Stage** can bring about its own set problems. I want to be careful here you should be able to deal with the different influences

239

in the **Life Line**, but that does not necessarily guarantee success or happiness. We have to look at life from the world and the different influences too.

(Illustration)

The news media presents the negative side of the stories, the disasters and personal problems. They also create the sensational side of the story. Very seldom do they present a positive story or something good that people do. There is so much good, but that does not make a good news story.

I think as you see the cross $+$ in your **Life Line**, we have hope for today, for tomorrow, the best part a person's destiny is sealed as a Christian. *"If God be for us who can be against us"*, **Rom. 8:31**.

The church you chose is another step in your Christian life the Sunday school class. How a person choses to worship and serve God can help a person handle the stress and the problems in their life.

It is a comfort to me to know that I am facing life as a Christian. I hope you have made this decision/choice and your destiny sealed, by accepting Christ as your Savior. If not we'll show you how.

Now I want to take a minute to talk about the last stage in your life, death or eternity if you please. Death is one of the biggest stresses a person deals with whether we're young or old, it can happen at anytime depending on the circumstance or illness. We as Christians do not have to worry because in:

John 14:1, 2

V-1 "Let not your hearts be troubled: ye believe in God, believe in me."

V-2 "In my Fathers house are many mansions if it where not true I would told you so, I go to prepare a place for you".

What a comfort as a Christian. At the same time:

John 14:5,6

V-5 "Thomas saith unto him, Lord, we know not whither thou goest;"? (verse 6) & he said:

V-6 "I am the way, the truth, and the life:"

LIFE LINE SKILLS

Life Line Axioms behaviors & patterns

How far are you willing to go in a relationship will determine whether you want to save a relationship or not, but then on the other hand how far is the other person or persons willing to meet the challenge? A person can only go as far as the other person will let them. There can be an impasse when nothing is happening. It can get to the point of <u>danger</u> and <u>damage</u> to the person it can affect their marriage relationship, the whole family, friends, and it can affect their work/job, our relations with our co-workers.

An Axiom, I have heard the term **50/50** in a **Relationship**. I believe in **50/50** as a good **axiom** if it works in a person's relationships, there is usually each person trying to gain the controlling edge, **51%** or more because it is (nature to think they're right) in some relationships it is out of balance some people want and expect a **75** to a **100%** control. It can be a (male or female) depending on the situation. You say why because in most cases each person has their strong points. With the women it should or could be kitchen, others like to control the check book. You get the idea? If each person is giving a **100%** you likely come up an agreement or the other saying let's try it your way first.

A controlling person wants it their way all of the time, that person has a serious problem; don't they?

Another Axiom, I strongly believe in is the **100%** approach240 Which in this case each PERSON IS GIVING & TAKING a **100%** in a situation when trying to solve a problem and/or making the relationship work. Each person is responsible to give a 100% for (his or her) own love and actions in a relationship) regardless of which **axioms** or **example** you use, be sure to look at both sides of the issues be for making a decision.

There are some common problems we all face as adults, young people, and even children. All of us have to face the realities in your life and relationships. The fact that a person's dreams don't always come true and their dreams can get mixed up with their realities.

As adults we look at life from a different perspective as young people they see their life developing right before their very own eyes, they begin to see how tough life can be. I still have the dreams as a child and young person my dreams have changed.

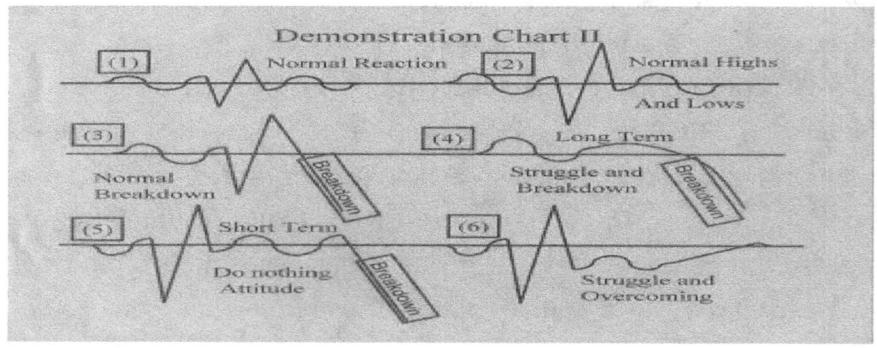

Formula – Scale from our Study-Guide:

Next we're going to break down the different types of **human behavior** from within and from without.

Now **Demonstration Chart II** <u>Graff Layouts</u> deals with the normal, abnormal emotional reactions and then three different kinds of **Breakdowns** to help us understand our **human nature**.

Go to Demonstration Chart II,

(1) Axiom: a normal reaction

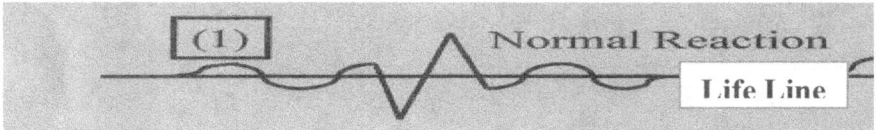

Now lets look at Cart II, (1). This is a **normal reaction** in a graph format, a reaction to any situation, stress, crisis, demand, need or desire, or emotional experiences. Also when you look at the chart you see small curves going down below the <u>line</u> with a small variance at the beginning and end the **Life Line**. Next, you see a sharp visual diagonal line going down and up with the same amount of variance above and below the **Life Line**. This is a **normal reaction** in process when a person sees the diagram it will help them understand their feelings and emotions a little better. I know it did when I saw the graph, now I see myself thinking about a situation in that light, and what the term means. The same variance before and after wards in an normal emotional reaction, a person's actions and reaction should tell them a lot about what's going on inside and out.

This term at this point is what we call an emotional reaction in relation to an experience. When we relate to love, joy happiness, or hurt, sorrow, crying, in the everyday emotional experiences. As we look at a **normal reaction** in a person's life we see that it is fairly quick and sharp, and a person's life goes back to normal fairly quickly or in a short period of time. There should be a normal pattern and rhythm before and after the experience, (if not), their life is not likely going into a normal pattern or rhythm afterwards it could depend on the severity of the circumstances.

Any **(human behavior)** can have more than one emotion and reaction at the same time. At this point it can have different meaning to different people at the same time. A decision/choice or problem can be difficult to understand and why someone said what (he or she) said, or why (he or she) did something is another. A person could think it to be one way and each person thinks they're right.

Titus 2:1-8 (36)

V-1 "But speak thou the things which become sound doctrine:

V-2 That the aged men be sober, grave, temperate, sound in faith, in charity, in patience.

V-3 The aged women likewise, that *they be* in behaviour as becometh holiness, not false accusers, not given to much wine, teachers of good things;

V-4 That they may teach the young women to be sober, to love their husbands, to love their children,

V-5 *To be* discreet, chaste, keepers at home, good, obedient to their own husbands, that the word of God be not blasphemed.

V-6 Young men likewise exhort to be sober minded.

V-7 In all things shewing thyself a pattern of good works: in doctrine *shewing* uncorruptness, gravity, sincerity,

V-8 Sound speech, that cannot be condemned; that he that is of the contrary part may be ashamed, having no evil thing to say of you.'

The next thing we look for is stress. How much stress was in the **normal reaction**, was there a crisis to deal with each person will know what a crisis when it comes whether its major or minor. Then, the demands in their life are when someone expects them to do something or tells them to do something, even life itself has demands, relationships, vocation, etc. Everyday needs and desires of the heart, mind, and flesh has stresses and demands.

Philippians 1:21-25 (37)

V-21 "For to me to live *is* Christ, and to die *is* gain.

V-22But if I live in the flesh, this *is* the fruit of my labour: yet what I shall choose I wot not.

V-23 For I am in a strait betwixt two, having a desire to depart, and to be with Christ; which is far better:

V-24 Nevertheless to abide in the flesh *is* more needful for you.

V-25 And having this confidence, I know that I shall abide and continue with you all for your furtherance and joy of faith;"

(Illustration) I thought a new marriage with a new person would mean a successful marriage and bring about happiness. I thought if I could start all over again with a new person that would bring about a successful relationship and for the most part it did, but when it didn't workout. I was more confused than ever. I wanted a successful marriage because I had failed before. Sometimes this is a driving force that causes a pattern if we're not careful it becomes away of life, a **down-hill-spiral**. Divorce maybe the only way out for some people. I'm not here to judge or criticize what is right or wrong that is between a person and God. I have faced the same things in my life. I can justify every marriage, divorce is the way of dealing with a bad relationship. In my case it may have been a matter of choosing the wrong person or was that the problem?

This is a part of my personal testimony & prayer life.

This for the most part was the way I looked at God's (will) before and I think I was wrong for the most part. I have found in the light of who God is He does the unexpected or I believe we should expect the super natural because He is God. His thoughts and ways are higher than our thoughts and the heavens are higher than the earth.

Isaiah 55:6-13   (38)

V-6 "Seek ye the LORD while he may be found, call ye upon him while he is near:

V-7 Let the wicked forsake his way, and the unrighteous man his thoughts: and let him return unto the LORD, and he will have mercy upon him; and to our God, for he will abundantly pardon.

V-8 For my thoughts *are* not your thoughts, neither *are* your ways my ways, saith the LORD.

V-9 For *as* the heavens are higher than the earth, so are my ways higher than your ways, and my thoughts than your thoughts.

V-10 For as the rain cometh down, and the snow from heaven, and returneth not thither, but watereth the earth, and maketh it bring forth and bud, that it may give seed to the sower, and bread to the eater:

V-11 So shall my word be that goeth forth out of my mouth: it shall not return unto me void, but it shall accomplish that which I please, and it shall prosper *in the thing* whereto I sent it.

V-12 For ye shall go out with joy, and be led forth with peace: the mountains and the hills shall break forth before you into singing, and all the trees of the field shall clap *their* hands.

V-13 Instead of the thorn shall come up the fir tree, and instead of the brier shall come up the myrtle tree: and it shall be to the LORD for a name, for an everlasting sign *that* shall not be cut off."

Because man can do things to influence his own thought process and destiny he makes his own decisions/choices. It can be very hard to know the difference between the (will of God) and the (will of man).

(Illustration), may I take another one of my own life experiences. When it came to my writing I didn't think I could do it, I wanted to do God's will, the main reason I didn't think I could do it I don't like to write or read. If I'm interested, I don't mind studying or even studying for a test, to set down for hours and read is not my "cup of tea". I like a short story format. Will guess what I'm doing? Just the opposite of what I thought I would be doing. In 1987 or along about that time, I was struggling with high-blood-pressure and heart problems. I was on the verge of having a heart attack. My arthritis was doing better about that time, the quality of live was not good. I started praying, trying to find God because I had gotten away from God over the years and didn't want anything to do with serving God. I was happy and content and had a good marriage at the time.

Now we're going into this thing of (Gods will) for my life. I have told this story before, but not in the relation to (God's will). I believe I was in God's presence for about 6 weeks; daily and in every thought, He was there speaking to me.

God said "write down the things I'm going to show you". (Man, I didn't know what to think, or know what to do when He said that), I said to God no one will listen to me. (I have an excuse.) I said I will do whatever, but surely you don't mean this about the writing, I just thought it was a phase and it would pass; it did for a while. Then in 1992 I even took some person notes when I was going through my last divorce and they got lost in moving at the time. I thought again that was okay because it can't be (God's will) for me to write about a divorce I still did not really craps the reality of what was going on in life until 1996. I started a support system in 1997 to help others but the burden to write always comes back stronger than ever. God spoke to me and dealt with for 5 years, in 1996 this time it was much clearer. I want you to write about what has happened. I said I don't know how, you must mean something else. This is a resulted in a series of studies.

Demonstration Chart II,

(2) Axiom is called normal Highs and Lows, again an emotional reaction/experience takes place.

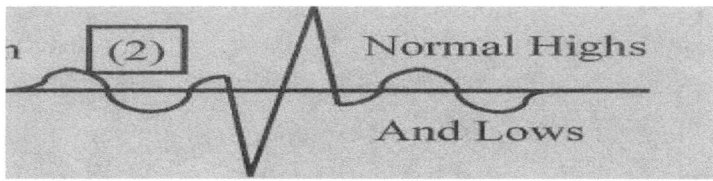

We are going to try and show the normal **emotional Highs and Lows** to anyone of a person's experiences or situations. This also has to do with normal reactions that reflect the **Highs** and **Lows**. When we are happy, even our body language shows it in our facial expressions like, (a smile) another is being unhappy our body language shows it could be (a frown) that tells a story. A normal high is when the sequence of events are emotional, like something that happens every day or looking forward for something good to happen. We don't get too excited or we are mentally prepared it doesn't shock a person. The stress level is usually above normal at this point and time.

Most of all **emotional Highs** and **Lows** are good in a proper balance. Proper balance has to do with your **emotional level** or **balance**. Now I hope I have not introduced terms that a person is not familiar with, it is probably a reaction a person doesn't think too much about, usually a person doesn't think about **normal reactions, emotional level,** and **balance** when things are happening in their life or in their everyday life and conversation. A person usually bases their decisions on what they believe to be right, emotions do enter into the decision; does that sound about right. Those three elements usually governs and rules in a decision? When there is an over or under reaction, in an emotional experience, is it too **High** or **Low**, that tell a person a lot about what has happened or going happen?

Another is the emotional reaction, (illustration) when a person is getting married or having a baby. Those are **highly** emotional experiences. There can be negative **Lows** in the emotional experiences such as illness and death causing **Abnormal Lows**. This again has to do with stress and the emotional level at the time. The time and effort should be short in nature and should not make it harder to get back to a **normal pattern** or **rhythm** in life. When a person has **Abnormal Lows**, a person may have a problem or experience depression, anxieties, and worry about what is going to happens especially when they are get down for any reason.

Now let's see what happens when it happens over and over again. At-the-lest, a person is looking at least an annoyance or it could be the starting of a pattern over along period of time, it may become a **down-hill-spiral**, a series of problems over a period of time, then it becomes a serious problem. **Normal reactions to normal Highs and Lows** are usually of no consequence at the time.

Again, when there is an over emotional reaction in a negative way, depression usually takes place a person can have exhaustion, fatigue, and/or burnout. When this happens a person's nerves are on edge, they're stressed-out, unhappiness etc. When a person notices this, they are **warning signs** taking place **Stop, Look,** and **Listen** it could be mental, physical, and/or emotional. It can cause health problem, or it is just around the corner. Even Christians get caught up in these emotional reactions because their **human** and to be **"human is to err"**. Sometimes people overload the mind an overreaction takes place it shows in their pride, arrogance, and sometimes a person thinks their special, God must really love me and He does, He may not like what He sees. This is a dangerous position, in some cases (I think too much) *"Pride comes before a fall"*, this is a paschal quote from The Bible.

(Illustration)

(A person may even joke about our success and think it's cute) (to the point of being arrogance). Yet a person needs pride and dignity as a person to be able to meet the challenges in their life. A person usually doesn't to brag for others to notice them. If a person does something right people usually don't pay attention, if a person does something wrong people have a tendency to notice their failures. We don't like that kind of attention. (Something is wrong when a person does things to get attention).

When this happens there is an "**improper balance**" we teach **Proper Balance** is a delicate balance between the right kind of **pride** and **humility** and *who we are* and/or what a person has done. A person needs to feel good without praise or pats on the back so to speak, they are always nice. We believe a person should spend time encouraging others.

When preachers preach on the subject of **pride** they usually speak on one side of the story every once and awhile we need to understand *who we are*. Our spouses do a pretty good job of keeping us humble (by letting us eat a little humble pie), once and while.

Proverbs has a lot say about **pride**; Solomon had a pretty good idea of **pride** not because he was the wealthiest person at that time. Read the book of Proverbs because he looks at **man**, the **human nature of man**, look at **Proverbs chapter 15** especially read **Prov. 15:30-33, Prov. 16:1-9**; and then (verses 16:10-17) again especially verses 18, 19 to the end of the chapter also **Prov. 22:4** about humility. The Bible uses the word proud to describe a person.

A good man shall accomplish much on earth, "*the steps of a good man are ordered of the Lord*" of **Ps. 37:23** and in the eyes of God, **Ps. 112, Matt. 25:14-30** the story of the talents given the servants, especially **Matt. 25:21-23** and one of my favorites is:

James 5:16 in part *"the effectual fervent prayer of a righteous man availeth much"*, also read (verse. 15) the whole chapter of **James Chapter 5** and book.

We have tried to present both sides of man in a realistic way, the responsibility of man to God and God responses to man. We are using Scriptural evidence of God's relationship to **man. (Pride)** can be feeling good about one's self.

There is one other point at this time about God and man, it is nothing new a person tend to think they are better than they really are especially when their successful. We are made in the image of God according to the Scriptures, we are in part like God, but we are **man**. This is another way that man can feel **(pride)**. We have the characteristics of God we're not God nor can we be our own god. Man needs to be mindful of himself **Prov. 4:23** *"keep thy heart with all diligence; for out of the issues of life."*

We have a tendency to think of God in our image (man) (that is why there is so many different churches and beliefs) or we tend to make ourselves into god. Why aren't we our own God?

Because God is the God of this Universe and man, is why we are mindful of Him and His power. We're in awe of His power, but God in His grace toward man is the defining difference and His love for **man**. In return we want to know this God in some ways we are like Him, how we do this and know the difference. Some want to be God and play like they are God, the real test of **man** is he wants to please God. Then God looks down on him in favor as **(men** and **women)**. That alone should humble us in gratitude toward a loving God.

There is a Scripture that says *"what is man, that thou art mindful of him"*? **Ps. 8:4** *"and the son of man, that thou visitest him."* Because He made man in His image; Body, Soul, and Spirit.

To live in this world is to live with the knowledge and presence of a (Holy and Righteous God).

What is our will in relation to God's love & will!

Now we want to look at the meaning of what has happened, (evaluate your self-image and self-worth) in the light of God's image, but also, be respectful of yourself because that pleases God too. He does not want a person to live beneath their means, or to be dominated by Satan and life. He wants a person to be in control of their destiny, God first, then others, and then themselves!

God's love is all encompassing in respect to God and man. **Love** is very much apart of the **10 commandments.** God is love **I John 4:7** " *Beloved, let us love one another: for love is of God; and every one that loveth is born of God.*" (**I John 4:17**) speaks of "*perfect love*". John was thought of by Jesus as the beloved. **I Corinthians 13** is the love chapter by the Apostle Paul. **I Cor. 13:1-4** "*THOUGH I speak with the tongues of men and of angles, and have not charity, I am become as sounding brass, or tinkling cymbal*"

I Cor. 13:2-4; 13

V-2 "And though I have the *gift of* prophecy, and understand all mysteries, and all knowledge; and though I have faith, so that I could remove mountains, and have not charity, I am nothing,

V-3 And though I bestow all my goods to fed *the poor*, and though I give my body to be burned, and have not charity, it profiteth me nothing.

V-4 Charity suffereth long, *and* is kind; charity envieth not; charity vaunteth not itself, is not puffed up," (verses 5 and on through 12) and then verse 13 sums it up

V-13 "And now abideth faith, hope, charity, these three; but the greatest of these is charity."

Now, let's get back to our responsibility and life. Another, thing we have to deal with is the way other people might see us, our friends, our relationships, etc. As we listen to other people and they give us advise based on what they see. Especially, (God will) or not, but whether yes or no, it is usually based on what we thought to be right. Sometimes, we ask God to do what we want and think, and think that is right rather than asking God for His will to be done:

Matt. 6:9, 10

V-9 *"Our Father which art in heaven, Hallowed be thy name"*.

V-10) "Thy kingdom come, Thy will be done in earth, as it is done in heaven".

Matt. 6:9 & 10, Luke 11:2 *"as in heaven, so in earth "*.

Sometimes, people think they are in God's will (most people want to know God's will for (his or her) life, or at least want His favor, and/or His blessings in what they do) people can be in God's will and still make the wrong decision/choice. This study is not about God's will as such but how it relates to our **human behavior**.

Some even go as far as to pray about it and seek God's will, there can have two people with different opinions both think it is God's will. (I have seen this happen in my own life and relationships).

Now what do we do? When I make a decision/choice based on my **emotional reaction**, **personal need,** or **desire**, and think that is God will for me, we're probably wrong based on what we thought to be right. Our purpose is to study **human nature** and the **will of man** as it reflects to our **reactions** and **emotions** in the light of God's Word and His will for man. *"God is longsuffering not willing that any should parish"* **2 Peter 3:9.**

We are going to be dealing with some other terms as we go on, that I think relate. Now we are going to be dealing with what is called **crossover tendencies**. This term is not used in Chart I layout that is why we need to discuss it now. We have actually been taking about **crossover tendencies** used in the Biblical terms. Now we will give personal meaning and why we need to define what they mean? This study is based on the **lifeline**. Those reactions and emotions that over-lap and relate to other **Axioms** which are called **crossover tendencies**. Then, the (positive or negative = +'s & -'s)

Introduction to Breakdowns

At this point we are going to **introduce 3 different kinds of Break Downs** and how they relate. I think it's important the order in which we have chosen these **Chart numbers**, they could appear in any order in a person's life, depending on the circumstances at the same time. They may seem like they are not in proper order now, let's wait and see. Any **human behavior** can have more than one **emotion** and **reaction** happening at the same time as we have just discussed. We try to use the logic of sequence as we look at any situation, a person may see them differently because they are dealing with the problems and that is okay. We are going to be dealing with **Break Downs** in any situation, stress, worry, crisis, demands, personal needs, despairs, the emotional reactions to them and how the **Break Downs** relates to a person's **behaviors** regardless of their Christian beliefs.

First a preview of **Demonstration Chart II (3) Axiom a normal breakdown**, second **(4-5)** are called **long-term breakdown** and **struggle, (6)** is **short** or **long-term breakdown, a do nothing attitude**.

Demonstration Chart II

(3) Axiom: Normal Breakdown

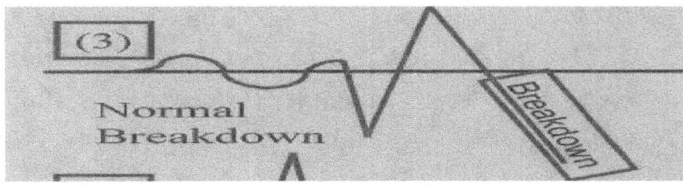

The **Axiom (3)** is a **Normal Breakdown** you're angry, you get mad at someone, or something; you get over it fairly quickly. It could be a conflict, stubbornness, or I just don't want to do it right now. **Axiom (4)** is a very bad one that deals with a person's (own will) or it could be two wills that lock horns.

Axiom (3) is defiantly a conflict of **will** and **will's, actions, reactions,** and **emotional** flare-ups, it could be that no one will give in and to what degree a person doesn't want to do something. This does not mean that life does not go on in a practical sense, it does the life has been altered, damaged, or abuse; the hurt is brief or for a short time. This breakdown may or may not have been resolved or repaired at this point, but life goes on without any or little variance before or afterwards you see nothing is done about it.

Now as we look at **Axiom (3)** you can see the sharp down, which in this case a **normal reaction** becomes a **breakdown**, you come back into the **Life Line** with a **breakdown** after it has happened it has a caused a conflict of the will or the conflict of two wills is a lot like **Axiom (1)** where you go back to a **normal reaction** in the life line, after the breakdown life will seem to have a **normal pattern**.

In this kind of breakdown has some damage, a person may think they have gotten over it, life goes on. This breakdown also has brought about breaking down a stress point, (you could have stressed-out) or a crisis, or it could have been a normal demand, (like yelling at the kids or spouse).

It is only a problem when it becomes a problem (or if it happens often or over the same type of situation) if you don't try to deal with it at the time. Even worse it could be a matter that you are not going to deal with at all. May I reemphasize that life goes on after a **normal breakdown** and what looks like a **normal pattern** or **rhythm** remember there has been some damage to say the least.

Under that normal **pattern** and **rhythm** there could be turmoil from something other than this particular breakdown there is disasters a head (a **time bomb** maybe ticking). Again the longer this festers and goes on the worse the hurt gets and the anger can build up, and even to the point of bitterness. This adds to some **normal reactions** that relate, that don't get resolved. You can have major problems to deal with in the future. Then (**boom**) one day it all comes to ahead anything can trigger the **explosion**.

The next is very important in life and relationships. I think this is where we need to pay-close-attention. We can get mad and so angry with someone at times, usually this is, "**Short Term**" or at least you had better hope its short term and again look at the problem closely to see if it fits into anyone these next **breakdowns**. A marriage relationship is one the most trying and stress related in a person's life.

Demonstration Chart II, Axiom (4):
Long Term Struggle & Breakdown

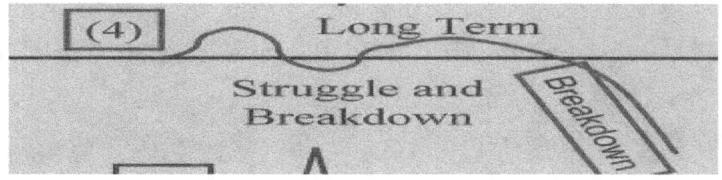

Now let's go on to **Axiom (4).** This has to do with a "**long term struggle** and **breakdown**", stress or stresses, a crisis, demands, or emotional **breakdowns**. It can happen during or after a **Normal Reaction.** Then, crash a major **breakdown** has happened and people are slow to recover, the hurt and damage has left a scare if has happened over a long period of time it can lead to depression. This is not a **normal reaction** in a person's life it could be a series of **normal emotional reactions** that have built-up over a period of time. That a person has struggled with, it could be a series of **Normal Breakdowns**, now a person is mad, hurt, anger, and bitterness has set in, that may have set in by this time, never-the-less this has been building-up over a long or short period of time.

It could be a particular crisis, circumstance, or situation that has prompted this **breakdown**. It could be a situation such as a job related situation, marriage, or relationship. Then **breakdown** finally happens (this kind of **breakdown**, could relate to burnout) and (depression).

Burnout this could be over worked, stressed out, a relationship, (where the fire and romance has gone out of a marriage or a bad relationship over a period of time).

It could be one situation over a long period of time (an illness can fit into this category too).

(We will use a person in the armed forces, this person has been in a battle zone, crisis situation and/or when battle fatigue sets-in).

Another (illustration), even life can be a battle, a struggle, and fatigue sets-in, depression, a person feels like giving-up, they think there is no hope. Then they are in real trouble.

Illness and mental illness, disabilities, and others fit into these situations and must be considered as a **Long Term Breakdown.**

Long Term Breakdowns can be some of the hardest to deal with in a person's life a person may even suffer depression over a long period of time and even want to die depending on what has happened and how bad the situation got (this is where suicides or a temped suicides come in) a person wants away out.

Life goes on life has been greatly altered in most cases the quality of life has been damaged, usually the struggle goes along with this kind of **breakdown**. It may take years to get over this kind of **breakdown** sometimes it is a life-long battle. In some cases people need professional help. If person doesn't get professional help and need it, get it if they can, we hope with our services can help find the right kind of help. Even with professional help, maybe our services can be of help to find a friend, "**Common-Ground Profiles**" that is someone who has gone through the same experience.

Yes, many Christians have faced trials and tribulations gone through a hell on earth, a "**long term breakdown**", and have found that their faith in God has helped them and a good church, Sunday school class, a good Christian friend, and/or Christian radio and TV program has helped them. It has given them hope and peace in the midst of a stormy situation. Let me encourage people with this thought, belief in God and then ourselves will help bring you through a situation or crisis.

I would hate to think where my life would be without my salvation; prayer and trust in the Holy Spirit to guide me. We do not want to close this part of our discussion without talking about the church and what it can mean in a person's life.

I have gone to church and have found a great deal of comfort there, preaching, classes, Bible studies, a place to worship and praise God, with Christian fellowship. I'm not saying some of these problems cannot be done outside the church and in addition to the church or Christian organizations. At this point may I say this it is up to the individual to choose what is best for (him or her) we would like to leave the door open until we get to the **6th Axiom**.

Demonstration Chart II, Axiom (5):
Short Term, the do nothing Attitude

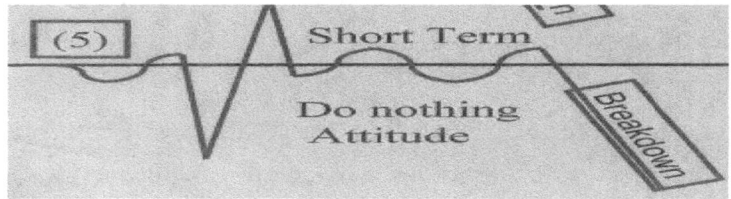

Axiom (5) has to do with **Short Term** server stress, crisis, demand or emotional breakdowns, **angry** and **getting mad, leading to a temper tantrum; actually lose control, cussing** and **swearing. That upsets the normal pattern and rhythm,** people who get mad at themselves have tendency to get mad at someone or something.

This is usually the one that gets people into some trouble and it is easy to recognize it is usually the hardest to control at the time. The reason it gives them trouble is because they think everything is alright, **because the before and after signs are normal**, people go on thinking its normal to feel this anger and frustration. Or maybe a person just hopes everything will work out by its self. That is the philosophy of the day we live in. It is a different reaction or emotion that causes this kind of **attitude** it shows up a person's **actions** and **reactions**. It can cause a great deal of trouble in a person's life and relationships. This is the way a person feels about themselves. (I think out-of-control unresolved anger or being mad is a good way to put it.)

Axiom (5) Do nothing Attitude, is when a person here's someone saying "they don't care", "there is nothing wrong with me I've always been like this". I did not know that anything was wrong by acting that way. (**Human nature** of **man**). This kind of person says people have to live with me as I am, how many times have I seen this happen in someone's life. It could be any reaction that causes this kind of **attitude** the **warning signs** were there.

A person don't see themselves that way because they have been this way all their life, they choose to ignore it, or even worse is when they don't care.

Sometimes, in other cases when the **breakdown** occurs it is too late. (Too much water has gone over the dam.) It could be a **short-term illness** or a **short-term problem** that doesn't work out.

Another, thing we deal with it may be alright when all it takes is a little time and see what is going to happen. That is alright too and that is why it is complex in nature. As a person sees the **<u>Life Line</u>** it started with a **normal reaction** that leads to **crossover tendencies**. The **<u>Life Line</u>** shows diagonals line going up and down people like to think nothing is wrong, and then the **breakdown** occurs they think why did this happen to me. That is the under lying problem in most situations they did not look at the under lying problems and took it seriously back when things happened and something could have been done. It is never too late, it much harder to deal with when things get bad.

We never know when a person has had enough and crossed the **breaking point**, sometimes that person does not know what will trigger one of these, **Short Term Breakdown**. As a person can see in **Axiom (5)** a person may go back to a normal pattern and rhythm in life. It may eventual cause a **Long Term Breakdown**. We have tried to deal with this subject in detail in this part of our study and in depth in all our study guides.

I would like to point out there could have been **several normal reactions** before this **Short Term Breakdown** occurs or it could be a particular flaw in a person's make-up and behavior pattern.

Demonstration Chart II, Axiom (6):
Struggle and Overcoming

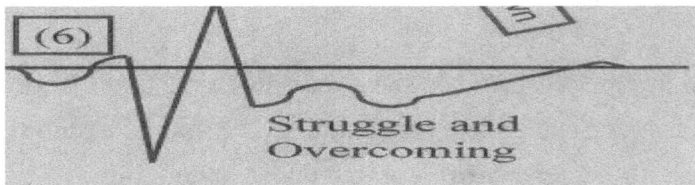

Now let's look at **Axiom (6)**, this is a good way to look at any reaction and then how to deal with any situation, is by recognizing the **stress** or **stresses, crisis, demand, wants need**, or **desire**, or any **emotional experiences**. It is probably the most important aspect of our studies on **human behavior** because it shows us how to deal with those **reactions** and **emotions,** and how a person could have or should have reacted to their experiences.

This will show a person how they should react to the situations or relationships. I think **Axiom (6)** is the most important of the **Demonstration Charts**. We need to understand the thought process of a struggle and overcoming in any reaction or emotions, it shows up in how they have dealt with their problems. Again may I reemphasize how society, family, church, and personal values, ethics, etc. play a role in the decision/choice process?

We believe a person needs to **stop, look**, and **listen**, from time to time and then evaluate. The idea here is to recognize the good and bad qualities in themselves as they relate to others, look for the good in people. If the bad over shadows the good then a person may have a problem maybe with their view of themselves). Try to identify with the good in people and their ability to get along with others. Contrary to what some believe.

If a person sees the bad in themselves and others, maybe they're dwelling too much on the personality treats in others or don't like in them, rather than seeing the person for who they maybe as a person.

1 John 5:1-13 (39)

V-1 "Whosoever believeth that Jesus is the Christ is born of God: and every one that loveth him that begat loveth him also that is begotten of him.

V-2 By this we know that we love the children of God, when we.

V-3 For this is the love of God, that we keep his commandments: and his commandments are not grievous.

V-4 For whatsoever is born of God overcometh the world: and this is the victory that overcometh the world, *even* our faith.

V-5 Who is he that overcometh the world, but he that believeth that Jesus is the Son of God?

V-6 This is he that came by water and blood, *even* Jesus Christ; not by water only, but by water and blood. And it is the Spirit that beareth witness, because the Spirit is truth.

V-7 For there are three that bear record in heaven, the Father, the Word, and the Holy Ghost: and these three are one.

V-8 And there are three that bear witness in earth, the Spirit, and the water, and the blood: and these three agree in one.

V-9 If we receive the witness of men, the witness of God is greater: for this is the witness of God which he hath testified of his Son.

V-10 He that believeth on the Son of God hath the witness in himself: he that believeth not God hath made him a liar; because he believeth not the record that God gave of his Son.

V-11 And this is the record, that God hath given to us eternal life, and this life is in his Son.

V-12 He that hath the Son hath life; *and* he that hath not the Son of God hath not life.

V-13 These things have I written unto you that believe on the name of the Son of God; that ye may know that ye have eternal life, and that ye may believe on the name of the Son of God."

Matthew 15:10-11   (40)

V-10 "And he called the multitude, and said unto them, Hear, and understand:

V-11 Not that which goeth into the mouth defileth a man; but that which cometh out of the mouth, this defileth a man."

James 1:12-23

V-12 "Blessed *is* the man that endureth temptation: for when he is tried, he shall receive the crown of life, which the Lord hath promised to them that love him.

V-13 Let no man say when he is tempted, I am tempted of God: for God cannot be tempted with evil, neither tempteth he any man:

V-14 But every man is tempted, when he is drawn away of his own lust, and enticed.

V-15 Then when lust hath conceived, it bringeth forth sin: and sin, when it is finished, bringeth forth death.

V-16 Do not err, my beloved brethren.

V-17 Every good gift and every perfect gift is from above, and cometh down from the Father of lights, with whom is no variableness, neither shadow of turning.

V-18 Of his own will begat he us with the word of truth, that we should be a kind of firstfruits of his creatures.

V-19 Wherefore, my beloved brethren, let every man be swift to hear, slow to speak, slow to wrath:

V-20 For the wrath of man worketh not the righteousness of God.

V-21 Wherefore lay apart all filthiness and superfluity of naughtiness, and receive with meekness the engrafted word, which is able to save your souls.

V-22 But be ye doers of the word, and not hearers only, deceiving your own selves.

V-23 For if any be a hearer of the word, and not a doer, he is like unto a man beholding his natural face in a glass:"

1 Corinthians 15:57-58   (41)

V-57 "But thanks *be* to God, which giveth us the victory through our Lord Jesus Christ.

V-58 Therefore, my beloved brethren, be ye stedfast, unmoveable, always abounding in the work of the Lord, forasmuch as ye know that your labour is not in vain in the Lord."

Another is the **human side** there is no one who is perfect, some expect too much out of themselves or sometimes they don't expect enough of themselves. A person can become overly judgmental, (too negative) they're disappointed because things don't go their way sometimes things don't turn out like they expected, everyday pleasures do not satisfy. There is not enough time and energy, too much stress, financial obligations, discouragement, worry and anxiety be patient with their expectations of themselves and others.

His grace is sufficient in all things. He does not want a person to struggle, or to feel bad; or "go begging". God loves us and cares for us, He does not want us to hurt either, He wants healing in our lives. He is willing to forgive us of all things. *"If we confess our sins, he is faithful and just to forgive us our sins, and to cleanse us from all unrighteousness."* **I John 1:9**

David said in **Ps. 103:11, 12**

V-11 *"For as the heaven is high above the earth, so great is his mercy toward them that fear him."*

V-12 *"As far as the east is from the west, so far hath he removed our transgressions from us."* David new something of God's forgiveness because he had taken Bath Sheba from another man. God will forgive at the same time and also hold a person accountable, His promise is to forgive and not hold them against a person; David wrote **Ps. 103**, in the light of forgiveness.

This is how a person needs to look at struggling and overcoming in their life. It is okay to struggle, but don't feel bad about a situation or problem they're dealing with, **it is okay to struggle**. The need to be the right kind of person should be the primary issue in dealing with any situation or problem. There is not a one that doesn't need to work on some part of our life.

We need to remember that we have a personal responsibility to God, then others and ourselves.

Think about the person you want to be and set out to improve in those areas that you feel need help; it could be a goal, a dream, or a destiny that is unfulfilled. In my case it was a combination of all these. It seemed like I need help in getting my life back on track. It was out of adjustment, and there were times when it was out of control. I felt bad about myself, another I felt God was judging me for what had I had done wrong (omission or than commission) when I looked myself thinking nothing I had done was right in the sight of God?

(Illustration), (I have had a back problem for a long time and had to have it adjusted) life is like that too. We may only need to make some adjustments. In my case it was a major overhaul (like when the engine of a car needs an overhaul, but you keep the same body).

Caution! Another thing that a person may not want to recognize about themselves some believe they don't need any changes, I'm happy with who I am; I didn't want to change things, I believed that at one time in my life. That is okay some people may want some improving in certain areas and that is (good sign).

In our Support, Outreach, SOS Life Enhancement Services, may be just what a person is looking for. These **Axioms** may have given you a better idea and understanding of how the process works.

The degrees of the ups and downs before and after success or even failure, being able to get back on track and go on and try again. Then being able to deal with the situation or problem is another aspect of the situation or problem. A person may want to deal with the situation or problem later, okay, don't forget the promise a person make to themselves.

If a do nothing attitude presets as is in **Axiom (5)**, what can a person do think how important it is to have better life. Is everything alright will it work it's self out in time? It could be that a person is a lazy thinker or they just don't want to uncover the past, in some cases it hurts too much maybe it's the wrong to think that way, it may be better to leave it in the past, if a person does, count the cost before a person goes on with their life. A person can by-pass that particular hurt or trauma if they want. I'm not saying that is wrong that person usually has problems associated with the by-pass method in the brain. A person usually has a basis and prejudges, they may have mental reactions to certain things in their past.

I felt I had to do something with the excess baggage, we can hid it or pretend that it didn't happen, (NO), I needed to put in the past, and put it in perspective with who I am, this can be some of the routes a person takes or it is someone else's fault, they may as much to blame in the hurt or trauma. What then? A person can make those decisions and go on with their life. I did and so can a person.

First, let me make this very clear that in no way do I suggest anyone do nothing, their not comfortable with. Do not dig into something a person is not willing to finish, don't open old wounds, that a person is not willing to face the consequences.

I hope I have answered some of the questions that **has do with the do nothing attitude**. There are no bad answers, only if a person lies to themselves.

Then do something about the hurt and pain, anger and/or bitterness by (Overcoming). Let me say this in every decision/choice these reactions will reflected in what is or has taken place. There is a problem when a person doesn't see a bad reaction happening or taking place. The b ad thing is "doing nothing

Axiom (6) Struggle and Overcoming

This will show up as we go on with our study on overcoming. This may take weeks, months, and even years in some cases depending on how sever the problem or trauma. It may take lots of support and study to get the real victory over just one problem, again depending on how bad a person the situation is their dealing with. After all of that a person still may have to deal with it the bad they have to live with the situation; life has its everyday problems too. When a person adds it all up, life is a (journey and a work in process as far as our studies are concerned).

One of the questions a person has to ask themselves *why me*? I think this is one of God's ways of getting a person's attention. If a person can find out the reason or *why* it happened, that may make it easier to deal with and live with. A person has to accept life, the responsibility and be accountable for it personally.

When we see the real problems and how they are affecting a person now a person has a good idea how to deal with them, when they don't, *then what*? Another thing is when a person sees a problem coming on, does a person duck their head, run and hide from it, do they face it, or hope it will go away. The problems in life are not always easy to see or do something about them because of their relationships or the circumstances surrounding it. Even if something turns out bad, learned from the experience. There is some good if a person looks for it.

When I dealt with my divorces and my health problems, I didn't like what was happening that made it even harder to deal with.

Another thing that does not keep a person from being successful and making mistakes (**being human**) in our successes and failures. In that light I wanted success in spite the cost for myself, was it what God wanted me to do. I do not believe in success at all costs.

I believe in personal ethics, values and guidelines. The right kind of success is important; I can be happy or sad because I believe in God's guidance gives me peace in my life.

Prov. 22:1-4 (42)

V-1 "A good mane is rather to be chosen than great riches, (and I like this part) and loving favour rather than silver and gold.

This is an equalizer

V-2 The rich and poor meet together: the Lord is the maker of us all. It doesn't say he made them that way, it says He made them both. Now let's talk about a wise person, in:

V-3 A prudent *man* foreseeth the evil, and hideth himself: but the simple pass on, and are punished.

Verse 4 gives us a key to life and happiness is Humanity

V-4 By humility *and* the fear of the Lord are riches, and honuor, and life".

I think this is a good lesson on **human behavior**. The inside of a (man or woman), is the heart and soul that makes them tick, that is what a person lives for. The part that makes them tick can be hurt so bad that they think life is not worth living at times.

Summary of Demonstration Chart II and Axiom (6)

When we use Biblical principle should take comfort in God, God is our hope, it is not cause bondage. That is a good way of knowing if it is of God. Christ came to set us free, *"ye shall be free indeed"*, **John 8:36** and **John 8:32**, *"and the truth shall make you fee"*.

During this time there is usually some confession, battling, and fighting it is hard to raise a family when that is going on, the children are affected by these influences. (It's hard to tell the Christians form everybody else, except on Sunday morning and sometimes the Sundays are no different). Then a person has their job and finances to worry about, if that is not enough. A person can get so busy they don't see the real problem.

A person needs to **stop** and find out what is causing the problems and confusion. We hope this part of these studies have helped a person find the real solutions to their problems in their life and how to deal with them. Then take steps to solve them or at least to some degree. We have some Biblical answers to these questions. We have just looked at a (man or woman), and some of their **human reactions**, **emotions** in a person's life, relationships, and God. I hope I hope you understand the **human side** of a (man or woman) and *who you are*?

We have gone through some of the details in Axioms 1 - 6.

Now we're going to dig a little deeper into, *who you are*? We are going to look at some the same issues from a different viewpoint. We have only scratched the surface as to *who you are*? We are going to look at ways *a person can help themselves & where they are going*? The third aspect of our studies is based on practical applications and profiles.

Demonstration Chart III Axioms, Studies, Information, & Profiles.
Link to! www.sosselfhelpbooks.info

SOS Bible studies (Means: Restoration) Studies & Information = being informed & tools to *help ourselves.*

(Means: Reconciliation) Surveys, Evaluations & **Check-ups** to see where you're going and how what you are doing,

(Means: Rehabilitation & Maintenance) Health-Awareness Programs improving the quality of our life and the health in our life!

Chapter 8

THE IMPACT OF RELATIONSHIPS

When there are two or more views involved!
Personal Relationships Jealousies & Co-dependencies / Self-will – Pride – Vanity & Ego/ and our Competitive-nature: (a. Spouse-Fiancé (b. Family (c. Friends (d. Marriage (e. Children (f. mixed Marriages (g. blended family's (h. stepchildren; others.

Let's look at the first relationship in The Bible.
First was the relationship of God and man in,
Geneses 1:26-28
V-26 "And God said, Let us make man in our own image, after our likeness:

> And let them have dominion over the fish of the sea,
> and over the fowl of the air,
> and over the cattle,
> and over all the earth"
> and over the creeping things.

And in **Gen. 1:27**, the writer sees fit to empathize
V-27 "created man in his *own* image, in the image of God created he him; male and female created he them."
V-28, "And God blessed them, and said unto them, Be fruitful, and multiply, and replenish the earth, and subdue it: and have dominion over"

Read the rest of **Gen. 1:28-30** is a repeat, and it describes all living things.

Again in these verses He/God uses the very same phases and connects them to creation.

Gen 2:7, 8; 18

V-7 "And the Lord God formed man *of* the dust of the ground and breathed into his nostrils the breath of life; and man became a living soul."

V-8 "And the Lord God planted a garden eastward in Eden; and there he put the man whom he had formed."

Gen. 2:9-17 gives place to its importance and credence to the garden itself.

V-18 "And the Lord God said,

It is not good that the man should be alone;

I will make him an help meet for him."

The first Relationship between (a man & a woman).

• Most of us know the story how Eve was created, some probably know it verbatim.

• Up to this point Adam had named every beast, fowl, and everything.

• God had made everything for Adam, it was a virtual paradise to live in.

• God gave him a women to keep him company. (help meet)

Gen. 2:23

V-23 "And Adam said, This is bone of my bones, and flesh of my flesh: she shall be called women, because she was taken from man.

(Profile the account & relationship)

1. We see is that they did spend much or all of their time together.

2. We know they must have at-leased discussed this one particular tree in the garden.

3. They had freedom to do anything, go anywhere and eat anything in the garden, but only one tree held

"the knowledge of good and evil".

4. They could not eat, or they would surely die.

(Profile of Eve)

1. She was tempted by the serpent.
2. She did discuss it with Adam and thy both agreed.
3. She was tempted was it a willful act with Adam.

Did Adam and Eve have a good relationship?

1. there was a breakdown in communication for sure.
2. they did not look at it the same way (the tree) in the same way.
3. they both finally agreed to eat of the tree "the knowledge of good and evil = (sin).
4. which brought about (disobedience/sin to themselves and to the whole world)

How dose Adam and Eve's relationship compare today's relationships?

1. They both had their own agendas.
2. They did discuss the problems before hand.
3. They had an easy life in the Garden of Eden.
4. Eve was hiding a secret in her heart.
5. They both loved each other to the point that they we're willing to suffer the consequences.
6. They stuck together.
7. They didn't give-up on each other, quit when the going got tough.

Question and answers about Adam?

    1. was Adam hen picked?   Yes _____ No _____

    2. was Adam overly protective? Yes _____ No _____

    3. was Adam a good husband under the circumstances?

                                Yes _____ No _____

The relationship between God and man changed!
Gen. 3:6-8

V-6 "And when the women saw that the tree *was* good for food, and that it *was* pleasant to the eyes, and tree to be desired to make *one* wise, she took of the fruit thereof, and eat, and gave also unto her husband with her; and he did eat."

V-7 "And the eyes of them both were opened,

    and they knew that they *were* naked;

    and they sewed fig leaves together,

    and made themselves aprons."

V-8 "And they heard the voice of the Lord God walking in the garden in the cool of the day:

This is one of the keys when it comes to unlocking the secrets in a person's childhood, and their relationship with their parents? Worst of all is when parents use them, playing head games, these are very revealing factors about their character is a parent controlling and manipulative? *How a person feels* about themselves will probably define the success or failure in their relationship; that is not all-inclusive. The couples morals, values and standards a-like, can they for-give others? What has happened to influence a person's love for someone? It could be that a person has crossed the line, crossed the bridge of no return.

(**An Illustration**) is that of Mary and Martha when Jesus came to their home? Look at the passage in this light Martha was a server her deeds were her make-up and character.

Mary's make-up and character was to love and be loving, probably not the servant type. Christ commended Mary because of her love in this case, but Martha was unhappy in her role as the servant/hostess she wanted to be with Christ.

Luke 10:40-42.

One, the old adage of opposites attract is there, it seems to me that some relationships (are based on opposite attractions) a quite shy person tends to fall-in-love with a person that is out going. Then on the other hand a wild person with a bad reputation will want a good moral person. In any relationship two people end up loving each other. In some cases it works out for the most part, it is the love for each other that makes the relationship work.

To make some more observations on opposites in some families children fellow in the parents foot-steps while other rebel and do the opposite of a parent / parents. This can happen from one generation to another when parents are stick the child will rebel and becomes the opposite type of parent. This is true in some cases when a child is raised in religious family, when they become adults they don't believe the Bible and what was taught them as a child.

First, there are some miss conceptions "love can cover multitude of sins". (True God can fore give sin) but love can on only go so-far when they are not abused there is loss of love because the abuse.

Second, some believe that "relationships are made in Heaven", "we have to live with them on earth." The humanity of a (man or women) is what we're dealing with. I'm not too sure that relationships or marriages are made in Heaven. We certainly believe God can lead a person in the right decision. I do believe a person should seek God's guidance in all matters. My hope is that your relationships/marriage is good one and blessed of God.

I hope (he or she) is an angle sent from God remember God love's both of you.

Here is another force **idealism's** we have to fight against self, self-will and deal with them! This happens so many times a person end up having to live with the situation and relationship whether it's **good** or **bad**. Why not try to make it better?

They love the person and they live with a bad marriage. There is that imbalance of give and take; usually people take on roles according to (male or female) roles.

One of the most important choices/decisions a person makes has to do with who they are going marry. Or "until death" that is not true in many cases it is until they separate or get a divorce.

Certainly jealousies and insecurities can come from either or both. In relationships it is usually critical because it can be demeaning to the other person. The idea is to make the other person feel like they are not as good as something or someone else.

That is what we are addressing in part of our study. No person wants to be looked down on or belittled. This is a very sensitive area form both sides of the relationship. I'm trying to present both views, step back and take a look at each other's motives and insecurities.

The natural conflicts, struggles, & warfare! =
    (**a.** Control - Controlled - Controlling – Out-of-Control,
    (**b.** Co-dependency/Addictions/Abuse = Alcoholism-Drugs
      -Pills-Smoking & Sexual-addictions/Adultery.
    (**c.** Anxiety, Depression, Bipolar, & Weight problems!

The psychologist spends much of their time dealing the different personal emotions and aspects of the reactions taking place.

Life is made of conflicts/struggles & in some cases warfare! The book of Job is based on a man and their conflicts, struggles / (troubles).

Job 14:1

V-1 *"Man that is born of a woman is of few days, and full of trouble."*

Job 5:6, 7 says about the same thing.

V-6 *"Although affliction cometh not forth of the dust, neither doth trouble spring out of the ground;"*

V-7) *"Yet man is born unto trouble, as the sparks fly upward."*

There is a natural harmony and yet a conflict between any two elements (examples) man/women, such as (man and his or her/will). The earth/heaven I guess the greatest of all conflicts is between God/Satan there is a warfare the battle between **good and evil.**

Eps. 6:11

V11 *"against the wiles of the devil"*,

Eps. 6:12

V-12 *"put on the whole armour of God"* and pray. Because we're in warfare mentally and spiritually.

    (a. Control - Controlled - Controlling – Out-of-Control, = out of balance.

    (b. Addictions = Alcoholism– Drugs– Pills– Smoking, & Sexual-addictions, Adultery, and pornography.

    (c. Anxiety, Depression, Bipolar, & Weight problems!

Let's discuss weight problems for a minute. Weight problems can result from any of the above elements, plus social disorders, or family traits. (It is usually no respecter of gender). Never-the-less, it is no less damaging than any other element that affects the body's metabolism and balance. It reflects in a person's personality (like laughing it off) and/or how it affects person's well-being. It is no laughing matter to those that have to deal with over-weight.

    (a. **Hurt**

    (b. **Anger**

(c. **Bitterness**

(d **Hostility**

Reactions to (a. through (d.

   (a. **Pain**

   (b. **Disappointments**

   (c. **Guilt.**

We are looking at 4. Major elements in (proper or improper feelings) behaviors (habits, patterns, etc.) they usually result in a negative reaction. The first four are steps downward:

   (a. **Hurt** (b. **Anger** (c. **Bitterness** (d. **Hostility**.

When a person has a problem with these four elements in their life and relationship. These four can become a major player in a person's down-fall they differently influence a person's feelings. One is when a person gets hurt it effects any of the other **Axioms,** it will reflect in **Demonstration Chart III axioms.**

Demonstration Chart III Axioms, Actions and Reactions to:

(a. **Hurt**

This is a very dangerous interaction because it can manifest its self outwardly like getting even or wanting to hurt a person in return. Sometimes when a person gets hurt, they take it out on others (like their spouse, family, or children) or others; or whoever is (handy). There are times when a person doesn't want to get into it with the person who actually caused the hurt. (A person has a tendency to transfer blame) & (sometimes unknowing). People do this a lot with their children and spouse as we discussed earlier. Another problem when others take it out on a family, people take loved ones for granted because they love them, is it okay? (No), a person needs to take time apologize.

Now, the other person can go back to a normal pattern or rhythm in the relationship. Now if we look at it from the child's point of view. They look at it in a different way because they feel the hurt they have their rights as a person. This could be a good example of all three **stages**.

When a person has a reaction or a combination of reactions relate to being hurt, anger, and then bitterness **stage**. This can go on for a short time, or a long period time, and even a lifetime. The one thing I want to point out be careful when an adult hurts they react differently. Even when a person fails God. Be for-giving and understanding in any case if it is not dealt with a person may experience a breakdown. We know if it happens over and over again, over a long period of time a person has a real problem.

When this happens it is not going to be a **Short-term Breakdown** / **stress** a person is going to be dealing with their hurt feelings. This kind of hurt could go on for a long time or a lifetime in some cases. Remember we called this a **Long-term Breakdown** / **stress**, crisis, demand, or emotional breakdown. When a person is hurt all of these reactions are taking place at the same time, in different stages, and different degrees of pain. This can take months and years to resolve and some cases it never gets resolved. I know of people that never have gotten over a bad relationship or death.

When someone hurts a (husband or wife), family or someone that they love it could be they are dealing with a bad relationship and family problems.

Depending on who or how many have hurt them. Someone has left a scare in most cases that kind hurt has a major affect the rest of their life. Another thing about these kinds of hurt in a person's life it usually affects the relationship with everyone in their life, even God.

This can even influence or prejudice their way of thinking about the person. This can even affect their emotional level and balance.

I have found that there is usually an **anger stage** when a person gets hurt. (Teens experience a **rebellious stage**) similar in nature to the **anger stage**. It could be for a brief second, go on for a short time, but if it goes on for months, or even a year or more. Every time the hurt is brought up the **anger** becomes deep seated a person can get mad just thinking about it. When something else goes wrong, they feel the pain all over again. They may not express their **anger** but it is there. There is a problem when they are not able to talk about it and they may think it's alright to feel that way.

Sometimes, it is better than hurting someone else, never-the-less, when people tend to hide it in their subconscious mind, or because it hurts too much to talk about it. I suggest they may need to talk to someone in some cases they will feel better and that is all they need to do. If it is a major hurt and pain, and it has led to the:

b. **anger stage**.

What happens when it reaches the anger stage? The best way is in **Ep. 4:26** says and it's a good principle to live by.
V-26 *"Be ye angry, and sin not: let not the sun go down upon your wrath"*.

Forgiveness and **forgiving** is two different things! A person says I forgive them, did they really mean it, in some cases they never forget. A person says I forgive them because that is what I am supposed to say. Is that really forgiveness? In some cases the more a person thinks about the situation the madder a person gets. I have set up some real situations that are very real, do they hit home in your life.

Forgiving is another matter.

Forgiving is a continuous act.

If this were to happen again could a person feel like forgiving them again, maybe not? This is not as easy as it sounds when a person make the statement. A person can harbor bad feelings. Is that really forgiveness and being forgiving? I don't think so or at least I wasn't satisfied in the way I saw the way a Christian should look at a person.

I have been there I have been angry, mad, and hurt all at the same time. I didn't want to forgive or forget. It felt good and I felt justified in my feelings. They had personally wronged me, I didn't do anything wrong. I was not happy and I didn't want them to be happy. I thought God should have judged them, instead I felt God was judging me. What about this approach? Was I wrong?

The Bible says in **Matt. 7:1, 2**

V-1 "JUDGE not, that be not Judged"

V-2 For with what judgment ye judge, ye shall be judged: and with what measure ye mete, it shall be measured to you again."

Read all of **Chapter 7 of Matt.** to understand the meaning of judging. *"Vengeance is mine; I will repay, saith the Lord". I will repay".* **Rom. 12:19**

c, **3rd stage is bitterness**. This emotion is different than **hurt** and **anger,** but similar in nature. A person can be **hurt, anger** they are the first two stages they are always a part of a person's feelings at the same time. This is where adults and children really have a hard time sorting out their true feelings. **Bitterness** is always **long-term.** When it goes too far the **anger stage** turns into **bitterness**.

When **bitterness** sets in, it can go on for years and even the rest of a person's life. Sometimes **bitterness** is the hardest to detect, most of the time a person doesn't realize how bad it is or if it's really there. It has become so much a part of a person it feels natural; it has become a part of the person's personality, (character/prejudices).

Even worse they don't realize it dominates their feelings, conversation, thoughts, and influences every relationship. I lived that way for serial years.

It is like **Chart 3; (3) Axiom Long Term Breakdown,** when it comes down to living life. This does not mean that people don't life together or work together. The worse thing about the **bitterness stage.** Some people didn't realize how it is affecting them day after day, week by week, and year after year. When **bitterness** gets **deep seated** it is hard to deal with **bitterness stage** varies in degrees as to how bad they are hurting.

Like a bad relationship, divorce, an illness, can cause this kind of reaction. Another, (illustration) is in wartime they live in a **hostile** situation over a long period of time a person may be dealing **PDST** toward the end their term it can happen to a person / nation, group of people, or religious sect.

Abuse is a definite act of extreme **human behavioral** or **action** not tolerated by the family, society, or church.

Then <u>Abuse</u> in any relationship is one the toughest things to deal with. There is always some miner abuse because a person's pride and ego, plus their own self-will. When a person looks at how bad the abuse is and how bad it gets. There are different kinds of relationships, family, and friends of course. The paramount question? What can a person do about abuse?

<u>Our   Social-Problems: Alcoholism-Drugs-Pills-Smoking-Divorce = Co-dependency & Substance Abuse / others</u>. These are some the common social disorders in our society, they can relate to abuse. Abuse can show up in any part of a person's life and reflect in the inner person. Even smoking could fit into this category. The ups and downs of these social disorders / diseases can be devastating

to deal with. In some cases they have been abused themselves and that is associated with the abuse in some way.

These people live through, "a living a hell on earth" while their family member goes through those diseases and so does the families. Sometimes it is a case of both people being involved. Every person suffers in those relationships. The wives-fiancé, children, mother and dad, the whole family. By society standards it a mental illness! It can destroy the brain cells and creates a mental in balance. They can't cope when it gets bad, they rely on drugs. There are all kinds of help and support groups out there to help them, they usually don't take advantage of the help I'm not sure they can be helped unless they want help.

We feel **SOS** has a <u>primary purpose</u> is to help find <u>support, information, encourage,</u> and <u>guide a person</u> in the right direction. <u>This is a place to start</u>! We get calls <u>looking for help</u> and <u>what kind of help is available</u>.

I found this to be very true in my life. How does a person deal with the impact of a problem or crisis? Then on the other hand how does it affect a person is a very important question?

How a person reacts to the abuse and what effect it has on their life in most cases there are two lives that are affected. One is the abuse to ones-self another the one who causes the abuse. The one who receives the abuse, what is going to happen to them? Sometimes they are very helpless individuals there is help out there.

We would like to help the person who can't move without the other person's approval. They have always had to deal with their anger and disapproval, even worse is their violent out-bursts. They usually feel trapped. Does this <u>sound familiar</u>? <u>Are you trapped in some way</u>!

We are asking a person to take a look at their relationship! To see if those <u>situations apply</u> and <u>to what degree</u>! A person needs to be able to <u>distinguish</u> between a person's <u>self-will</u> and <u>abuse</u>.

You are your own judge. This can happen to a (male or female). Children and young people have to deal with adults the person's within the situation. These are some of the same trademarks of a bad relationship. A person's inadequacies, insecurities, abuses and the need for love, adds to the situation of course. A person's childhood influences are tangled up in all of this does this fit you or your relationship?

Divorce

Divorce is a whole different story and we're going to dedicate this section of the book to those who would like or need help in this area of marriage, divorce problems.

We find that a lot of support groups are unable to help people. We feel that **SOS services**, has a <u>primary purpose</u> and that is to <u>inform,</u> <u>encourage</u> and <u>guide a person</u> in the right direction. <u>Support</u> <u>Outreach Services is a place to start</u>!

We get calls from people <u>looking for help</u> and <u>what kind of help</u> <u>is available</u>. I found this was true in my life. How does a person deal with the impact of a problem or crisis?

How a person reacts to the abuse and what effect is it going to have on their life is very important. This puts the counselor right in the middle, trying to deal with both sides of abuse, we as counselors are to report the abuse to the authorities when it comes to children. We have two lives that are affected. One is the abused then the one who causes the abuse, and what is going to happen to them. Sometimes both parties are very helpless in the situation the problem boils down to the individuals and how to be able to help them.

We're on the side of right, we are likely going to point out both sides of who is right. As a counselor we point out other alternatives as we have done in section on abuse, can the abused person make a decision based on their feeling at the time. We're going to support the person who comes to us whether we think they are right or wrong. We will inform them as to what needs to be done. The main thing we want emphasize is their right to make a choice.

If we, or some other counselor or organization, wants to be apart of our support-group we will try to help them, we want them to understand the need <u>professional help and support</u>.

In server cases of assaults taking place, the person is so glad when it's over because they have live in consent fear of the next assault and how bad is it going to be at the next time. Sometimes they are <u>beaten</u> or at least <u>threatened</u> to the point of death. Not knowing when the next attic will take place and for what reason. They walk on eggshells so-to-speak, because any little thing can trigger an attic on them. We find this to be very true most ABUSE cases and how it affects the relationship.

Put all of those elements together. The person is dealing with **hurt**, **anger**, **bitterness** and the ever day stress of a family and job. Yes, a person can go to church and be a Christian with all of these elements of abuse in their life.

By design we put things in our programs and services to help people. In this case the glass can be 2/3 full or even 7/8 full of bad elements the rest of the glass has very little good elements.

A person can be doing all the right things for the wrong reasons. Depending on how good or bad the elements are in a person's life. The glass is always is full, it is a matter of what kind of elements are filling the glass. We are talking about the heart and soul of a (man or woman). The motive behind why they do what they do.

The bitterness stage affects relationships and tares a person apart inside.

I have been there and I know what I'm talking about. All of this happened to me it didn't happen overnight. The worst thing about **bitterness stage** it affects everything in a person's life what a person do to help themselves? It took a lot of effort on my part and sticking to it to get past the bitterness and see the other side. I never wanted to give up I knew I needed help. Where did I find the answers to my problems? There is a reason for everything and I didn't understand everything that happened? I made my decisions //chooses and believe that some good could come out of it. I know that maybe over simplifying the ways at this point there is a Biblical principal there.

Remember there are no easy short cuts in decision making!

At this point in my life I had a lot bad feelings about myself we are **human,** it only made me feel worse I used the excuse of being human is to err.

There is only one person who can change your life. God can't change your life unless you want a change. I hear people say I knew God could not do it, I still feel the same. Believe me, I have said the same thing myself a few times. The worst thing about being **hurt** is feeling sorry a person's guilt makes them think they deserved to be **hurt**. In my case I went to Christian group sessions until I got victory over feeling hurt. I saw how bad others felt, I didn't want that to happen to me.

Hostility

When a person has been hurt, the anger stage may set in, there will be evidence of a conscious **hostility stage**, which may only last for a short time, the **bitterness stage** is long-term, in some cases lasts for a lifetime. When these feelings set in, a person has some deep rooted problems to deal with. Not only to the one who has hurt them, as a result they have their own set of problems, because it hurts them in the process. When it comes to criticism, constructive disagreement can be good, if it is taken in the right way.

We have dealt with the angry stage, and how this affects a person's feelings. Anger is a very strong emotion when a person has any major situation in their life, the hurt can turn to anger. This leads to **hostility** and then **bitterness**, which plays a big part in a person's emotional level being out of balance. Another problem is when a person doesn't want to talk about these emotions or do anything about the **hurt** and **anger stage**, now the **hostility** has led to **bitterness**. A person tends to burry things in the subconscious because it hurts too much, if this goes on for years it will take a while to heal.

These emotions relate to the hurt, anger and **hostility builds to bitterness**, when all four of these are going on at the same time the reality of these are hard to accept because they are under the surface of the person's inner feelings. By the time they realize how bad it has gotten, and to what degree it is affecting them. Even worse, when they don't realize any one really cares, they become dominating factors in their life, it affects their relationships. This can influence their relationships, because of the severity and degree it has taken over time, and finally, it affects their **personal-well-being**. That was the state I was in.

Each time a person gets victory over a problem the easier it gets and if not the harder it gets the next time. Remember at any time a person loses control they fall back into that old pattern and become defeated. Believe me I could not have changed without having a way to deal with my problems. We are going to be dealing with all these aspects as we continue this study. We want to help a person by applying these principals they will play a big part in the rest of our study.

The Bible says in:

Ephesians 4:16-32 (KJV)

V-16 "From whom the whole body fitly joined together and compacted by that which every joint supplieth, according to the effectual working in the measure of every part, maketh increase of the body unto the edifying of itself in love.

V-17 This I say therefore, and testify in the Lord, that ye henceforth walk not as other Gentiles walk, in the vanity of their mind,

The Gentiles were proud people, as the Jews had great scholars did the gentiles, Aristotle and Roman philosophers of that day, speaking to those on Mares Hill.

V-18 Having the understanding darkened, being alienated from the life of God through the ignorance that is in them, because of the blindness of their heart:

V-19 Who being past feeling have given themselves over unto lasciviousness, to work all uncleanness with greediness.

V-20 But ye have not so learned Christ;

V-21 If so be that ye have heard him, and have been taught by him, as the truth is in Jesus:

V-22 That ye put off concerning the former conversation the old man, which is corrupt according to the deceitful lusts;

V-23 And be renewed in the spirit of your mind;

V-24 And that ye put on the new man, which after God is created in righteousness and true holiness.

V-25 Wherefore putting away lying, speak every man truth with his neighbour: for we are members one of another.

V-26 Be ye angry, and sin not: let not the sun go down upon your wrath:

V-27 Neither give place to the devil.

V-28 Let him that stole steal no more: but rather let him labour, working with *his* hands the thing which is good, that he may have to give to him that needeth.

V-29 Let no corrupt communication proceed out of your mouth, but that which is good to the use of edifying, that it may minister grace unto the hearers.

V-30 And grieve not the holy Spirit of God, whereby ye are sealed unto the day of redemption.

V-31 Let all bitterness, and wrath, and anger, and clamour, and evil speaking, be put away from you, with all malice:

V-32 And be ye kind one to another, tenderhearted, forgiving one another, even as God for Christ's sake hath forgiven you."

A person needs to learn how to control and have discipline over these matters. When it comes to balance and control of a person's emotions and actions.

This is not the way a Christian is supposed to act or anyone else. I know people get **angry** at times that is normal. The **old nature** is still there it may not change unless a person bring it under subjection, even God cannot do anything without a willing heart.

(Illustration),

(What if there is infidelity in the relationship or addictions) can they bring it under control, the Scripture says *"bring our bodies under subjection"*, **Rom 12:1**, if you are going to do something about it. Prayer will help, that usually means you have acknowledged the problem when people want to do something about it. It is up to the person to bring it under control. The way to do this by discipline take action do it on daily bases, pray about it daily, (our Christian walk works the same way), in any kind of decision/choice in a person's life.

Let's see what the scripture says in

Gal. 6:3-9

V-3 *"For if a man think himself to be something, when he is nothing, he deceived himself."*

V-4 *But let every man prove his own work and then shall he have rejoicing in himself along, and not in another."*

V-5 Servants, be obedient to them that are *your* masters according to the flesh, with fear and trembling, in singleness of your heart, as unto Christ;

V-6 Not with eyeservice, as menpleasers; but as the servants of Christ, doing the will of God from the heart;

V-7 With good will doing service, as to the Lord, and not to men:

V-8 Knowing that whatsoever good thing any man doeth, the same shall he receive of the Lord, whether *he be* bond or free.

V-9 And, ye masters, do the same things unto them, forbearing threatening: knowing that your Master also is in heaven; neither is there respect of persons with him.

Here is some more about the ego it can apply to **"the law of sowing and reaping"**

Galatians 6:7-10

V-7 "Be not deceived; God is not mocked: for whatsoever a man soweth, that shall he also reap.

V-8 For he that soweth to his flesh shall of the flesh reap corruption; but he that soweth to the Spirit shall of the Spirit reap life everlasting.

V-9 And let us not be weary in well doing: for in due season we shall reap, if we faint not.

V-10 As we have therefore opportunity, let us do good unto all *men*, especially unto them who are of the household of faith.

I have spent some time on **self-control** and finished with the **6th Chapter** of **Galatians** it is one of our models.

Chapter 9
WHAT A PERSON THINKS & FEELS ABOUT THEMSELVES?

This is a significant part of the study about self and a person's **self-image, self-esteem, self-worth**. When I talk about a person, what do they think in the term self? If we were to say self, what does a person think when I say self, you would probably think I'm talking "about real me" and what am I thinking about? There is a Country Song by Toby Keith that says "I want to talk about me, 'me-me-me'!" That has a lot to say about a person and what they what and think of themselves. It is (me) first!!! And then others.

Now let's look at other issues in a person's life:
(d. **Hostility**

(1) The benefit of peace with God (verse 1). As a result of our justification by faith, Paul writes, we have "**peace with God**" (verse 1). "**Peace with God**" is very different from the "**peace of God**" (**Philippians 4:7**). The peace "**of God**" is that inner tranquility which God gives to the Christian, even when there is external turmoil. It is that peace which marks the end of a person's hostility toward God in (**Ephesians Chapter 2**).

(2) The benefit of an introduction, by faith, into a standing in grace (verse 2a). Justification opens the door to God's dealing with men on the basis of grace not on the basis of works (**Ephesians 4:16**). This standing in "**grace**," which justification accomplishes, is merely the beginning. Paul calls it an "**introduction**." Justification removes the wrath of God and gives us peace with God. A person is taken out of the arena of performance and placed in the arena of divine grace.

A whole new world commences as a man is justified by faith as time passes, more and more of God's plans and promises are unveiled before the wondering eyes of the believer.

(3) The benefit of the jubilant hope of a glorious conclusion (verse 2b). Justification by faith is a glorious beginning, but this same justification by faith is also the basis for our confidence in a glorious conclusion. Through the justification which God accomplishes on our behalf, we have confident assurance and joyfully exult in the **"hope of the glory of God"** (verse 2).

(4) The benefit of a jubilant hope in present tribulation (verses 3-8). Paul does speak of the present circumstances in the Christian also has peace and prosperity, health and wealth. Paul characterizes the normal Christian life as Jesus and the apostles did a life in which one encounters tribulation (**Matthew 13:21; John 16:33; Acts 14:22; 2 Corinthians 4:17; 6:4; 7:4; 8:2; Colossians 1:24; 1 Thessalonians 1:6; Hebrews 10:33; compare 2 Timothy 3:12**).

(e. **Pain**

In the New Testament these aspects are spoken of in a number of ways. Regarding the putting off of sin Paul says that we need to 'put to death the deeds of the body' (**Rom. 8:13**) or 'put to death your members which are on the earth' (**Col. 3:5**). There is to be a continuous mortification of sin. The phrase "put to death" means to render inoperative, to completely eliminate sinful deeds. In **Galatians 5:24** Paul says that 'those who are Christ have crucified the flesh with a person's passions and desires". A rejection of sin and former manner of life must be a relentless, uncompromising rejecting sin. Similarly, Jesus taught the necessity of self-denial saying, "let a man deny himself and take up His cross and follow Me" (**Mk. 8:34**).

The putting off sin involves personal sacrifice. How often does our Lord require putting off sin? *"Jesus says that every Christian must take up his cross daily"* (**Luke 9:13**).

(f. **Disappointments**

We believe God is the healer of all our problems no matter how BIG or small. One of the most helpful things is letting go of the passed disappointments, and betrayals. God is not like us being human within our human capabilities in all our relationships. God is faithful and just. Jesus walked this earth so that we can talk to Him through the Holy Spirit about our trials here on earth.

(g. **Guilt.**

You do not have to feel **guilty** about being depressed. It is not a sin (this is what everyone believes before they become a Christian, God loves everyone), the doubting process can build a strong foundation for you to re-build on.

He knows if a person is doing the right thing for the wrong reason chances are the task they are doing will not get done properly. Doing something out of a sense of drudgery, duty is a far cry from doing the same thing out of a willing gratitude. In some ways people try to get away with the minimum amount of effort. We should be doing our best in every situation.

It is our gratitude to God for his mercy that Paul wants Christian's to be motivated in our obedience to Christ. Notice that it does not say *"In view of God's fearsome judgement"*. Nor, In view of your **guilty conscience** you desire to fit in, and to make the world a better place, offer ourselves to God, wrong motivation will stifle our very relationship God, He wants us to have with Him.

It is because of God's mercy we are forgiven, set free from the penalty our sin it should set us right with Him. The discipline of having our mind on God, Paul has been keen to point out this from the start, Paul says to grow with the right view of God's mercy.

Comparing psychology and The Scriptural view of psychology

Profile of Self-Esteem

I believe in **Self-Esteem**, my parents reinforced that belief all my life. They always said "a person can do anything or be anything they want if they're willing to work for it" I believe there is a great deal of truth in that statement, especially in America. I have lived my life by that belief. Let's look at **Self-Esteem** and see if there is any value in believing in one's self, of course there is always extenuating circumstances, of course God's will, old saying "the lords willing and the creek don't rise", "come from my nick of the woods".

Improving Self-Esteem   Pages 1-6   [13]

"If you lack self-confidence in certain areas, take classes or try out new activities to increase your sense of competence (for example, take a math class, join a dance club, swimming lessons.

A person's past experiences, even the things they don't usually think about, are all alive and active in a person's daily life, in the form of an **Inner Voice**. Although most people do not "hear" this voice in the same way they would speak to another person, it is there in many ways it acts in a similar way, constantly repeating those original messages of what we need to do.

Dr. John C Barrett Jr. PH-D

196

• Most people's feelings and thoughts are about themselves somewhat based on their daily experiences. The grade you get on an exam, job, etc; how your friends treat you, your ups and downs in a romantic relationship-all can have a temporary impact on your wellbeing.

• It can create anxiety, stress, loneliness and increased likelihood for depression.

• It can cause problems with friendships and relationships.

• It can seriously impair academic, job, etc - performance.

• It can lead to underachievement and increased vulnerability to drug and alcohol abuse.

Ask for Support from Friends

• Ask friends to tell you what they like about you or think you do well.

• Ask someone who cares about you to just listen to you "vent" for a little while without

• trying to "fix" things.

• Ask for a hug.

• Ask someone who loves you to remind you that they love you too.

Get Help from Teachers & Other Helpers

Go to professors or advisors or tutors to ask for help in classes if this is a problem for you. **Remember**: They are there to help you learn!"

http://www.utexas.edu/student/cmhc/booklets/selfesteem/selfest.html   3/12/05

On Improving Self Esteem
Articles – On Improving Self Esteem   Page 1-2   [14]

"We must learn to value ourselves, and try to be valued for who we truly are, not the false fronts we present because of who we think we "should" be. This means dropping our focus on what we are "too much" or "not enough" of and focusing instead on what is the authentic truth, what a person really does or wants to be and do: shooting for (and keeping steadily focused on) their positive goals instead of avoiding negative ones, giving themselves credit when they do things that give them pleasure or bring them closer to their goals, turning off that infernal judge and critic inside them who so often sound remarkably like Mom or Dad, Gramma or Grampa, Sister or Big Brother.

It also means creating environments, friendships as well as in our intimate relationship, in which we will get positive feedback. When we get a lot of criticism or negative feedback as children, we tend to be drawn to situations in which we continue to get it-- we tend to be most comfortable with familiar patterns, even if they aren't inherently nurturing. A person needs to take responsibility for their behavior that elicits validation. A person has want to change the way they feel about themselves, a person also needs to be drawn to a positive solutions in which people will validate them

298

appreciate them, and tends to give them positive feedback no matter how bad they feel about themselves at any given moment of time. (This is not to say that a person should avoid criticism, that a person should learn to focus less on avoiding criticism and more on getting even if it means asking having a positive "attitude.")

http://www.1-in-2-1.co.uk/articles/selfesteem/   3/15/05

Christians Athletes

I think we can create a problem when we use people to benefit our **self-esteem**, this is done in the world, and Christian's are also guilty of doing things for their own good.

A few years ago I went to see Kurt Warner and his wife at a Saint Louis Cardinal Baseball game. It was "Christian day" at the park. He was the National Football League's Most Valuable Player the year before! A few years before no one wanted him to hear him speak. He was playing in the arena league, and in the World Football League. He was never a great quarterback in college, the poor teams overlooked him. He finally got his chance in 2000 when he was a backup quarterback for the Saint Louis Rams.

The starting quarterback was hurt for the season because of an injury. Kurt Warner stepped in and dazzled the fans, the league and his peers, as he led the Rams to a Super Bowl Championship. Kurt Warner never gave up on himself. He never stopped believing in himself. Sure there were failures and setbacks along the way to winning the Super Bowl. Self-Confidence was one of them, believing in his ability, he could do it. Even, if he was not a high drafted pick out of college, he didn't focus on his failures and short comings. He kept his eye on his goal of being a quarterback in the NFL, always believing he would succeed.

He always gave Christ the credit for his success! I think there is a good lesson there.

The most successful baseball players have over a .300-batting average. A few of the great baseball player hit .390 -.400. In fact .400 is pretty awesome. That means a "successful" baseball player only hits the ball 30-percent of the time. He fails 70-percent of the time. But, he doesn't focus on the times he misses. A great hockey player will score 50-goals in a season. That means out of 80 + games he will score in slightly more than half of them!

When a person is batting .000 in life or a woman doesn't feel good about herself then they need to look at WHY?

Successful people are not successful all the time, is the point we're making. If they don't focus on their failures, this helps create self confidence that propels them to greater success.

To develop their <u>mind power</u> and feed their <u>subconscious</u> a daily dose of positive thinking that increases their <u>self-esteem and confidence</u> is good when it not over done one way or the other.

Scriptural view of Self-esteem

Self-Esteem is God's business whether you and I believe it or not, He loves building up and taking care of us.

Comparing the modern age of psychology and The Scriptural view
Self-image, has to do with the character of a man or women.

Main Entry: self-image   {}
Function: *noun*

       : one's conception of oneself or of one's role

          <changing the *self-image* which many petty offenders have

-- Irwin Deutscher>
http://www.merriam-
webstercollegiate.com/cgi/Eleventh?book=Dictinary&witness
3/4/05

Profile of Self-image

Self-Image can be understood as the aggregate of positive perceptions and representations held by an individual in their feelings, reference to particular characteristics of a (man or women) and/or prefers to the attribute they project in their self. It forms an expression, as in the context of well-being in which one can be viewed. Self-image can be perceived in a macro context in which exists as a sum of the individual's innate characteristics that together make up the personal perception of one's self. It can be seen in a micro context in which individuals can be perceived in the analysis of one's self. Both, of these contexts require consideration in the examination of **Self-Image**, how it forms, and the consequences of one's actions.

WHAT ARE THE DIMENSIONS OF SELF-IMAGE?

To comprehend fully the multiple dimensions of SELF-IMAGE implicated in the preceding definitions, it is important to array its dimensions in a model that will enable practitioners to understand feature the concept of one's self, the relationships that make each dimension relevant to the others. The model developed of **self-image** as the product of:

(1 an environment compromised of multiple forces
that influence the exchange of resources between
different entities of the person,

301

(2 inputs in the form of needs, desires and expectations
   that carry charactertics from the environment a
   person is raised or lived,

(3 attributes to performance that facilitate or retard
   personality responsiveness to the external presence
   by influencing important decisions related to the
   activities in life,

(4 a conversion process that transforms a person's needs,
   desires, expectations, as it relates to the environmental
   stimuli into personal **self-image**,

(5 outputs that carry the results in multiple environments,

(6 communication that involves formal and informal
   procedures for disseminating information about
   outputs of personal preference,

(7 feedback that transmits public perceptions relative to
   the outputs produced by one's self back to the
   conversion process as the inputs in the person. Each
   dimension interacts with the others.

Now the phrase is linked with the feel-good do it in some philosophies, **self-esteem** has a negative connotation.

Self-esteem can be an empty value if it's not tempered with a sense of responsibility and social awareness.

Self-Esteem philosophies ignores the value of good mental health: the ability to "delay gratification" and "tolerate frustration".

Some argue that the push for **self-discipline** is the opposite to **self-esteem** it is more semantics than a real change in what parents need to do to help their kids growing into successful adults: Offer "unconditional love and acceptance" is a huge step in getting your child to feel loved and accepted.

302

- Now the phrase is so linked with the feel-good do it in some philosophies, **self-esteem** has a negative connotation.
- **Self-esteem** can be an empty value if it's not tempered with a sense of responsibility and social awareness.
- One of the popular **self-esteem** philosophies ignores the value of good mental health: the ability to "delay gratification" and "tolerate frustration".
- Some argue pushing for self-discipline is the opposite to **self-esteem** it is more semantics than a real change in what parents need to do to help their kids grow into successful adults:
- Offer "unconditional love and acceptance" is a huge step in getting your child to feel loved and accepted.
- Empathy when others are hurting. **Rom. 12:15**
- Christ likeness in **1 Cor. 15:49; Eph. 5:1; 1 Thessalian's. 1:6; 1 Cor. 4:17; Php. 3:17;**
- Alert watching for a snare or temptation. **1 Cor. 16:13; Eph. 6:18; Php. 3:2; 1 Th. 5:6**

Profile of a child

As a child they may have been teased a lot. This child as an adult may become timid, they may develop an inferiority-complex, very determined, or become aggressive in nature. They feel hurt, angry, or mad as they become adults because of their treatment as a child, if they felt it was personal abusive/tormenting to the child. On the-other-hand they may have taken in the wrong spirit.

(Natural **Self-Esteem**) has to do with an person's nature and temperament, and helps shape their self-concept.

(Rhythm and balance) is another thing that shapes self-concept.

(Actions and reactions) of others may also help shape their self-concept.

(Social messages) others also influence our self-concept.

(Social esteem) is how others values a person, this will influence their self-concept.

Some people cannot control the (**old nature** it can show up in the **new creation**). A person will be able to detect these by their examples of the (**old nature**), the **old nature** can **dominate/control their attitude, emotions/feelings, actions** and **reactions.**

What happens when a person fails before and after a falling away, then what?

There are all kinds of influences that inhibit a person's progress and growth.

The meaning of Self-Esteem

Self-will is doing what a (man or women) wants that also has to do with the central character of a person being able to **love** in the right way, then to **love** is not a new term, **self-love** is new in the fact that we put the two words together which means **esteem.**

A term that needs more explanation includes a person's **self-esteem** another is another way describing a personal characteristic which means man **esteem** it is good if used in the right way, again **esteem** is another very good term when is found in the Bible **Self-esteem** is another characteristic of the **human behavior** in any person whether their a Christian or not. When people feel bad about themselves it shows up in their attitude toward themselves and their love for others. This is brought to light in modern psychology when a person is negative about one's self they are more likely to be depressed, show signs of anxiety and uneasy about a situation or in general their overall outlook on life.

This can happen to Christians as well. When we get through with this study we hope to show people a better way when they are dealing with their **self-esteem**. God loves a person no matter how bad the situation or how bad a person has sinned, to do this a person must follow along and get the perception of one's self, and how to love. When a person gets these three things in line they're going to see a new person that is what this section of this study is all about.

The word **self-image** is used by modern psychology and it is based the New Testament, **image** is used time after time in the Old Testament referring to **the image of God**, and **man's image**, it is not a bad term, some people like to think it is a fairly new term, all we need to do is go back to **Genesis** to find the word **image**.

When you add **self** to the word **image** we are talking about one's self, in general we usually have a problem when someone says, (I) did this or that. The big (I) is a problem, we usually associate the word **esteem** as it takes on a different meaning. When we add the word **self** it seems to have some miss conceptions, or are they miss leading themselves as we think about the truth, to prove a point.

If that is true there are deferent kinds or degrees of **esteem**, we must understand the value of **love** to understand **self-esteem** of a person and God's love, to understand the English language, look at the terms concerning one's self:

Now the three characteristics of a person, we are going look at what the Bible has to say about these characteristics.

Scriptural view of self as it describes the image of a person

Few would disagree with the following statement: What people think of themselves to a large degree determines how they will think of others is true, what a person thinks of God, how a person applies these principles set forth in the Scriptures will show how a Christian's attains and maintains their relationships and God.

That also true, **one's self** how a person feels tells a lot about a person's relationship with man and God. That will largely determine their discipline, and decision making.

First, there is no area of a person's life that will not be directly or indirectly affected more than their perception of one's self, by the way how a person views themselves. What they think of themselves is important, that is not an absolute truth in life. There are two different views on the subject of **self**.

Secondly, is the image they show forth as a person, and the life they live? The Scripture spends as much time on bringing man, that a person will see their sins in relation to God and salvation; the other is spent in how to redeem fallen man.

Thirdly, is absolutely contrary to human reasoning because the unbeliever thinks they have no sin. People think of themselves as being a good person both are true statements. Both are significant in man knowing *who he or she is*. Depending on which side of the sin question their looking at as a Christian or unsaved person.

The modern age of methodology in terms of the Scriptural view of each:
  A. Down-hill-spiral exposes the weaknesses in man.
  B. Down-hill / from a Christian's point of view means sin
  C. Burnout - Depression - Anxiety in Christian's,
The personal view of each down-hill-spiral exposes the weaknesses in a person-Christian.

Personal view of down-hill-spiral

In the last chapter we gave a **Chart II Layout of Breakdowns**. Now a personal view of **down-hill-spiral** life is not always perfect at its best. That is how I felt having to deal with a disability, crippling arthritis, it has left a crippling of the fingers and toes. I got to where I couldn't walk at different times that was not the least of my problems, I had heart problems that made it even twice as hard to overcome.

It was a **down-hill spiral**, is a series of **Breakdowns** and setbacks, a twisting of the joins, each set of new problems meant another attack on my health and another catastrophe to deal with. Then, they're were all of the personal pitfalls, the normal ups and downs. Add all them up it is going to be a difficult to restore my health. All of these problems and obstacles were just about all the body, mind, and spirit could handle at the time they have gotten worse over the years.

 Something had to change or I was going to be a cripple for the rest of my life and I am, I haven't let it get me down. I'm not sure what turned my life around, I think it was a combination of all of these things working against me, not just one thing.

God was always been there for me, I think the most profitable aspect was knowing what kind of Christian I wanted to be, I had to gotten some control of my health. I wanted to do something about the circumstances and change them, how am I going to it? There was even a big question in the back of my mind, will I be able to do this, my faith was weak because I had failed God. I had a vision and insight plus a purpose in life. If this works I'm on track in my life, I'm letting people know it can be done, it is by God's grace and mercy, and prayer, I'm going to give God all the praise for it. That is reason for writing the expositions about what happened.

I have a kind heart that has caused me problems because people seem to be taking advantage of my kindness. I am a gentle kind person, take my word for it is this a weakness in character? I am thankful because this is the nature of my mother.

I am also like her in the fact I'm honest, loyal, and very sincere person as get to know me. I have never tried to force the issues on someone else, myself or anyone.

The wisdom and the enlistment of life comes from the pearls and pit-falls that a person has to face along the way. The best way to describe a series of problems is a **down-hill-spiral** to a degree it was my fault, it was a challenge because I blamed myself. I never did anything real bad I was just human enough to make bad choices. I heard one lady say, when her investment went bad, "what if my investment had turned out good, I'd be a wealthy person today", but they didn't.

This has brought about some pretty extreme situations and experiences. I even thought I was going to have heart attack at the age 45. There will always be those specials times and places, and oh yes, those special people that have meant so much to me and made life worth living.

This is one of the classic stories from the Old Testament it is about Samson, very true to life as far as a **down-hill-spiral**. There are lots things that brings a person to their knees, bad relationships, health, drugs, alcohol, addictions, and other devices. In book of Judges is the story of Samson and Delilah the truth about being caught up in the wrong kind of a women and her taking advantage of Samson. Most people have to reach the bottom before they look up as we see in Samson's case; it cost him his life.

Judges 15:16 (43)
V- 16 "And Samson said, With the jawbone of an ass, heaps upon heaps, with the jawbone of an ass have slain a thousand men."
Judges 16:6-9

V-7 "And Samson said unto her, If they bind me with seven green withs that were never dried, then shall I be weak, and be as another men." [but he lies to her]

V-9 "And De-li'-lah said unto Samson, Behold, thou hast mocked me, and told me lies: now tell, I pray thee, where with thou mightest be bound" [they put ropes around him he broke them] "like a thread".

Judges 16:15-18

V-15 "And she said unto him, How canst thou say, I love thee, when thine heart *is* not with me thou hast mocked me three times, and hastnot told me wherein thy great strength *lieth*.

V-16 And it came to pass, when she pressed him daily with her words,and urged him,, *so* that his soul was vexed unto death;

V-17 That he told her all his heart, and said unto her, There hath not come a razor upon mine head; for *have* been a Nazarite unto God from my mother's womb:

V-18 if I be shaven, then my strength will go from me, and I shall become weak, and like any *other* man."

Judges 16:21 & 28

V-21 "Then the Philistines seized Samson and gouged out his eyes; and they brought him down to Gaza and bound him with bronze chains, and he was a grinder in the prison."

V-28 "And Samson called unto the Lord, and said, O Lord God, remember me, I pray thee, only this once, o God, that I may be at once avenged of the Philistines for my two eyes."

Read the whole story of Samson in **Judges Chapters 13-16.**

You shall have a son, and when he grows up he will begin to save Israel from the hand of the Philistines. Your son must never drink any wine or strong drink as long as he lives. And his hair must be allowed to grow long and must never be cut, for he shall be a *"Nazarite under a vow to the Lord."*

In the Old Testament we know of women giving their child to God, when a man gave himself to God, he was forbidden to drink wine, as a sign, his hair was left to grow long while the vow or promise to God was upon him. Such a person a was called a Nazarite, a word which means *"one who has a vow"*; and Manoah's child was to be a Nazarite, and under a vow, as long as he lived.

In this case the child was named Samson. He grew up to become the strongest man at the time according to the Bible. Samson was not a general, like Gideon or Jephthah, he was called out by his people and led them when they went to war. He did much to set his people free; all that he did was by his own strength.

Samson would not take his wife's sister. He went out very angry; determined to do harm to the Philistines, because they had cheated him. He caught all the wild foxes he could find, until he had three hundred of them. Then he tied them together in pairs, by their tails; and between each pair of foxes he tied to their tails a piece of dry wood which he set on fire. These foxes became firebrands he turned them loose among the fields of the Philistines when the grain was ripe. They ran wildly over the fields, setting the grain on fire, burned it; and with the grain of the olive trees in the fields.

Samson did this to set his people free; he might have done much more, if he had led his people, instead of trusting in his own strength; if he had lived more for God, and not done his deeds as though he was playing pranks. There were some deep faults in Samson, at the end he sought God's help, and found it, God used Samson to set his people free. A person to look at who failed God:

Matthew's account Judas Iscariot
Matthew 26:20-21   (44)
V-20 "Now when the even was come, he sat down with the twelve.
V-21 And as they did eat, he said, Verily I say unto you, **that one of you shall betray me.**
Matthew 26:48-49;
V-48 "Now he that betrayed him gave them a sign, saying, Whosoever I shall kiss, that same is he: hold him fast.
V-49 And forthwith he came to Jesus, and said, Hail, master; and kissed him."
Matthew 27:3-8
V-3 "Then Judas, which had betrayed him, when he saw that he was condemned, repented himself, and brought again the thirty pieces of silver to the chief priest and elders,
V-4 Saying, I have betrayed the innocent blood. And they said, What *is that* to us? See thou *to that.*
V-5 And he cast down the pieces of silver in the temple, and departed, and went and hanged himself.
V-6 And the chief priest took the silver pieces, and said, It is not lawful for to put them into the treasury, because it is the price of blood.
V-7 And they took counsel, and bought with them the potter's field, to bury strangers in.
 V-8 Wherefor that field was called, The field of blood, unto this day."

Judas may have repented???

Chapter 10
BURNOUT, DEPRESSION, & STRESS

CHRISTIAN BURNOUT & STRESS –MINISTRY
BURNOUT – Avoiding Christian Burnout
Avoiding Burnout   Pages 1-5   [15]

"Many Christians who reach out to others can do burn out quickly because they launch out into a ministry before they have establish themselves in the foundation being committed to God. Discouragement, despair, boredom, and frustration often occurs if they don't recognize first their called is to God.

(…)

This reward is twofold:

(1 The Holy Spirit communicates God loves we are to obey Him.

(2 We become a vessel through which the Father's can use for Jesus it flows back to Him. This twofold reward keeps a person invigorated, and they can avoid much of the burnout.

God fashioned us to receive love and to be vessels through which His affection flows through Him. It just feels right when a person experience His love in the moments of weakness and distress. At such times we can have the Father's affection for Jesus pulsating through a person heart toward God.

(…)

God has many blessings for the believer. There are physical, emotional, and intellectual pleasures, all of which are ordained by God. No pleasure is more intense than the pleasure that comes when God communicates Himself to the human spirit.

When God communicates His passion to the believer, people experience what life is all about. It is life at its very best.

There are tender moments with God and spiritual awareness to be filled with the Holy Spirit. Of course, we do not experience an unbroken sense of God's love in our life. Such dramatic touches of God's presence tend to move a person to higher things. Only in heaven will we enjoy the continual ecstasy of his presence. I said to myself and to God, 'Oh yes, we have an awesome God!'

As God pours His love, that same love flows through a person back to Him. As I am loving Him back, greater revelation of His affection and beauty comes, the cycle just gets richer and richer. Just like anyone else, I am a person, saved and kept by His grace. I experience seasons of spiritual blessings, then I go through times of dryness, wherein I loss the joy, glad, and feel all of the other human emotions.

Burnout occurs when we do not experience the pleasure of the Christian life found in a loving relationship with God. I try to be careful not to loss the intensity of such encounters with the Holy Spirit, I don't want to discourage a person in reaching for a particular experience while seeking after God Himself and letting Him reveal Himself to any individual. This is important because getting focused on unrealistic spiritual expectations can actually lead to feeling unworthy, discouraged, and leave them doubting whether God loves them or not.

However, feeling loved - a little bit - and feeling God's love- even more. God has a dramatic powerful impact upon the human spirit. I cry out this message because I want to be a noble soldier for God. I'm committed to sharing this message, to crying out the necessity of putting the commandments of God first, I've experienced a reality that the body of Christ has within our reach. We must refocus on souls; we must put God first, first to realize the awesome spiritual power in Christ. (…)

Love Reduces Strife

I do not always respond positively to such attacks, even when I am in a season in which I am sensing the communion of the Holy Spirit. But when I have that little bit of happiness that comes from feeling the embrace of God's love. It reminds me of how I felt when I first met my wife. I was so lovesick with infatuation that if some guy had stolen my car, I would have said, 'You can have my car, do you want my wallet, too?' Satisfied people just fight less.

The body of Christ simply will not function properly until the first commandment is where it is supposed to be, in first place. This is absolutely imperative to the health of the body of Christ. I appreciate people whose number one drive is the Great Commission and relationships. I also know that until being a lover of God becomes their first priority, they will burn out, be tempted, and become entangled in strife.

Driven by Love

The apostle Paul said, "*The love of Christ constraineth us*" (**2 Cor. 5:14**). The word constrain means "to grip tightly." Paul was motivated by Christ's love working in him and through him. God's love became a driving force in all he did. It is the very power of living in godliness. I encourage people to focus on enjoying God more, not trying harder to overcome sin.

(…)

The Holy Spirit pours God's affection into the human heart regardless of their personality type or history of bondage, regardless of where we've been wounded or how we've been broken. It's a supernatural love that transcends the human experience.

As Paul says, "*Now hope does not disappoint, because the love of God has been poured out in our hearts by the Holy Spirit who was given to us*" (**Romans 5:5**). When we become worshipers we will not become warriors. Through Christ's loving embrace, He will show us when we become a bride we become united with Christ.

The conformation of the spiritual heart, soul, and mind. Revelation 20:11-12

V-11 "And I saw a great white throne, and him that sat on it, from whose face the earth and the heaven fled away; and there was found no place for them.

V-12 And I saw the dead, small and great, stand before God; and the books were opened; and another book was opened, which is *the book* of life: and the dead were judged out of those things which were written in the books, according to their works."

The saved have already been raptured in **I Thess. 4:17** caught up together in the air. (…)

This was created in man in the original creation in Adam. It passes on genetically the proof of this is coming to light in a person's DNA. You can trace a person's DNA for generations if they have a (particle of hair or specimen of any kind) if they had the equipment and technology it would go back to Adam.

If you remember John saying don't worry about remembering these things, the Holy Spirit will bring these things back to your remembrance in **John 14:26**."

http://www.homestead.com/raywatsonsecretplace/Articles2/Christian_burnout_stress.htm   3/16/05

The Scriptural view of Anxiety
Luke 12:22-27 (45)

V-22 "And he said unto his disciples, There for I say unto you, Take no thought for your life, what ye shall eat; neither for the body, what ye shall put on."

V-23 "The life is more than meat, and the body *is more* than raiment."

V-24 "Consider the ravens: for they neither sow nor reap; which neither have storehouse nor barn; and God feedeth them: how much more are ye better than the fowls?

V-25 "And which of you with taking thought can add to his stature one cubit?"

V-26 "If ye then be not able to do that thing which is least, why take ye thought for the rest?"

V-27 "Consider the lilies how they grow: they toil not, they spin not; and yet I say unto you,that Solomon in all his glory was not arrayed like one of those."

Profile of General Depression and Moods

Being honest with yourself about changes in mood, mood swings, or the intensity of negative feelings as they occur will help a person identify with the possible sources of depression or stress. A person should examine their feelings and try to determine what is troubling them in their relationships such as a spouse, family, or friends. The financial responsibilities, and so forth. Discussing problems with the people involved or with an understanding friend can sometimes bring about a resolution before a critical stage of stress is reached. When a person deals with mild depression it should be dealt with if it interferes with their effectiveness to get to get things done.

A person might try to:
- Changes in your normal routine by taking a break for a favorite activity or something new, even a weekend trip if you feel like it.
- Exercise to work off tension, take a walk, do some yard work, the exercise will probably improve your ability to sleep.
- Avoid known stresses.
- Avoid making long-term commitments, decisions, when you are in a bad mood, or changes that make you feel trapped or confined; it is better to put them off until you feel you're are better able to cope.

Being there for them:
- Do not try to "cheer them up." be empathic!
- Do not criticize or shame them, feelings of depression cannot be helped.
- Do sympathize and claim your feels in the same way as (he or she) does, **UNLESS** a person has been diagnosed by a doctor having depression too.
- Try not to get angry with the depressed individual.
See a physician/doctor, if physical complaints persist.

Depression information and treatment Pages 1-3 [16]

"Depression is one of the most common psychological problems, affecting some personal experiences, through depression in a family member. Each year over 17 million American adults experience a period of clinical depression. The cost in human suffering cannot be estimated because depression can interfere with normal activities, frequently causes problems at work, causing social and family adjustment.

It causes pain and suffering not only to those who have a disorder, but also to those who care about them. Serious depression can destroy family life as well as the life of the depressed person.

Impact of Depression:
- Causes tremendous emotional pain
- Disrupts the lives of millions of people
- Adversely affects the lives of families and friends
- Reduces work productivity and absenteeism

Has a significant negative impact on the economy, costing billions every year, depression and bipolar depression are presented separately on this website because of the unique problems encountered with bipolar disorders. Individuals interested in information about bipolar disorders should review the information on depression, bipolar disorders usually include depressive episodes as well. Bipolar disorder was formerly called manic-depressive disorder. It is a type of depression, and it is characterized by the presence of mood swings, especially 'manic highs' that often result in high risks in self-damaging behavior. Most individuals with bipolar disorders have both depressive episodes and hypomanic episodes.

Depression is a psychological condition that changes how a person thinks and feels, it also affects social behaviors and a lake of physical well-being. We have all felt sad at one time or another, but that is not depression. Sometimes we feel tired from working hard, or discouraged when faced with serious problems. This too, is not depression. These feelings usually pass within a few days or weeks, once a person adjusts to the stress. If these feelings linger, intensify, and begin to interfere at work, school affecting family responsibilities, it may be depression.

Depression can affect anyone. Once identified, most people are diagnosed with depression are treated. Unfortunately, depression is not always diagnosed, many of the symptoms are diagnosed as a mimic physical illness, such as sleep and appetite disturbances. Recognizing depression is the first step in treating it.

Nearly two-thirds of depressed people do not get proper treatment:

- The symptoms are not recognized as depression.
- Depressed people are seen as weak or lazy.
- Social stigma causes people to avoid needed treatment.
- The symptoms are so disabling that the people affected cannot reach out for help.
- Many symptoms are misdiagnosed as physical problems
- Individual symptoms are treated, rather than the underlying cause.

Clinical depression is a very common psychological problem, and most people never seek proper treatment, they are misdiagnosed with physical illness. This is extremely unfortunate because, with proper treatment, nearly 80% of those with depression can make significant improvement in their mood and life adjustment."

http://www.psychologyinfo.com/depression   3/16/05

What is depression   Pages 1-2 [17]

"Depression can affect the whole-body" illness, involving your body, mood, and thoughts. It affects the way you eat and sleep, the way a person feels about them self, and the way they think about things. A depressive disorder is not the same as a passing blue mood. It is not a sign of personal weakness or a condition that can be willed or wished away.

People with depression cannot merely "pull themselves together" and get better. Without treatment, symptoms can last for weeks, months, or years. Appropriate treatment, however, can help most people who suffer from depression.

The symptoms of depression may vary from person to person, and also depend on the severity of the depression. Depression causes changes in a person's thinking, feeling, behavior, and physical well-being.

• Changes in Thinking – A person may experience problems with concentration and decision making. Some people report difficulty with short term memory, forgetting things all the time. Negative thoughts and thinking are characteristic of depression. Pessimism, poor self-esteem, excessive guilt, and self-criticism are all common. Some people have self-destructive thoughts during a more serious depression.

• Changes in Feelings - They may feel sad for no reason at all. Some people report that they no longer enjoy activities that they once found pleasurable. They might lack motivation, and become more apathetic. They might feel "slowed down" and tired all the time. Sometimes irritability is a problem, they may have more difficulty controlling t heir temper. In extreme depression, is characterized by feelings of helplessness and hopelessness.

• Changes in Behavior - Changes in behavior during depression are reflective of the negative emotions being experienced. A person might act more apathetic, because that's how they feel. Some people do not feel comfortable with other people, so social withdrawal is common. A person may experience a dramatic change in appetite, either eating more or less. This is known as chronic sadness, excessive crying.

• Some people complain about everything, and act out their anger with temper outbursts. Sexual desire may disappear, resulting in lack of sexual activity. In extreme cases, people may neglect their personal appearance, even neglecting basic hygiene. Needless to say, someone who is this depressed does not do very much, their work productivity and household responsibilities suffer. Some people even have trouble getting out of bed.

• Changes in Physical Well-being - We already talked about the negative emotional feelings experienced during depression, but these are coupled with negative physical emotions as well. Chronic fatigue, despite spending more time sleeping, is common. Some people can't sleep, or don't sleep soundly. These individuals lay awake for hours, or awaken many times during the night, and stare at the ceiling. Others sleep many hours, even most of the day, they feel tired. Many people lose their appetite, feel slowed down by depression, complain of aches and pains. Others are restless, and can't sit still.

Now imagine these symptoms lasting for weeks or even months. Imagine feeling this way almost all of the time. Depression is present a person experiences many of these symptoms for several weeks. Of course, it's not a good idea to diagnose yourself. If you think that you might be depressed, see a psychologist as soon as possible. A psychologist can assess whether you are depressed, or just under a lot of stress and feeling sad. Remember, depression is treatable. Instead of worrying about whether you are depressed, do something about it. Even if you don't feel like it right now."

http://www.psychologyinfo.com/depression   3/16/05

Causes of depression   Pages 1-2   [18]

"You may have heard talk about chemical imbalances in the brain that occurs in depression, suggesting depression is a medical illness, without psychological causes. However, all psychological problems have some physical manifestations, and all of the physical illnesses have psychological components as well. In fact, the chemical imbalances occur during depression it usually disappears when they complete psychotherapy for depression, this can happen without taking any medications to correct the imbalance. This suggests that the imbalance is the body's physical response to psychological depression, rather than the other way around.

Some types of depression do seem to run in families, suggesting a biological vulnerability. This seems to be the case with bipolar depression, and to a lesser degree, severe major depression. Studies of families, in which members of each generation develop bipolar disorders, found those with bipolar disorders have a somewhat different genetic makeup than those who are diagnose through genetic testing, DNA.

However, the reverse is not true. Not everybody with the genetic makeup causes this vulnerability to a bipolar disorder. Additional factors, such as stress when other psychological factors are involved in its onset. Likewise, major depression also seems to occur, generation after generation, in some families, but not with a frequency that suggests clear biological causes. In Addition, it also occurs in people who have no family history of depression. While there may be some biological factors that contributes to depression, it is clearly a psychological disorder.

A variety of psychological factors appear to play a role in vulnerability to these severe forms of depression. Most likely, psychological factors are completely responsible for other forms of mild and moderate depression, <u>especially reactive depression</u>. <u>Reactive depression</u> is usually diagnosed as an <u>adjustment disorder</u> during treatment.

People who have **low self-esteem**, they are consistently viewed as pessimistic, who are overwhelmed by stress, and are more prone to depression. Psychologists often describe social learning factors as being significant in the development of depression, as well as other psychological problems. People learn both adaptive and maladaptive ways of managing stress and responding to life's problems within their family, educational, social and work environments.

These environmental factors can be influence psychological adjustments and development, this is one way people try to resolve problems when they occur. Social environment factors also explain why psychological problems appear to occur more often in family members, from generation to generation. If a child grows up in a pessimistic environment, in which discouragement is common and encouragement is rare, that child will develop a vulnerability to depression as well.

A serious loss, chronic illness, relationship problems, work stress, family crisis, financial setback, or any unwelcome life change can trigger a depressive episode. Very often, a combination of biological, psychological, and environmental factors are involved in the development of depressive disorders, as well as other psychological problems. When a person feels depressed, and doesn't know where to turn, talk to someone who can help.... a counselor, psychologist or therapist."

http://www.psychologyinfo.com/depression   3/16/05

Depression information from Christian perspective

What is depression?

"Depression can be called a disease of the emotions. It's classification as a mental illness does not make it any less real or painful. It is a common disease, one in twenty people suffer from depression.

Depression is a disturbance in mood characterized by varying degrees of sadness, disappointment, loneliness, hopelessness, self-doubt, and guilt. These feelings can be quite intense lasting for a long period of time. Daily activities may become more difficult (...). The individual may be able to cope with them. It is at this level, the feelings of hopelessness can become so intense that suicide may seem to be the only solution.

A person experiencing severe depression may experience extreme moods, feelings and even a desire to completely withdrawal from their daily routine and the outside world. Depression is nothing to be ashamed of, it is not a sign of weakness. It is treatable, medications can cause depression, at this point a person may need or want therapy and counselling, or both. God answers prayer, persistent prayer facilitates the process of emotional healing.

For the depressed Christian whose world has fallen apart, prayer may not seem like an option. In this case, the persistent prayer of close friends or relatives will help.

What depression is not

Depression is not "Just in your mind." It isn't a made-up illness, it isn't laziness, or a couple of days of feeling sad or blue. It isn't

PMT, or stress. It is not rejection by God, or abandonment. If it is from God, as a result of a specific sin (i.e. refusal to end an adulterous affair), you will know it. You will not be left wondering.

Some causes of depression
(This is not a complete list, there are other causes)
Physical Causes:
- Pre-menstrual and postnatal hormone changes
- Some types of manic depression have been shown to have a genetic basis
- Hormone deficiencies (such as thyroid disturbances)
- Generalised illnesses such as kidney or liver disease
- Lack of natural light during winter in some susceptible people
- Alcoholism
- Drug dependency
- Food allergies and strange reactions to medicines, chemicals or food additives.

Mental Causes:
- Unconscious impulses (from Freudian and Jungian psychology)
- Learning the wrong way to cope with difficulties
- Learned helplessness (from behaviouristic psychology)
- Overload or stress

Spiritual Causes:
- (most likely in NON Christians) Sense of despair/futility of life; death of a loved one.

Symptoms
- Lethargy (everything seems just too much trouble to do)
- disturbed sleep (early waking, difficulty getting to sleep)
- waking up tired after a "normal" night of sleep)
- lack of concentration
- irritability
- exhaustion
- lack of sexual drive
- sensation of utter despair
- sense of hopelessness or uselessness of everything
- fear of death
- phobias
- obsession behavior
- permanent sense of anxiety
- feelings of wanting to cry, but inability to do so
- thoughts of suicide, or fear of committing suicide
- change in appetite and weight
- other symptoms, this is not a definitive list

Likely effects of depression in Christians
John Lockley says:

> Christians, spiritual effects follow from the
> pression, and seldom the other way round. I repeat -
> Christians, nearly always the depression comes first,
> llowed by a sense of remoteness from God, rather
> an depression being the result of "falling away.
> l *Practical Workbook for the Depressed"*

Being a Christian doesn't offer immunity from trials, troubles or illness.

This does not make a person holy and perfect, this may involve dealing with a person's past. It is not an overnight process, and it may be painful. We may have leftover baggage from the past hurts suffered, wrong attitudes, incorrect information and so on. This can slow us down, and can be a source of depression."
http://www.gosplecom.net/cdp/info/.hmtl   3/16/05

The Scriptural view of depression
Moses
Numbers 11:13-15;   (46)
V-13 "Whence should I have flesh to give unto all this people? For they weep unto me, saying, Give us flesh, that we may eat.
V-14 I am not able to bear all this people alone, because *it is* too heavy for me.
V-15 And if thou deal thus with me, kill me, I pray thee, out of hand, if I have found favour in thy sight; and let me not see my wretchedness."

Joshua
Joshua 1:9
V-9 "Have not I commanded thee? Be strong and of good courage; be not afraid, neither be dismayed : for the Lord thy God *is* with thee whithersoever thou goest."

Hannah
I Sam. 1:9-11;   (47)
V-9 "So Hannah rose up after they had eaten in Shi-loh, and after they had drunk. Now E'-li the priest sat upon a seat by a post of the temple of the Lord.

V-10 And she *was* in bitterness of soul, and prayed unto the Lord, and wept sore.

V-11 And she vowed a vow, and said, O lord of hosts, if thou wilt indeed look on the affiction of thine handmaid, and remember me, and not forget thine handmaid, but wilt give unto thine handmaid a man child, then I will give him unto the Lord all the days of his life, and there shall no razor come upon his head."

David

Psalms 9:9-10;   (48)

V-9 "The Lord also will be a refuge for the oppressed, a refuge in the times of trouble.

V-10 And they that know thy name will put their trust in three: for thou, Lord, hast not forsaken them that seek thee."

Psalms 30:5

V-5 "For His anger *endureth but* a moment; in his favour *is* life: weeping may endure for a night, but joy *cometh* in the morning."

Psalms 46:1

V-1 "God *is* our refuge and strength. A very present help in trouble."

Psalms 107:6

V-6 "Then they cried unto the Lord in their trouble, *and* he delivered them out of their distresses."

Psalms 107:8, 9

V-8 Oh that *men* would praise the Lord *for* his goodness, and *for* his wonderful works to the children of men!

V-9 For he satisfieth the longing soul, and filleth the hungry soul with goodness."

Isaiah 41:10, 11

V-10 "Fear thou not; for I *am* with thee: be not dismayed; for I *am* thy God: I will strengthen thee; yea, I will help thee; yea, I will uphold thee with the right hand of my righteousness.

V-11 Behold, all they that were incensed against thee shall be ashamed and confounded: they shall be as nothing; and they that strive with thee shall perish."

Christ

Matthew 6:28-30 (49)

V-28 "Come unto me, all *ye* that labour and are heavy laden, and I will give you rest.

V-29 Take my yoke upon you, and learn of me; for I am meek and lowly in heart: and *ye* shall find rest unto your souls.

V-30 For my yoke *is* easy, and my burden is light,."

Paul

II Cor. 4:8-10

V-8 "*We are* troubled on every side, yet not distressed; *we are* perplexed, but not in despair;

V-9 Persecuted, but not forsaken; cast down, but not destroyed;

V-10 Always bearing about in the body the dying of the Lord Jesus, that the life also of Jesus might be made manifest in our body."

James 3:13, 14

V-13 "Who *is* a wise man and endued with knowledge among you? Let him shew out of a good conversation is works with meekness of wisdom.

V-14 But if ye have bitter envying and strife in your hearts, glory not, and lie not against the truth."

Anxiety

Everybody worries or gets a case of butterflies in the stomach. **Anxiety** is a part of life, it is built into our **nature**. People miss out on an opportunity for happiness, because of their fears and worries. Can **anxiety** interfere with a person's life? While moderate **anxiety** can be limiting, severe, or acute **anxiety,** it can be crippling. **Anxiety** currently afflicts more than 20 million Americans a year, making it the most common mental illness in the US. Find out if you're feeling **anxious.**

Let's talk about anxiety disorders

American Psychiatric Association   Pages 1-4 [20]

or is it anxiety. It will determine whether you should consider seeking help, and to what degree.

Let's Talk Facts About . . .

Anxiety Disorders

"That first date, an important job interview, the big speech, a critical test (. . .) times when most people feel a little anxious. Sweaty palms and "butterflies" in the stomach during challenging situations are normal. Anxiety disorders, however, are considered medical illnesses they differ dramatically from normal feelings of nervousness. The symptoms of these disorders often occur without warning and can make the simplest of life's routines sources of unbearable discomfort.

What Are Anxiety Disorders?

Anxiety disorders are common emotional disorders, annually affecting more than 20 million Americans (approximately one in nine). Symptoms of anxiety disorders can include:

- Overwhelming feelings of panic and fear
- Non controllable obsessive thoughts
- Painful, intrusive memories; recurring nightmares
- Pausea, sweating, muscle tension, and other uncomfortable physical reactions

Anxiety disorders differ from normal feelings of nervousness, as the symptoms often occur for no apparent reason and they do not go away. Rather than functioning as a call to action, these alarming reactions can make everyday experiences sources of potential terror. If left untreated, anxiety disorders can propel people to take extreme measures (such as refusing to leave the house) to avoid situations that may trigger or worsen their anxiety. Job performance and personal relationships suffered as a result.

Fortunately, these illnesses generally respond well to treatment, and the majority of patients receiving treatment experience significant relief from their symptoms. Unfortunately, many people with anxiety disorders do not seek treatment because they do not recognize their symptoms as a sign of illness or they fear the reactions of co-workers, family, or friends.

Types of Anxiety Disorders
Panic-Disorder

The core symptom of panic disorder is the panic attack, an overwhelming fear of being in danger, during which the individual may experience:

- Pounding heart or chest pain
- Sweating, trembling, or shaking
- Shortness of breath or sensation of choking
- Nausea or abdominal pain
- Dizziness or lightheadedness

- Feeling unreal or disconnected
- Fear of losing control, "going crazy," or dying
- Numbness
- Chills or hot flashes

Because these attacks occur unexpectedly and seemingly without reason, people with panic disorder often first believe that they are having a heart attack."

http://www.psych.org/public_info/anxirty.cfm   3/16/05

The Scriptural view of anxiety

Pray as the early disciples did, "Lord, increase my faith". FAITH is the opposite of **anxiety**. Faith not only pleases God, but keeps us trusting in God's fatherly care. As you have read I am a witness to God's grace and mercy!! Praise God "*from whom all blessing flow*"!

Psalms 37:1-11   (49)

V-1 "Fret not thyself because of evildoers, neither be thou envious against the workers of iniquity.

V-2 For they shall soon be cut down like the grass, and wither as the green herb.

V-3 Trust in the LORD, and do good; so shalt thou dwell in the land, and verily thou shalt be fed.

V- 4 Delight thyself also in the LORD: and he shall give thee the desires of thine heart.

V- 5 Commit thy way unto the LORD; trust also in him; and he shall bring it to pass.

V-6 And he shall bring forth thy righteousness as the light, and thy judgment as the noonday.

V-7 Rest in the LORD, and wait patiently for him: fret not thyself because of him who prospereth in his way, because of the man who bringeth wicked devices to pass.

V-8 Cease from anger, and forsake wrath: fret not thyself in any wise to do evil. Do not fret it only causes harm.

V-9 For evildoers shall be cut off: but those that wait upon the LORD, they shall inherit the earth.

V-10 For yet a little while, and the wicked shall not be: yea, thou shalt diligently consider his place, and it shall not be.

V-11 But the meek shall inherit the earth; and shall delight themselves in the abundance of peace."

Psalms 131:1, 2

V-1 "LORD, my heart is not haughty, nor mine eyes lofty: neither do I exercise myself in concern myself with] great matters, or in things too high for me.

V-2 Surely I have behaved and quieted myself, as a child that is weaned of his mother: my soul is even as a weaned child."

Psalms 127:2

V-2 "It is vain for you to rise up early, to sit up late, to eat the bread of sorrows: for so he giveth his beloved sleep: eating the bread of anxious toil; for he gives to his beloved sleep."

Anxiety   (50)

Proverbs 12:25

V-25 "Heaviness in the heart of man maketh it stoop: Anxiety in the heart of man causes depression; Anxiety in a man's heart weighs him down]: but a good word maketh it glad."

Proverbs 24:19-20

V-19 "Fret not thyself because of evil men, neither be thou envious at the wicked:

V-20 For there shall be no reward to the evil man; the candle of the wicked shall be put out."

Jeremiah
Jeremiah 17:7-8

V-7 "Blessed is the man that trusteth in the LORD, and whose hope the LORD is.

V-8 For he shall be as a tree planted by the waters, and that spreadeth out her roots by the river, and shall not see when heat cometh, but her leaf shall be green; and shall not be careful anxious in the year of drought, neither shall cease from yielding fruit.

Matthew
Matthew 6:24-34   (51)

V-24; "No man can serve two masters: for either he will hate the one, and love the other; or else he will hold to the one, and despise the other. Ye cannot serve God and mammon.

V-25 Therefore I say unto you, Take no thought for do not worry about; do not be anxious about your life, what ye shall eat, or what ye shall drink; nor yet for your body, what ye shall put on. Is not the life more than meat, and the body than raiment?

V-26 Behold the fowls of the air: for they sow not, neither do they reap, nor gather into barns; yet your heavenly Father feedeth them. Are ye not much better than they?

V-27 Which of you by taking thought [NKJV: worrying; RSV: being anxious] can add one cubit unto his stature?

V-28 And why take ye thought for So why do you worry about; And why are you anxious about raiment? Consider the lilies of the field, how they grow; they toil not, neither do they spin:

V-29 And yet I say unto you, That even Solomon in all his glory was not arrayed like one of these.

V-30 Wherefore, if God so clothe the grass of the field, which today is, and tomorrow is cast into the oven, shall he not much more clothe you, O ye of little faith?

V-31 Therefore take no thought do not worry; do not be anxious, saying, What shall we eat? or, What shall we drink? or, Wherewithal shall we be clothed?

V-32 (For after all these things do the Gentiles seek: for your heavenly Father knoweth that ye have need of all these things.

V-33 But seek ye first the kingdom of God, and his righteousness; and all these things shall be added unto you.

V-34 "Take therefore no thought for the morrow do not worry about tomorrow; do not be anxious about tomorrow for the morrow shall take thought for the things of itself for tomorrow will worry about its own things; for tomorrow will be anxious for itself. Sufficient unto the day is the evil thereof, Sufficient for the day is its own trouble; Let the day's own trouble be sufficient for the day."

Philippians 4:6, 7

V-6 "Be careful for nothing Be anxious for nothing; Have no anxiety about anything; but in every thing by prayer and supplication with thanksgiving let your requests be made known unto God.

V-7 And the peace of God, which passeth all understanding, shall keep your hearts and minds through Christ Jesus."

Self-Esteem

Philippians 2:3   (52)

V-3 "*Let* nothing *be done* through strife or vainglory; but in lowliness of mind let each esteem others better than themselves."

Luke 16:14-17   (53)

V-14 "Now the Pharisees, who were lovers of money, also heard all these things, and they derided Him.

V-15 And He said to them, You are those who justify yourselves before men, but God knows your hearts. For what is highly esteemed among men is an abomination in the sight of God.

V-16 The law and the prophets *were* until John. Since that time the kingdom of God has been preached, and everyone is pressing into it.

V-17 "And it is easier for heaven and earth to pass away than for one title of the law to fail."

Profile of Self-love.

It is implied that we should be able to love ourselves. How can a person love someone when they don't love themselves? That shows a person does not have the love of the Father in them. There is a self-love which is corrupt of course, which is the root of sins, it must be put off and mortified: (crucified), there is a self-love which is natural, and the rule of the greatest duty of man, and it must be preserved in sanctification through Christ, and that is not of themselves. A person must love themselves, that is, a person must have a due regard to the dignity of a person's own nature, and a due concern for the welfare of their own souls and bodies, before they can help someone else. (Right)

Ephesians 4:2-16   (54)

V-2 "With all lowliness and meekness, with longsuffering, forbearing one another in love;

V-3 Endeavouring to keep the unity of the Spirit in the bond of peace.

V-4 *There is* one body, and one Spirit, even as ye are called in one hope of your calling;

V-5 One Lord, one faith, one baptism,

V-6 One God and Father of all, who *is* above all, and through all, and in you all.

V-7 But unto every one of us is given grace according to the measure of the gift of Christ.

V-8 Wherefore he saith, When he ascended up on high, he led captivity captive, and gave gifts unto men.

V-9 (Now that he ascended, what is it but that he also descended first into the lower parts of the earth?

V-10 He that descended is the same also that ascended up far above all heavens, that he might fill all things.)

V-11 And he gave some, apostles; and some, prophets; and some, evangelists; and some, pastors and teachers;

V-12 For the perfecting of the saints, for the work of the ministry, for the edifying of the body of Christ:

V-13 Till we all come in the unity of the faith, and of the knowledge of the Son of God, unto a perfect man, unto the measure of the stature of the fulness of Christ:

V-14 That we *henceforth* be no more children, tossed to and fro, and carried about with every wind of doctrine, by the sleight of men, *and* cunning craftiness, whereby they lie in wait to deceive;

V-15 "But speaking the truth in love, may grow up into him in all things, which is the head, *even* Christ:

V-16 From whom the whole body fitly joined together and compacted by that which every joint supplieth, according to the effectual working in the measure of every part, maketh increase of the body unto the edifying of itself in love."

Ephesians 5:1-2 (55)

V-1 "Be ye therefore followers of God, as dear children;

V-2 And walk in love, as Christ also hath loved us, and hath given himself for us an offering and a sacrifice to God for a sweetsmelling savour."

Matthew 6:24

V-24 "No man can serve two masters: for either he will hate the one, and love the other; or else he will hold to the one, and despise the other. Ye cannot serve God and mammon."

This book is about (Reconciliation) **II Corinthians 5:17-21** Paul says the same thing and uses the same word (reconciled) us in Christ.

Romans 5;8-13 (56)

V-8 "<u>God commendeth his love toward us,</u>< ><u>in that, while we were yet sinners</u>< ><u>Christ died for us</u>".

V-9 we are "justified by his blood"

V-10 states > <u>we were reconciled to God by the death of his Son</u>< and in

V-9 Much more then, being now justified by his blood, we shall be saved from wrath through him.

V-10 For if, when we were enemies, we were reconciled to God by the death of his Son, much more, being reconciled, we shall be saved by his life.

V-11 And not only *so*, but we also joy in God through our Lord Jesus Christ, by whom we have now received the atonement.

V-12 Wherefore, as by one man sin entered into the world, and death by sin; and so death passed upon all men, for that all have sinned:

V-13 (For until the law sin was in the world: but sin is not imputed when there is no law.

A person needs a mental awareness *as to who they* are and how are they handling things. This section of our study guide deals with a person's mental state, the mind is vital link to the life system. Stress-Factors and Pressure-Relief are vital links to a person's Mental-Will-Being.

Everyone has to deal with STRESS in different way. Our main goal is for a person to keep a stress balance and have check points set up in their life. Then be aware of the emotional needs in their life. We call this part of our study STRESS-FACTORS and PRESSURE-RELIEF. This is important part of this study guide.

When a person is stressing out they may be out of control or may be they don't have a serious problem or a crisis for a person to call us. The president has his "Hot Line". We have the panic button. That is when a person needs to call us or a partner. PLEASE DON'T TAKE IT OUT ON SOME ONE ELSE. Let the stress out and talk to someone. I have been so angry and even out of control of my life a view times. We hope that SOS services can help a person get back on track.

It's normal to feel anxious when facing a challenging situation, such as a job interview, a tough exam, or a blind date. If a person worries and fears seem overwhelming and interfere with their daily life, they may be suffering from an anxiety disorder. There are different types of anxiety disorders—and effective treatments and self-help strategies. Once a person understands how to deal with anxiety disorders, there are steps a person can take to reduce the symptoms and regain control of their life.

1. Learn to recognize the signs, symptoms, and types of anxiety recognize how anxiety affects the whole body with a wide range of physical symptoms.
2. Make it a priority to connect support face-to-face with supportive people.

3. Move frequently—don't sit for more than an hour.

4. Get the full amount of restful sleep that is required

5. Learn and practice relaxation techniques

Anxiety attacks, are also known as panic attacks, are episodes of intense panic or fear. Anxiety attacks usually occur suddenly and without warning. Sometimes there's an obvious trigger like getting stuck in an elevator, for example, or thinking about the big speech a person has to give—in other cases, the attacks come out of the blue.

Anxiety attacks usually peak within 10 minutes, they rarely last more than 30 minutes. During that short time, the terror can be severe, they feel as if they're about to die or losing control. The physical symptoms of anxiety attacks are frightening people believe they're having a heart attack. After an anxiety attack is over, they may be worried about having another one, particularly in a public place where help isn't available or they feel they can't escape.

If a person identifies with **several** of the following 7 signs and symptoms, and they won't go away, a person may be suffering from an anxiety disorder:

1. Is a person constantly tense, worried, or on edge?

2. Does a person's anxiety interfere with your work, school, or family responsibilities?

3. Are they plagued by fears that you know are irrational, but can't shake?

4. Do they believe that something bad will happen if certain things aren't done a certain way?

5. Do they avoid everyday situations or activities because they cause you anxiety?

6. Do they experience sudden, unexpected attacks of heart?

7. Does a person feel danger and catastrophe are everywhere?

Anxiety

If you have anxiety that's severe enough to interfere with your ability to function, medication may help relieve your symptoms. However, anxiety medications can be habit forming and causing unwanted side effects, be sure to research your options. Many people use anti-anxiety medication when therapy, exercise, or self-help strategies would work just as well or better there are side effects and safety concerns. It's important to <u>weigh the benefits and risks of anxiety medication</u> so you can make an informed decision.

How to deal with these human factors:

1. The stress point and how a person react to **stress** is one of the most common problems a person faces.
2. When there is a **crisis** the stress point is goes up.
3. There are so many **demands** in life that we will not be able to count all of them.

How a person responds is very important. That will determine whether they are dealing with a major or minor factors. These are some of the easiest to see, on the other hand they are complicated by the stress evolved.

4. The point is how much stress can a person take before they bend or break. When there is too much stress and too much bending over time there are reactions taking place.

A person can only take so much before the breaking point, sometimes something has to give. Sometimes it only takes a push or shove to bring out the breaking point.

I worked as a maintenance foreman in a power plant. We measured the amount of wear on a part and the stress point on a part, if there was too much wear we would have to replace it with a new part.

Our lives take on some of the same principles we can fix some of the problems, we cannot replace the body. The wear and tear on a person's life gets to be too much. That is when they need a doctor to replace or fix the damage in their life, can they change or fix their life, to the point of having a new life? (YES) Stay with me and see how we do this!

Stress

When there is too much stress! There can be the breaking point and this can be very dangerous. When a person has drastic human or physical failures taking place, if it is not a life treating situation, or it is very serious when people can't do anything or say anything, at this point people need help.

If there is a cure most people would want the cure what if there no cure this can be devastating. That can cause a person to hit the panic button what does that mean? We have spent a great deal of time dealing with the personal side of life now we want to deal with the positives aspect of a person's self-actualization.

Stress is your body's way of responding to any kind of demand or threat. When a person feels threatened, the nervous system responds by releasing stress hormones, including adrenaline and cortisol, which arouses the body calling for emergency and action. A person's heart pounds faster, muscles tighten, blood pressure rises, breath quickens, their senses become sharper. These physical changes increase a person's strength and stamina, speeds up or slows down their reaction time. This is known as the "fight or flight" or mobilization of stress responses this is the way the body protects a person.

When stress is within your comfort zone, it can help you to stay focused, energetic, and alert. In emergency situations, stress can save a person's life—giving them extra strength to defend themselves. For example spurring a person to slam on their brakes to avoid an accident. Stress can also help a person rise to meet challenges. Stress is what keeps a person on their toes during a presentation or at work, sharpens a person's concentration. Beyond their comfort zone, stress stops being helpful when it is over loaded it can cause major damage to a person's mind and body.

The body's nervous system often does a poor job of distinguishing between daily stressors and life-threatening events. If a person is stressed over an argument with a friend, a traffic jam on their commute home, or a mountain of bills, for example. A person's body can still react as if they're facing a life-or-death situation.

Social engagement has always been the most evolved response to life's stressors. It's no surprise that people with a strong network of friends and family—with whom they're comfortable sharing their emotions—are better able to tolerate stress. On the flip side, the more lonely and isolated a person feels, the less opportunity they have for social engagement and a greater vulnerability to stress.

Whether a person is trying to build their tolerance to stress or cope with its symptoms, when a person has control over their stress than they might think. Unfortunately, many of us try to deal with stress in ways that only compound the problem.

Chapter 11

SELF-ACTUALIZATION & DISCIPLINE

Discipline can be equated and leak of faith in:
II Timothy 3:14-17 (57)

V-14 "But continue thou in the things which thou hast learned and hast been assured of, knowing of whom thou hast learned *them*;

V-15 "And that from a child thou hast known the holy scriptures, which are able to make thee wise unto salvation through faith which is in Christ Jesus."

V-16 "All scripture *is* given by inspiration of God, and *is* profitable for doctrine, for reproof, for correction, for instruction in righteousness:"

V-17 "That the man of God may be perfect, throughly furnished unto all good works."

SELF - ACTUALIZATION - IMPROVEMENT
Image   Worth   Esteem
"Self-Image, Self-worth, & Self-Esteem / Ego.
Self-Discipline, Self-Control & Motivation – Pride/Vanity, & Self-identity.
Motives, Discipline, Self-Control, and Attitudes

I am making a personal observation of Christians. They are leaking in personal discipline as well as Christian discipline in their Christian walk and talk, and their testimony. This erosion has come over the last few decades because we have had an easier way of life. It reflects in a person's life style and dress, the economy especially in American's life style is so much better than those of the Depression of the1930's & 40's.

I am going to give a "C" for **Self-Control** because I don't think for the most part people have improved in the area of **Self-Control / Motives**. People still get angry and lose their temper, use bad language, and use God's name in vain.

Profile of Self-Control
Example

I substitute teach and find that most Christian young people do not have good personal discipline skills or **Self-Control** over their personal life. They want their "**cake and eat it**" at the same time. They want to play at studying to them life is a game, and at the same time they want good grades. They don't want to study, they don't have good study habits resulting in poor **Self-Discipline** as I have discussed. They don't want to work for good grades, especially no homework, because that is their personal time. It is sad to say that hard work is not a part of their vocabulary.

Self-Control is another aspect of their life that is out of control, it doesn't take long to see they don't have **Self-Control,** they want talk and use their I-phones. Their out bursts in class and leak of **Self-Control** shows up in their lack of respect for others. They are very **self-centered**.

The last two are also reflected in their motives, they are selfish and self-willed, it doesn't mean they don't care for others, they have selfish motives as long as it befits their personal happiness. What has happened, "live for today and let tomorrow take care of its self". Motives come under the heading of motivation / will, "how bad do you want something". If a person has to work for something, it is out of the question, most go home to video games, TV, socializing, and talking on the phone.

This is where I really have a problem it is in a person's **Attitude**, they think they are special they are taught that as a young child and it shows up in a **selfish attitude**. We are special in the sight of God, that should humble a person in His sight, it should make us proud not boastful, we have to live with others, and how a person relates to themselves and others reflects in their **attitude**.

Let's put this into prospective, how about "God first" "others second" and "me last" that is what should be taught. We need to put it into practice having a humble spirit, and should have a little humility in our lives.

I don't see a lot of that in our young people and even adults reflect these same attitudes, I see where it is coming from.

It does mean a person should not be **self-sacrificing** to the point of letting someone abuse them or their children. Young people lives should be about being a good a person, a good Christian seems to be old fashioned, the ideas of feeling bad about oneself is not good.

That being the case a person needs to work on being balanced in all four of these areas. This is where psychology has come into prominence by recognizing and categorizing these four areas, by using methods that do help bring **Motives**, **Discipline**, **Self-Control**, and **Attitudes** into balance and under control in a person's life.

Scriptural view of self.
I John 2:12-16   (59)
V-12 "I write unto you, little children, because your sins are forgiven you for his name's sake.
V-13 I write unto you, fathers, because ye have known him *that is* from the beginning. I write unto you, young men, because ye have overcome the wicked one. I write unto you, little children, because ye have known the Father.

V-14 I have written unto you, fathers, because ye have known him *that is* from the beginning. I have written unto you, young men, because ye are strong, and the word of God abideth in you, and ye have overcome the wicked one.

V-15 Love not the world, neither the things *that are* in the world. If any man love the world, the love of the Father is not in him.

V-16 For all that *is* in the world, the lust of the flesh, and the lust of the eyes, and the pride of life, is not of the Father, but is of the world.

V-17 And the world passeth away, and the lust thereof: but <u>he that doeth the will of God abideth for ever</u>."

James 4:1-10   (60)

V-1 "From whence *come* wars and fightings among you? *come they* not hence, *even* of your lusts that war in your members?

V-2 Ye lust, and have not: ye kill, and desire to have, and cannot obtain: ye fight and war, yet ye have not, because ye ask not.

V-3 <u>Ye ask, and receive not, because ye ask amiss,</u> <u>that ye may consume *it* upon your lusts</u>.

V-4 <u>Ye adulterers and adulteresses</u>, know ye not that the friendship of the world is enmity with God? whosoever therefore will be a friend of the world is the enemy of God.

V-5 Do ye think that the scripture saith in vain, The spirit that dwelleth in us lusteth to envy?

V-6 But he giveth more grace. Wherefore he saith, God resisteth the proud, <u>but giveth grace unto the humble</u>.

V-7 <u>Submit yourselves therefore to God</u>. Resist the devil, and <u>he will flee from you</u>.

V-8 <u>Draw nigh to God, and he will draw nigh to you</u>. Cleanse *your* hands, *ye* sinners; and purify *your* hearts, *ye* double minded.

V-9 Be afflicted, and mourn, and weep: let your laughter be turned to mourning, and *your* joy to heaviness.

V-10 <u>Humble yourselves in the sight of the Lord, and he shall lift you up</u>."

We have given some scriptures on **Self-Control** now we will give some definitions and symptoms of mental disorders. We have tried to give a balance of scriptures, psychological terms, and how to deal with behaviors.

Definition of Psychosomatic {14}

Function: *adjective*

Etymology: International Scientific Vocabulary

Date: 1863

1   : of, relating to, concerned with, or involving both mind and body

<the *psychosomatic* nature of man – Herbert Ratner>

2   : of, relating to, involving, or concerned with bodily symptoms caused by mental or emotional disturbance

<*psychosomatic* symptoms>

<*psychosomatic* medicine>

Definition of Neurosis {15}

Main Entry: **neu·ro·sis**

Function: *noun*

Inflected Form(s): *plural* **neu·ro·ses**

Date: circa 1784

: a mental and emotional disorder that affects only part of the personality, is accompanied by a less distorted perception of reality than in a psychosis, does not result in disturbance of the use of language, and is accompanied by various physical, physiological, and mental disturbances (as visceral symptoms, anxieties, or phobias)

Definition of Psychosis {16}
Main Entry: **psy·cho·sis**
Function: *noun*
Etymology: New Latin
Date: 1847

: fundamental derangement of the mind (as in schizophrenia) characterized by defective or lost contact with reality especially as evidenced by delusions, hallucinations, and disorganized speech and behavior

Definition of Intitutionalze {17}
Main Entry: **in·sti·tu·tion·al·ize**
Function: *transitive verb*
Inflected Form(s): **-ized**; **-iz·ing**
Date: 1865

1 : to make into an institution
: give character of an institution
to <*institutionalized* housing>; *especially*
: to incorporate into a structured and often highly formalized system <*institutionalized* values>
2 : to put in the care of an institution <*institutionalize* alcoholics>

Definition of Psychiatry {18}
Main Entry: **psy·chi·a·try**
Function: *noun*

Etymology: probably from French *psychiatrie,* from *psychiatre* psychiatrist, from *psych-* psych- + Greek *iatros* physician -- more at -**IATRY**

Date: 1828

> : a branch of medicine that deals with mental, emotional, or behavioral disorders

Definition of Psychotherapy {19}

Function: *noun*

Etymology: International Scientific Vocabulary *psych-* + *therapy*

> **1 a** : treatment of mental or emotional disorder or maladjustment by **psychological** means, especially involving verbal communication (as in **psychoanalysis**, nondirective psychotherapy, reeducation, hypnosis, or prestige suggestion)
>
> **b** : a particular school or method (as Freudian **psychoanalysis**) of psychotherapy <the bewildering proliferation of self-improvement manuals and popular *psychotherapies* -- R.D. Rosen>
>
> **2** : any alteration in an individual's interpersonal environment, relationships, or life situation brought about especially by a qualified therapist and intended to have the effect of alleviating symptoms of mental or emotional disturbance

Definition of Theist {20}

Main Entry: **the·ism**

Function: *noun*

Date: 1678

> : belief in the existence of a god or gods; *specifically*

: belief in the existence of one God viewed as the creative source of the human race and the world who transcends yet is immanent in the world

Definition of Mentally ill {21}

Function: *adjective*

Etymology: Middle English, from Late Latin *mentalis,* from Latin *ment-, mens* mind -- more at **MIND**

Date: 15th century

　　1 a : (1) of, relating to, or affected by a psychiatric disorder <a *mental* patient>

　　　　　<*mental* illness>

　　　　: (2) **mentally** disordered

　　　　: MAD, CRAZY

　　　b : intended for the care or treatment of persons affected by psychiatric disorders

　　　　　<*mental* hospitals>

　　3 : of or relating to telepathic or mind-reading powers

Definition of Humanistic {22}

Main Entry: **hu·man·ism**

Function: *noun*

Date: 1832

　　1 a : devotion to the **humanities**

　　　　: literary culture

　　　b : the revival of classical letters, individualistic and critical spirit, and emphasis on secular concerns characteristic of the Renaissance

　　2 : HUMANITARIANISM

　　3 : a doctrine, attitude, or way of life centered on **human** nterests or values; *especially*

: a philosophy that usually rejects supernaturalism and stresses an individual's dignity and worth and capacity for self-realization through reason

Definitions of Hallucinations   {23}

Main Entry: **hal·lu·ci·na·tion**

Function: *noun*

Etymology: Latin *hallucination-, hallucinatio, alucination-,*

1 a : perception of objects with no reality

: experience of sensations with no external cause usually arising from disorder of the nervous system (as in delirium tremens or in functional psychosis without known neurological disease)

b : the object of a **hallucinatory** perception

2   : a completely unfounded or mistaken impression or notion

: <u>DELUSION</u> <that popular *hallucination*, from which not even great scientists are ... free -- Lewis Mumford>

Definition of Confrontation   {24}

Function: *noun*

Inflected Form(s): **-s**

Etymology: French, from Medieval Latin *confrontation-, confrontatio* comparison, boundary, from *confrontatus* (past participle of *confrontare* to bound) + Latin *-ion-, -io* -ion

: the act of **confronting**

: the state of being **confronted**

: as

a : <u>MEETING</u>; *specifically*

: the bringing face to face of an accused person and his

352

accusing witnesses -- used especially in the phrase *right of confrontation*

b : the clashing of forces or ideas : CONFLICT

c : COMPARISON

Definition of Genetic   {25}

Main Entry: **ge·net·ic**

Function: *adjective*

1 a : relating to or determined by the origin, development, prior history, or causal antecedents of some phenomenon

: CAUSAL, HISTORICAL, EVOLUTIONARY

<the *genetic* factors in juvenile deliquency>

<the *genetic* features of rocks -- L.V.Pirsson>

<the *genetic* development of a legal doctrine>

<traces the *genetic* development ...

of his neurotic conflict

-- Lionel Ovesey>

b : based on or determined by evolution from a common source

<the relationship ... is not causal but *genetic* ...

both are derived from a common source, a literary

convention -- F.H.Ellis> --

used especially of relations among languages or among

words and grammatical forms of languages

<classes of words ... relied upon in establishing *genetic*

connections between languages -- M.J.Andradel

c : concerned with or seeking to explain, interpret, or

understand (as a literary or psychological phenomenon)

in terms of its origin and development or of its causal

antecedents

<what we call the evolutionary approach or the
historical attitude is technically labeled the *genetic*
method –
John Dewey> <*genetic* psychology>

2 : of or relating to **genetics**
: characterized or produced by the agencies and
Operations of **genetics**
: employed in the processes of **genetics**
<*genetic* studies>

3 : of, relating to, produced by, or being a gene
: GENIC <*genetic* combinations>

Definition of Axiomatic   {26}
Function: *adjective*
Etymology: Middle Greek *axiōmatikos,* from Greek, dignified,
honorable, from *axiōmat-, axiōma* honor, axiom + *-ikos* -ic
: of or relating to an **axiom** or **axioms**
: as
a : taken for granted
: SELF-EVIDENT <an *axiomatic* truth>
b : APHORISTIC <*axiomatic* wisdom>
c : POSTULATIONAL, HYPOTHETICO-DEDUCTIVE
Merriam-Webster's Collegiate Dictionary Eleventh Edition 2/15/04

Name two sources of the so called "mental illness"
(1) Non-organic (2) autogenic

Rather than change, the habit dominated person will **endeavor** to continue to resort to **bizarre behavior** as his solution. If the pattern is not broken, their **behavior** will eventually become set in the end and **become dominate that in the end they will need to institutionalize**.

His social contacts are broken off, the **society** which (he or she) drifts away and as they **hide** from it. The problem has become known as **catatonic schizophrenic**. At this stage they have begun to act **bizarre** and discovered they believe they have **thrown** everyone off **track**.

People in this condition are trying to hide behind the **illness** in much the same way a grammar school child will from an illness, when they don't want to take a test for which they have not prepared for adequately.

When people are approached by those who held them **responsible,** they usually **responded** by trying to hide their feelings, it can be hard to understand what a person is thinking when they are going through a bad situation.

Schizophrenia is a serious disorder which affects how a person thinks, feels and acts. People with schizophrenia may have difficulty distinguishing between what is real and what is imaginary; they may be unresponsive or withdrawn; and may have difficulty expressing normal emotions in a social situations.

Contrary to public perception, schizophrenia is not a split personality or a multiple personality. The vast majority of people with schizophrenia are not violent and do not pose a danger to others.

Schizophrenia is not caused by childhood experiences, poor parenting or lack of willpower, symptoms are similar for a person.

The cause of schizophrenia is still unclear. Some theories about the cause of this disease include: genetics (heredity), biology (abnormalities in the brain's chemistry or structure); and/or possible viral infections and immune disorders.

These symptoms are called "positive" because they are *additions* to that person's normal behavior. They can include:
- Hallucinations, like seeing, hearing, or even feeling things that aren't there
- Delusions, which are beliefs in something even when it's proven to be false
- Thought disorders, like disorganized thinking or not making sense
- Movement disorders like involuntary movements or catatonia, which is no movement

These are called "negative" because they are things that have been *subtracted* from that person's normal behavior. Sometimes they can be mistaken for depression or other disorders. They can include:
- "Flattened" behavior where a person's face or voice doesn't show emotion
- A loss of interest in things they used to enjoy doing
- Neglecting personal appearance and cleanliness

There is a possibility that some bizarre behaviors are looked at in the same way they may appear and act like a **schizophrenic** person, it could also stem from **organic roots** or **drugs**. A number of those who are currently labeled as **"schizophrenics"** could no longer be considered "mentally ill" (as if their judgment were impaired) they could be reclassified as **perceptually ill.**" The problem can be determined by chemical testing.

Name three reasons for the rejection of transference as a tool in counseling.

First, that counselors become in tune with the client, as the counselor and counselee both agree in employing such transference.

Secondly, Even if a counselor simply sits back in an accepting manner without making nouthetic responses to their attitudes or statements, without knowing the counselor becomes a party in condoning of the problem, in the eyes of many clients. The important point is acceptance of the problem.

Thirdly, to agree to use transference that can find a means to an end and justify the means.

Of course, one might also ask, does transference really help? The answer is either (yes) or (no) if they don't change their attitude and behaviors is never helpful.

Controlling You and Your Environment.

I want to help a person control their conflicts / environment if a person is not in control of their situations are others controlling a person. How to deal with the different aspects **self-control**? I know I would not be where I am today without being a disciplined person. How was I able to deal with the anger and how can a person manage one's self and control the situations in their life? When you are able to this a person will have to control their mind-set and master their environment the way to do this is using **Self-Help Principles**.

This study I have clearly define some of the basis in one's beliefs about **self-control** this will include a person's own **self-control**. Personal discipline is ultimately controlling ones' self-will, sacrifice, and **self-gratification**.

I will take into consideration a person's ability to control their desire to overcome personal failures and yet that is another aspect of overcoming in a person's life.

Self Assurance

Everything in your life starts with you. **Self Assurance** will lead to improvements in a person's life. The foundation in your life, the decisions that you make, the actions you take, they are what creates your life. If your life is not the way you want it to be then only you can change it. Yes you can get help from other people, only if you accept the right kind of help.

It is often difficult for a person to accept the fact that they are totally responsible for the condition of their life. I mentioned this briefly because Fear and Failure go hand and hand, they usually don't lead to Success, I believe Failures are stepping stones to expand a person's self-confidence.

Laying blame at a person's own feet for what they have done shame on a person for letting other people and things control them. The fastest route to losing control is when they place blame outside themselves. They are saying someone else has more control than them than they do. A good illustration is like a leaf in the wind, blown all over the place, by letting others influence a person's desires and whims. How can a person change their life?

Motives & Direct behavioral signs:

- Assaultive: physical and verbal cruelty, rage, slapping, shoving, kicking, hitting, threaten with knife or gun.
- Aggression: overly critical, fault finding, name-calling, accusing someone of having immoral or despicable traits or motives, nagging, whining, sarcasm, prejudice, flashes of temper.

- Hurtful: malicious gossip, stealing, trouble-making
- Rebellious: anti-social behavior, open defiance, refusal to talk

Direct verbal or cognitive signs:
- Open hatred and insults
- Contempt and disgust
- Critical: "If you really cared about me, you'd…"
- Suspicious: "You haven't been fair…"
- Blaming: "They have been trying to cause me trouble."
- Revengeful: "I wish I could really hurt them."
- Name calling

Research has found that 'flying off the handle' or 'letting it rip' with anger actually escalates anger and aggression does nothing to help a person resolve the situation. In fact, none of the responses listed above do anything to help solve a problem. These unhealthy responses to anger serve only to destroy personal relationships, undermine a person's work, life and job effectiveness and damage their physical and emotional health.

A person also has to watch for the **patterns** in their life. There are **patterns** in how a person lives or deals with their **stress,** because it's important in measuring the **stress level** in a situation and as a person develops **stress patterns, demand patterns,** and **crisis patterns,** and watch how life changes when there is too much **stress.** These **patterns** have been developing since childhood, now a person becomes sat in their **patterns** which relate to how they feel, gravened by good or bad responses.

The worst thing about **pattern's** the person becomes unaware of how they are **controlling** them, and they don't realize what is happening, or least I didn't.

There are other aspects in **patterns** such as **selfish motives** and **despairs**, a person doing the right thing with **wrong motives**. When they know it is the right thing to do, also knowing something is wrong and don't know why, and they still end up doing it any way.

(Attitude) is also a reflection of one's self, it is very much like a mirror in a person's life. When a person looks at their reflections there can be a problem because they tend to see only what they want to see, in the way they view a problem. In a mirror they may not see the real problems, or their own personal (attitude).

I am going to be looking at the PRIMARY INFLUENCES first. To do this I need to develop the precept of what is important. To do this we must examine a person's MOTIVES because they are a major **influence**. This is going to be a reflection of how a person is dealing with things. These **primary influences** will relate to their personality for instance their family's moral values. These **influences** can become a part of a person, destroy their life, and have a lasting effect on their relationships.

It also points out a good (example) of good **patterns**. I was DETERMINED not to make the same mistakes over again, but I did. I tried different ways, I ended up with the same problems as a result. I want a person to look at the **patterns** in *their* life, and see them. Now I want *you* to see the PRIMARY INFLUENCES, and how they are affecting a person or may be how they are **controlling** a person's life. We want a person to Break through those chains that are holding them captive.

Accepting Control

This does not mean that a person never let others be a part of their life don't let them control you, or do you? When a person gets a job their boss will tell them the hours to work, police officers will control a person's actions, so will traffic signals. In fact when a person looks at it a large part of their life it is controlled by other people and things. A person is still responsible, you say how can I control my life. It is still your decision whether to accept their control or take control of your life. Most of the time these outside controls are good and you accept the control because it benefits yourself and others.

A good illustration is when a person gets stuck in traffic, there had been an accident and a police officer was directing traffic onto a different route. When I drove up he waved for me to turn left, I refused to accept that control. He started to get annoyed and waved even harder. Then I pointed to the nurse who was pushing a wheelchair across the intersection, he understood.

What if I had blindly followed his control and hit those pedestrians, who would have been responsible? A person may say he made me do it, who is really to blame in that situation! If someone was having a heart attack and you were driving them to the hospital would you sit and wait at the stop lights?

This is a major step in **Self-Control** accepting full responsibility for your life and how you affect others. (Right)

Controlling the Uncontrollable

Are there circumstances that you don't have control over? Apparently so, floods, fires, accidents, health issues etc. You are still in control of your reactions to them. You can let them defeat you as implied earlier, or you can face them head on and handle them.

How about when someone is close to you dies, a person does not have control over that a person does over their initial reactions. To what degree is a person controlled by the situation? What do they give up if it doesn't work out like they think, usually people end up dealing with some form of grief. Some stop living while others keep on trying, while others don't seem to care, why? If a person let's things get to them, they have just ended two lives, maybe even dishonored their memory by blaming them for what has happened in the past.

Wouldn't it be so much better to thank them for the time you had together, look for the good and don't let it ruin a life. Would they want a person to give up the memories and say it would have been better if they had never known them; of course there is a lasting memory. Honor their memory if it is good, if it is a bad one, here is a good way to deal with that, by living your life to the fullest even do some things that you have always wanted to do.

I will show a person how much more control they have over their life than they realized, let us continue with **self-achievement**.

Here are some obvious steps to **self-actuation**, exercise, better diet, education and so on. The fact that you are reading this information shows that you are on the right track.

How about tackling some of the areas that you know you are weak in. I used to be very shy at social gatherings I would usually sit in a corner hoping no one would not notice me. I would have to know someone before I would initiate a conversation. The thought of talking to a crowd of people was terrifying, I enjoy doing it now.

Shyness is a very uncomfortable and limiting behavior. I decided to face it head on, I went to college. I chose public speaking courses or anything that would put me in front of an audience. It took a little time, after teaching and public presentations I started to enjoy it.

Now I love standing in front of an audience, class, or group. I am even better at one to one communication because of my degree in counseling and psychology.

A simple self-improvement technique is to do something new every day or at least once a week. It does not have to be big, take a different route to work, try some different kinds of food, shop and do-something-for-yourself.

Self Improvement includes:

1. Your identity.
2. Your thoughts
3. Your feeling
4. Your home and work

"And do not be conformed to this world, but be transformed by the renewing of your mind, that you may prove what the will of God is, that which is good and acceptable and perfect."

Romans 12:2

When you feel like a loser you act like a loser!

A Step in the right direction

You may have ideas about false beliefs about what could have made you like you are. A person may have developed good or bad behaviors. I believe people have these beliefs firmly fixed in their mind because of all the things they have experienced in their life. The apostle Paul urged us to avoid the world's bad influences. A person's belief's is not being conformed to this world because it shows a person the way the world would have them look at themselves.

These false beliefs are so much a part of a person's thinking; this can cause them to react to life's situations in harmful ways.

Have you ever found yourself saying?

"Why in the world did I do that?"

"Wow, that just goes to show what a dummy I am,"

"I feel like a real loser,"

"I'll never be able to do that correctly,"

"Nothing in my life ever turns out right"?

Have you made these remarks in some way or to yourself in response to an unpleasant situation you found yourself confronting?

Try to remember an unpleasant situation you found yourself in recently.

How did you feel?

_____

_____

_____

Describe the situation briefly.

_____

_____

_____

Which of these statements describes how you felt at that time?

☐ I felt as if I were a failure.

☐ I felt as if someone were rejecting me.

☐ I felt guilty about what I said or did.

☐ I felt shame because nothing changed because of what I did.

☐ Other

Review these false beliefs before we move on in this study how these false beliefs affect a person, let's review them. Now I want a person to think about these false beliefs. Feel free to go back to the list if you need a little help.

1. I must meet my expectations to feel good about myself.
2. I must have the respect of others to feel good about myself.
3. Those who (including myself) and others are unworthy of my love and devotion.
4. I am who I am, can I change who I am or who I want to be?

Self Worth

Name three things you like about yourself?

1. _____
2. _____
3. _____

Name three things you don't like about yourself?

1. _____
2. _____
3. _____

What would you change about yourself?

_____

_____

_____

Mark T (true) F (false)

_____ 1. **I am glad of who I am.**

_____ 2. **I love the way I am**

_____ 3. **I like being who I am**

_____ 4. **I have a healthy sense of self worth**

_____ 5. **I see changes which I need to make in my life**

_____ 6. **I am eager to change things**

_____ 7. **I believe I need more discipline to make changes**

Self-Evaluations

Again, everything in your life starts with you. **Self-Evaluations** will lead to improving your life. You are the foundation for every decision you make it either builds character or destroys confidence, the actions you take are what influences your life.

It is often difficult for a person to accept the fact that they are totally responsible for the condition in their life. I mentioned this briefly in this study, but I will expand on it here.

I will show a person that they have more control over their life than they realized, see Creative Visualization. For now let us continue with an **self-evaluation** and **improvement**:

There are many obvious ways like education and so on.

I enjoy speaking to crowd and I like doing videos.

Deal with shyness or being an introverted.

A simple **self-evaluations** and **self-improvement** techniques do something, challenging to see if you can do it. This is a way of disciplining yourself and in better ways.

I would like to reemphasis how discipline leads to **self-control** and **self-improvement**, there are other technique a person can try in their own life, by doing something for others, do something a person doesn't like to do will give a person discipline and perseverance.

This is the basis for our studies on the Well-being of a person.

I think faith, hope, and love are the foundation for our inner Well-Being. To evaluate these and other fundamental elements is crucial to a person's Well-Being.

I want a person to build on **Self-Control**?

Definition of Self-Control: {27}

Main Entry: **self-control**

Function: *noun*

> : control of oneself
>
> : restraint exercised over one's own impulses, emotions, or desires
>
> <his anger blazed out and burned up his *self-control* – H.E.Scudder>
>
> <passionate and rebellious, she never learned *self-control*

Definition of Control: {28}

control : *noun*

> **1 a** : to check, test, or verify by evidence or experiments
>
> **b** : to incorporate suitable controls in
>
> **2 a** : exercise restraining or directing influence overregulate
>
> **b** : to have power over
>
> **c** : to reduce the incidence or severity of especially to innocuous levels

Merriam-Webster's Collegiate Dictionary Eleventh Edition / (date 5/24/04

I want reemphasis a person can do anything if they want if they want to bad enough or if they put their mind to it and put some effort into it, all of that depends on how bad a person wants to accomplish anything, is that also true in solving a problem. I have two wonderful profiles of people with handy caps who achieved great things in their life, read book SOS SELF IMPROVEMENT on "Self-Worth & Determination", the first person is a contemporary story of about Ray Charles and the second is Fanny Crosby.

We will be dealing with one's **"will power"** a person's personality and character will reflect in their attitude toward life. It will show up in how a person lives and gets things done in their walk and talk, and in their daily conversation at work and in their relationships.

There is evidence that testifies to the fact that people who know how to manage their own feelings well, who read, and deal with them effectively have an advantage in life, whether its romance, and they usually have intimate relationships with others. People who are **emotional stable** govern themselves, and are will organized in handling their **emotional skills** they are successful in their personal life and in their vocation. They are more likely to be content and happy, mastering their habits of the mindset, plus being productive. People who cannot master to some degree their **motivation** over fear, anxiety, battling their ability to focus on life and their job, etc.

Delaying gratification and stifling impulsiveness underlies accomplishments of every sort. Being able to get into the "flow" enables outstanding performance. People who have this skill tend to be more highly productive and effective in whatever they undertake.

Profile on Motivation.

I want to help a person have a better understanding how **self-control** is one thing that can help a person deal with **self-discipline**. Some of these methods have to with **motivation**, which are in fact the **principles** I use every day. I want to challenge a person to take control, by not being controlling. I will use modern methods in psychology, proof's and evidence verifying this part of the study.

Definition of Motivation   {29}

    a : the act or process of <u>motivating</u>

    b : the condition of being <u>motivated</u>

  1   : a motivating force, stimulus, or influence

      : <u>incentive, drive</u>

      : the act or process of giving someone a reason for doing something : the act or process of motivating someone

      : the condition of being eager to act or work

      : the condition of being motivated

       : a force or influence that causes someone to do something

Merriam-Webster's Collegiate Dictionary Eleventh Edition / (date 11/24/16

A person must want to change their own environment and **self-will** to do this it will take a changed heart and mind-set, living a life to the fullest; this study will change your world and the way you look at the world around you.

I am not going to give you any set plan for happiness and success, because each person has their own gifts and qualities which is either limited or enhanced by their personal abilities. I hope to be able to help a person identify the successful areas in their life; that people need to deal with every day. It is up to the person to identify with their qualities and goals, more than that if a person doesn't know how to be in control or be disciplined, a person will not be able to help themselves. Nor is anyone else going to able to help them, in reality they are unable to help themselves.

Another problem comes when they are not facing the real issues in their life, God knows the heart and the intent of every person. God only expects the best a person can do and so do I.

Being a realistic person, I found it harder live to up to what was expected of me, then to live up to my expectations according to my expectations of myself. There is so much more to living than just saying, I want to be successful and live a better life, the challenge comes when a person learns to discipline and what they want to be.

We are not puppets on string; we are an intelligent creation, we are left here to rule over our own lives and not to be deceived by their own devices. I believe to do that a person has to control and discipline their life. There is another law of sowing and reaping, what a person sows "they shall also reap".

I believe a person can do whatever (he or she) wants and they can get by with it for a while, some believe they can get by with anything and at the time they are willing to pay the price for what they do every person has to deal with control issues in one way or the other. Does that rule apply to everybody? (Yes) The best alternative is to define things before they do them. The real issue is a person willing to pay the consequences for what happens.

How is Creative Thinking Involved in Solving Problems
    1. **What is Creative Thinking?**
       Negative Attitudes Block Creativity or Critical Thinking
       & Problem Solving.
       Mental Blocks to Creative or Critical Thinking and
       Problem Solving
       Myths about Creative Thinking or Critical Thinking
       and Problem Solving
    2. **Critical Thinking creates a good Attitude.**
    3. **Critical Thinking involves Problem Solving**

There is more to be added to our Christian Psychology study. I call it **will power** and how a person accepts **(Accountability)** & **(Responsibility)** as they deal with it in a personal way. I feel it is important to study a person's **attitude** before and after changes are made. I don't want a person to take anything away from their experience its theirs to enjoy, because that is one of the most important steps in the process; looking back is a good way to refresh what has happened think things through before they happen. Let me point two definitions at this time.

What is Success?
Definition of Success   {30}
Success
Function: *noun*
    1 obsolete **:** something that ensues the OUTCOME,
        CONSEQUENCE, ISSUE
        <what is *success* --Shakespeare>
    2 obsolete a **: COURSE, SEQUENCE, SUCCESSION**
        b : a group that proceeds in temporal sequence;
    specifically : LINEAGE

3 a : the degree or measure of attaining a desired end

: kind of fortune <the poor *success* of the book

Disgusted him – Aldous Huxley>

<the *success* of the performance is judged by its

Volume and enthusiasm – *American Guide Series*

: *Florida>*

b : a succeeding fully or in accordance with one's desires

: favorable termination of a venture

<I believe very little in the fortune ...

to which men attribute their *successes*

and reverses -- George Meredith>

<in pursuing this task she had, at first, cheering hopes

of *success* – Matthew Arnold>

specifically

: the attainment of wealth, position, esteem, favor,

or eminence

<the first book has been published and had a great

success -- L.L.Day>

4 a : a person achieving success <as a dance student ...

was .., an immediate *success* -- *Current Biography>*

<*a success* as a rich man's wife –

Pearl Buck>

b : an undertaking that succeeds or confers success

<the play was an immediate *success*>

<a remarkable series of *successes* in

experimentation>

2005 by Merriam-Webster, Inc.   9/10/2005

Gardner's influential 1983, book *Frames of mind* was a manifest
to refuting the IQ view.

"He proposed that not just one, monolithic kind of intelligence is crucial for life's success, but rather a wide spectrum of intelligences, with seven key varieties. His list includes two standards:

- Verbal = communication
- Mathematical-logical = alacrity
- Spatial capacity = outstanding art or architect

Kinesthetic genius = displayed in the physical fluidity and grace of a Martha Graham

- Interpersonal skills = like those of a great therapist such as Carl Rogers or a world- class leader such as Martin Luther King Jr.

"Intrapsychic" = capacity that could emerge, on the hand, in the brilliant insights of Sigmund Freud or with less fanfare, in the inner contentment that arises from attuning one's life to be keeping with one's true **feelings**."

Copied   9/10/2005

Optimism and hope are a like; and can be learned as will and dealt with as a part of life's experiences.

In the terms of motivation, when people believe in what they are doing they are much more likely to succeed.

Self-Confidence

When people believe in themselves they have a dipper meaning of self-confidence and a jump in self-consciousness; their very notions of themselves involves improving. One of the greatest specific blows to a person's social self-esteem and confidence, shows in how they make and keep friends. It is at this juncture, Hamburg points out, that it helps immensely to bust boys and girls' abilities to build close relationships and navigate crises in friendships, and build their **self-confidence**.

Confidence is a continuum in believing in who they are, it has no beginning and no end, it endures, or it can fad with a blow to the ego. It can never be taken away from a person as long as they do not take it away from themselves. There is no end to it as long as they believe in themselves. It is utterly safe, there is no danger when a person doesn't let it control them. Therefore, to give of one's self is to contribute to others without a loss of control. In the true sense of the word, self-control is fulfilling in giving of ones self. In the best sense of life a person should control their own feelings without having to fight or be afraid of one's self. This must truly please the heart of God as He made a man, when they come to Him.

There is an opposite effect, when false self-control of one's self is miss used (bondage):

- They are more sensitive to others' feelings
- They are better at understanding the consequences of their behavior
- They have increased ability to "size up" interpersonal situations and plan appropriate actions
- They have higher self-esteem
- They are more pro-social in their behavior
- They are sought out by others for help
- They are better able to handle the transitions in life
- They are less antisocial, self-constructive, and socially ordered behavior, even when followed up in life.
- They have improve learning-to-learn skills

They are better at self-control, social awareness, and social decisions at work and in the home.

The individual who does not believe in others as equals, if they have to own and control a person to the extent they believe it to be necessary to hold on to the other person. Being a controlled person losses their value of life, the fear of losing someone or being able to control someone leads to a false narrative of their own well-being.

Which in return brings about withdrawal, indifference, non-involvement, non-commitment, numbness of feelings, separation, and a refusal to let others live their life. This can happen to a person or in a marriage.

When a person is involved in their distortion of values, they cannot see the true picture of others it basically comes down to their insecurity. They must not associate their lack of freedom. Even if intellectually they know better, emotionally they cannot experience the mutual freedom and trust.

This mode of perception sacrifices accuracy relying on first impressions, reacting to the overall picture or the most striking aspects of a relationship. They take people for granted, as a whole, reacting without taking the time for thought or time to analyze why they act the way they do. Vivid elements can determine by their impression, out-weighing a careful evaluation of the details. The great advantage is how the **mind** reads their **emotional reality** (he's angry with me; she's lying; this is making him sad) in an instant, making the intuitive or snap judgments that tells them who to be leery of, who to trust, or who's in distress.

Such a struggle cannot be resolved without understanding how the mind works, knowing the spirit and will of a person relates to their view of others. Activate the heart of the person by expressing how to give of yourself fearlessly, without fear of being controlled. Express your desire to feel and experience the oneness and freedom, granted to each other let the experience grow and flourish. This can happen in personal relationships.

We have tried to in able a person by establishing the necessary sense of integrity and **self-acceptance**. When a person discovers the more they give the more they get back in return and selfhood grows and flourishes. WOW isn't that great news. If you express this possibility as a formulated thought, then activate your inner powers and experiences, you must come out of whatever problem you may find yourself.

A person's loneliness, fears, and conflicts, in one way or another come down to this: a person needs to look for a purpose in a situation. Another thing look for divine guidance that will help a person through it, the real fulfillment is a product of being in control, for the heart and soul of a person can indeed help in solving problems, if a person lets it happen and then give God the praise. This can only help you when a person calls their inner spirit.

It is the inner being that knows and understands the "process" of life; the freedom to give of one's self. The second is giving and receiving love in your relationships. Your outer self is what you want others to see in you if you don't understand this concept you are missing what life is about. You cannot produce a healthy state of mind if you do not truly comprehend freedom of choice. Your inner self can help you call on it when you need it.

The Architecture of the Mind

For this reason, it is absolutely essential a person "processes the data in the brain" when a person is receiving accurate information, appropriate and interpreted correctly. When a person receives bad data information, they can make inaccurate interpretations, and ultimately, wrong decisions. Therefore, a person must make sure they are receiving the right data information, to avoiding making the wrong decision. Being able to develop these skills of processing and interpreting what needs to be done. That will usually lead to the right kind of decisions. God-pleasing, and productive transform in a person's life. The real sense of the situation is finding real joy and happiness.

A person's mind is like the wide-screen TV. A person cannot choose what the news broadcasters has to say, a person can choose what channels they are going to watch in their home.

This is why a person must take ownership of their mind, and win the battle over the "remote." Because whatever a person allows to fill their mind will eventually show up in how they think.

Proverbs 4:23

V-23 *"Keep your heart [mind] with all diligence, for out of it spring the issues [experiences and events] of life."*

Show me your mind-set, and I'll show you your future. You cannot fill your mind with worldly thinking, ungodly entertainment, unclean language and images, and fear-filled imaginations, then expect life to be filled with the blessings and promises of God.

The first step to renewing a person's mind and taking ownership of their own thoughts. The truth is that we are powerless to change anything for which we refuse to accept responsibility. Becoming aware of what and how a person thinks is an important first step to developing a new mind-set. Their thoughts should reflect on God. When a person limits and has defeating thoughts they find themselves returning to self-defeating thoughts during the day?

When a person is alone do their thoughts, patterns of thinking or do they find their mind drifting on things of the world? Does a person keep their life full of good activities or are they afraid of their own thoughts, feelings, and fears? These are all signs in some way show a person they need to regain control of their thoughts.

Mind-sets are hard to change. This is a good thing if a person's mind-sets are positive, helpful, and based on the Word of God. A godly mind-set affords great peace and strength. In order to change a wrong mind-sets, a person needs to exchange their old thoughts for new ones. To keep those right images in their mind until they replace the old mind-sets. Paul goes on to instruct the believer about what kinds of "negative" worldly thoughts and behaviors need new thoughts and actions.

Romans 12:1-3 (61)

V-1 "I beseech you therefore, brethren, by the mercies of God, that ye present your bodies a living sacrifice, holy, acceptable unto God, *which is* your reasonable service.

V-2 And be not conformed to this world: but be ye transformed by the renewing of your mind, that ye may prove what *is* that good, and acceptable, and perfect, will of God.

V-3 For I say, through the grace given unto me, to every man that is among you, not to think *of himself* more highly than he ought to think; but to think soberly, according as God hath dealt to every man the measure of faith."

Titus 3:1-8 (62)

V-1 "Put them in mind to be subject to principalities and powers, to obey magistrates, to be ready to every good work,

V-2 To speak evil of no man, to be no brawlers, *but* gentle, shewing all meekness unto all men.

V-3 For we ourselves also were sometimes foolish, disobedient, deceived, serving divers lusts and pleasures, living in malice and envy, hateful, *and* hating one another.

V-4 But after that the kindness and love of God our Saviour toward man appeared,

V-5 Not by works of righteousness which we have done, but according to his mercy he saved us, by the washing of regeneration, and renewing of the Holy Ghost;

V-6 Which he shed on us abundantly through Jesus Christ our Saviour;

V- 7 That being justified by his grace, we should be made heirs according to the hope of eternal life.

V-8 *This is* a faithful saying, and these things I will that thou affirm constantly, that they which have believed in God might be careful to maintain good works. These things are good and profitable unto men."

Believe it or not, the Bible teaches us to meditate on the Word of God. The practice of biblical meditation is nothing like the meditation taught by the Gurus and religions of the Far East. In those religions, one is taught that meditation is the emptying of the mind. The Bible never tells us to empty our minds! Instead we are to fill out thoughts with His Word. Biblical *meditation* is the practice of focusing a person's mind on Jesus Christ, the wonderful promises He has given to us, in the teachings of the Bible. Where most non-Christian philosophies teach meditation is a skill that takes years to master, the simple truth is that mediation is a practice each of us *already do every day of our lives.*

When we think about things for an extended period of time, a person creates a "perception" in the mind. The perception has a way of dominating a person's perspective thoughts, eventually making a person to have feelings about things that others have the same type of "feelings." Positive or negative, right or wrong, blessing or cursing, the focus of a person's meditations will begin to affect their feelings that are tuned into actions.

When a person meditates on something long enough it will begin to control their thinking, impact their decisions and choices, and becomes apart of their experience even if it never happens. *Whatever a person thinks about over time, then a person began to act.* The mind begins to draw associations and reinforce a person's beliefs that causes a person to fixate on the things they think. This is why it is so important to develop the right thought process.

The result of the right kind of thinking will bring about God's peace. In fact, one way to know whether or not your thoughts are moving in the right direction is by checking your *peace of mind*. If a person's thoughts are fixed on God, His Word, as a person trusts Him with their problems, they will have real inner peace.

This peace is not the result of everything in your life being perfect, or all your circumstances going well. It comes from relying on the Lord that should put a person's mind at peace. In fact this peace will stay the same regardless of how bad the circumstances.

Building a healthy mind-set is an important part of growing spiritually and renewing your mind. When a person moves in a new direction, they need to associate with people who are believing t he same way. Often this requires a person to lay aside the relationships that tie them to their past ways of thinking. If you want to get to California, you don't get on a bus going to Boston. God uses people who are heading in the right direction.

Sometimes a person become stagnate in their spiritual growth. A person's mind gets locked into patterns of thinking and feeling that prevents them from moving forward. When this is the case, it is important to take time to examine a person's thoughts and feelings. Often the real reason a person gets "stuck and doesn't move on" they need to examine their old patterns of thinking as they reflect on the past. David writes in:

Psalm 139:17-24   (63)

V-17 "How precious also are thy thoughts unto me, O God! how great is the sum of them!

V-18 *If* I should count them, they are more in number than the sand: when I awake, I am still with thee.

V-19 Surely thou wilt slay the wicked, O God: depart from me therefore, ye bloody men.

V-20 For they speak against thee wickedly, *and* thine enemies take *thy name* in vain.

V-21 Do not I hate them, O LORD, that hate thee? and am not I
grieved with those that rise up against thee?
V-22 I hate them with perfect hatred: I count them mine enemies.
V-23 Search me, O God, and know my heart: try me, and know my
thoughts:
V-24 And see if *there be any* wicked way in me, and lead me in the
way everlasting."

False control creates (walls of separation). To eliminate these
(walls) by contacting the deeper and vaster faculties of the mind;
even while the (walls are still present) your concern should be to
open the keys to the mind, the brain centers the activity in a person).
How a person deals with their feels will govern what happens.

A resourceful person formulates their wants, needs, and desires.
To activate and fill a person with understanding, with constructive
outlooks and energies. The mind will become a person's strength. In
so many different ways the will manifests how truly a person is
commitment to themselves and trust within themselves. Trust your
judgements and feelings in the process of making good decisions.

Romans 8:4-9 (64)

V-4 "That the righteousness of the law might be fulfilled in us,
who walk not after the flesh, but after the Spirit.
V-5 For they that are after the flesh do mind the things of the flesh;
but they that are after the Spirit the things of the Spirit.
V-6 For to be carnally minded *is* death; but to be spiritually minded
is life and peace.
V-7 Because the carnal mind *is* enmity against God: for it is not
subject to the law of God, neither indeed can be.
V-8 So then they that are in the flesh cannot please God.
V-9 But ye are not in the flesh, but in the Spirit, if so be that the
Spirit of God dwell in you. Now if any man have not the Spirit of
Christ, he is none of his."

Chapter 12

As I stated at the beginning of this study I said we would spend some time on the personal aspects of a person's life. As we come to the end of this study, I want to remind people this is one of 4 Bible studies and 3 self-help study guides.

Look for our books on, Amazon, Kindle / e-books, Barnes & Noble. There are videos, digital downloads, and other media that focus on Bible studies who support learning and agrees with what you are wanting to experience and learn.

Our ministry is to help people arrive at the right places in life. By applying psychology to Christians living for God. When believers really care, take the time to encourage, and pray for each other, we believe in an environment for growth in a person's life.

Support Outreach Services & Ministries SOS LLC, Self Help Books & Bible Studies

3 Self-Help study Guides
SOS Life Enhancement

SOS Self Improvement

SOS New Beginnings

Our Family Biography
Facing The Real Me

4 Bible Studies

How Does God Answer Pray?

We are Ambassadors for Christ.

Opening the Door to Christian Psychology.

Applying Christian Principles

Dr. John C Barrett; PH-D Program - Coordinator, & SOS Publications.

**Faith Based
Evangelistic Meetings
Conferences – Seminars
Workshops & Training Manuals:**

Mentoring & Coaching & Discipleship

Leadership Training

The Road to Recovery

SOS PROGRAMS & SERVICES

1. TO INSPIRE
2. TO ENCOURAGE
3. TO STRENGTHEN
4. TO SUCCEED.

THE KEY INGREDIENTS IN **SOS** STUDIES & PROGRAMS.
(PATIENCE) (COMPASSION) (UNDERSTANDING)
IN OUR LIFE ENHANCEMENT PROGRAMS TOOLS TO
WORK WITH.

    1. EXPRESS YOURSELF,

    2. TALK ABOUT YOUR SELF,

    3. STUDY TO SUPPORT YOURSELF.

          OUR LIFE ENHANCEMENT PROGRAMS
@OUR EXPERIENCES
@OUR STUDIES
@OUR PROGRAMS.

IN OUR LIFE ENHANCEMENT EVALUATIONS & SURVEYS
  A. PERSONAL - PPROFILES
  B. PERSONAL - EVALUATIONS
  C. STRESS - EVALUATIONS
  D. HEALTH & FITNESS - EVALUATIONS

Our motto is: BEAR YE ONE ANOTHER BURDENS.
It means sharing with another in a sincere attitude.
These three steps may be very helpful when (SOS) deals with a person:
HEALTH - AWARENESS (Booklet I - Video)
STRESS- RELIEF (Booklet)
INTORDUCING SUPPORT OUTREACH SERVICES (Booklet)

One-to-One = Common Ground
www.sosselfhelpbooks.info
Individual or Group Sessions,
Counseling Sessions 417 204-8022
Email <u>drbarrettphd@yahoo.com</u>

Information (Booklets, & Manuals)

BOOKs

One book $15.00
Two Books $25.00
Three Books $35.00
DVD's $10.00
Study materials: $5.00
Shipping up to: $10.00

Order books from me: **Email**

drbarrettphd@yahoo.com

Amazon, Kindle, / Barnes & Noble

Dr. John Barrett Bachler of Science in Theology; Masters Degree in Counseling, & PH-D in Psychology.

No Gimmicks, No Pressure Tactics

COMMON SINCE GUIDE LINES.
A. Don't go over-board. (use good judgment, DON'T OVER REACT)
B. Don't get in a hurry, WAIT. (take your time and THEN SOME!)
C. Don't give up to soon. (LOOK for the right answers)
D. Don't ever say I won't. (be willing to except THE RIGHT ANSWER)
E. Don't get discouraged. (in will doing except THE CIRCUMSTANCE)
    WAIT can become one of the longest words in the dictionary.

SOS Life Line News Letter

Our newsletters are a vital link between **SOS** and the person. We will have two different newsletters. One, **SOS Life Line News**, we will have information that adults can identify with, whether they are single or married and whatever your relationship is with your children. Secondly, SOS Youth Views, we will have information pertaining to teens and college age young people. We definitely deal with relationships and how to deal with them.

SOS links

www.sosselfhelpbooks.info

Home| Support | Outreach | Services | SOS Self Help Books | Newsletter | Contact us

YOUR SOURCE FOR SUPPORT

Links to! **SOS** Intro-Booklet   SOS Directory Service   Mission Statement

Into - Pages 1, 2   Personal Surv. 3,4   Co-PartnerSurv. Pages 5, 6

I. Support helping & healing

II. Outreach Common-Ground Matching Profiles

Conferences & Retreats

III Services

Rehabilitation & Maintenance

SOS Information Network0

SOS Life Line News Letter

Support Outreach Service - Directory Service

Directory 2000 Directory Network = a referral-oriented services that helps everyone.

Directory 21st Century

Book: "SOS LIFE ENHANCEMENT", Reconciliation Surveys & Evaluations
Restoration Studies & Information

Book My Family Biography & Memories = FACING T HE REAL ME

BOOK Three, Studies-guide = Reference Profiles (Book & Booklets)

SOS Personal Surveys & Evaluations = (Means Health-Awareness)

Personal survey,
Personal Relationships / Co-dependencies Evaluations,
Sv-Relationships
Support, Christian Living + Profiles & Studies.
Personal Testimony
My Mediation & Prayer life
Christian Principles

Communication Network = talking to someone who cares, one to one.
SOS Directory Network = a referral-oriented services that helps everyone.
Into Pages 1, 2
Personal Surv. Pages 3, 4
   Support-partner survey **Co-Support-partner Pages 5, 6**
SOS Intro Booklet

A personal look at my life and how all this fits together. I have reflected on my thoughts and feelings at different times in my life, in our family biography "FACING THE REAL ME, Run John Run". A view from my mountain and from the different vantage points on the mountain as I go up and down the mountain.

Christian Methods and Principles for Christian living book APPLING CHRISTIAN PRINCIPES how the fit into our Bible Studies. Also how these 4 books fit together? They go hand and hand they fit like a glove. Now you're getting the total picture as it took place in my life.

I go into my life experiences in different sections of our studies, and how the inner dependence fits into my health and fitness in **Life Enhancement**. Those are some of the major victories I have shared with you, why it is so important to understand these concepts of Christian Psychology. I have gone into how this book fits into our other studies on Personal and Mental-Awareness, and how they fit into my life "OK'!

I have used lots of grafts, charts and **illustrations to aid us, my hope is they have given a clear-cut picture to go by in "**OPENING THE DOOR TO CHRISTIAN PSYCHOLOGY.**"**
Believe it or not it gives SOS a chance to work in your life.

Our motto is: BEAR YE ONE ANOTHERS BURDENS.

It means helping someone else! That will add a new meaning to your life. The key is how to love and help others. I have shown you the concepts of these, "WE ARE AMASSADORS FOR CHRIST" and now this will give you a unique opportunity to help yourself and share in someone else's life at the same time. I can't think of anything any more exciting than that! Can you?

Another way to help a person is from your own home and it doesn't take much time or anything away from you or your family.

This is away to check on them. This is personal mentoring or coaching and another way is using our LIFE ENHANCEMENT PROGRAMS you do this by accessing our website and see for yourself how it works, it is strictly up to you.

I use the priority of the situation, as a person trains for "MENTORING / COACHING, & DESCIPLESHIP TRANING". This how to help a person deal with their life. I will present another study Manuals on personal problem solving "THE ROAD TO RECOVERY" as a person deals with person issues. They may want to go on as I present the different alternatives.

I hope you have stopped from time to time to get your breath before going on. Each of us can only take in so much at one time. Then stop! You will be able to go on without missing anything. There is a joy in helping others, don't forget yourself at the same time. There will be breaks before going on.

I hope we have given you a better understanding of our **SOS** Bible studies and workshop manuals. The best is yet to come, our SOS LIFE ENHANCEMENT – self-help information and study guides. There is going to be more fun and interesting studies, workshops, books, and manuals. There are some exciting concepts as we take you through others studies! We hope you will want our complete set of studies. You always have the option of some of our studies or the programs you want to be a part of:

I. Support

II. Outreach

III. Services.

We will present our human behavior studies. Then how our Christian Methods and Principles help in Christian living, how Biblical principles fit in. These can fit together and go hand and hand they will fit like a glove.

Our motto is: BEAR YE ONE ANOTHERS BURDENS.
There is a joy in helping others, don't forget yourself at the same time.

Services *Directory 21 Network* – *Referral Oriented Service that helps everyone.*
How do we deal with the problems and situations? We have broken them down into sections, by subject matter. If you would like check them out to see how they could fit into your life.

SOS Life Enhancement Studies & Information (Means: Restoration) = being informed & tools to *help ourselves*
The Challenge of dealing with one's self, **Mental**, **Emotional**, **Spiritual**, & **Physical**, LIFE!
Principal 1: Personal-Attention & Care: *Who am I?*

One to One personal attention and **support.**
Pride & Self-will: A look at the personal influences?
Emotional Reactions, the ups & downs, how to apply these Axioms to:
(Mentally – Emotionally – Physically)
Social-Behavior & Personal Problems,

Common-Ground round in-home help, there are Conferences, Seminars if people would like to attend.

You are going to see this better as we go along with our other studies and let you participate in our workshops and services. We want to remind you there is more to come, we will use these same **axioms profile charts** in our videos and other books/booklets and studies.

REVIVALS

CONFERENCES - SEMINARS

TEACHING MANUALS & WORK SHOPS

SOS Leadership Training for "Group Sessions"

Support Group Sessions

"Leadership Training"

The "Leadership Team"

Unlocking the doors to Assessments, Self-Concepts

The "Roots of Leader The "Empowerment of Change"

Manual

Manual
Mentoring & Coaching
/Discipleship

One to One Support

Manual
Mentoring Program

The Road to Recovery

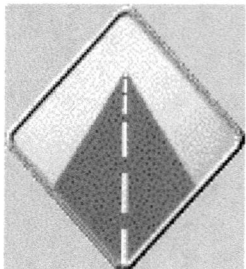

Appendix A WEB REFERENCES

C. S. Lewis sets the tone for modern Christian psychology. [1] P. 30
Carl Roger's Personal Centered Approach TO PSYCHOLGY
Pages 1 – 2 [2] P. 30
Key Theorists in Psychology –CARL ROGERS, 1902-1987
Page 1 of 3 [3] P. 33
Association for Humanistic Psychology Pages 4-8 [4] P. 33
Aristotle's Challenge: Pages 1-2 [5] P. 39
Re-training abnormal brainwaves Page 1 [6] P. 40
Brain School 101 [7] P. 50
The Pictorial View and Brake Down of the Brain. [8] P. 56
Neurological and Struck Pages 1-3 [9] P. 61
The Central & Peripheral Nervous System Page 2 -5 [10] P. 69
CGG Bible Study: Overcoming (Part 4): Self-will
Pages 1-4 [11] P. 92
Laying down our self-will Pages 1-4 [12] P. 95
Improving Self-Esteem Pages 1-6 [13] P. 295
Articles – On Improving Self Esteem Page 1-2 [14] P. 298
Avoiding Burnout Pages 1-5 [15] P. 312
Depression information and treatment Pages 1-3 [16] P. 317
What is depression Pages 1-2 [17] P. 319
Causes of depression Pages 1-2 [18] P. 322
General Depression information from Christian perspective
Page 1-4 [19] P. 324
American Psychiatric Association Pages 1-4 [20] P. 330

Appendix B   DEFINITIONS

Definition HOMEOSTASIS?   {1} **P. 71**
Definition of Physiology: *Noun*   {2} **P.82**
Definition of Psychic : *Noun*   {3} **P. 84**
Definition of psychology : *noun*   {4} **P. 84**
Definition of soul : *noun*   {5} **P. 85**
Definition of heart : *noun*   {6} **P. 86**
Definition of self- and will,   {7} **P. 87**
Will   {8} **P. 87**

Free+will+problem - Merriam-Webster Page 1 of 1 {9} **P. 88**

Definition of Esteem   {10} **P. 107**
Definition of Image   {11} **P. 108**
Definition sovereignty   {12} **P. 169**
Definition of Foundation: {13} **P. 234**
Definition of Psychosomatic   {14} **P. 348**
Definition of Neurosis   {15} **P. 348**
Definition of Psychosis   {16} **P. 349**
Definition of Intitutionalze   {17} **P. 349**
Definition of Psychiatry   {18} **P. 349**
Definition of Psychotherapy   {19} **P. 350**
Definition of Theist   {20} **P, 350**
Definition of Mentally ill   {21} **P. 351**
Definition of Humanistic   {22} **P. 352**
Definitions of Hallucinations   {23} **P. 352**
Definition of Confrontation   {24} **P. 354**
Definition of Genetic   {25} **P. 353**
Definition of Axiomatic   {26} **P. 354**
Definition of Self-Control: {27} **P. 367**
Definition of Control: {28} **P. 367**
Definition of Motivation   {29} **P. 369**
Definition of Success   {30} **P. 371**

Appendix C   BIBLE REFERENCES

John 12:24-27	(1) P. 8
Ephesians 4:20-24	(2) P. 11
Luke 15:11-32	(3) P. 16
John 1:7-11	(4) P. 17
Luke 15:1-10	(5) P. 22
2 Peter 1:19-21	(6) P. 27
John 16:1-16	(7) P. 28
2 Timothy 3:17	(8) P. 29
2 Timothy 4:6-8	(9) P. 78
1 Peter 4:12-16 -	(10) P. 89
Matthew 10:37-39 & 42	(11) P. 103
John 15:12-15	(12) P. 104
John 19:25-27	(13) P. 104
I Corinthians 13:1-13	(14) P. 106
II Timothy 3:1-5	(15) P. 112
Psalm 8:1-9	(16) P. 120
Romans 1:1-32	(17) P. 124
Romans 2:1-29	(18) P. 127
2 Peter 3:8-18	(19) P. 161
Acts 17:31-34	(20) P. 162
Hebrews 4:1-16	(21) P. 163
Galatians 5:8-26	(22) P. 167
Romans 11:1-11	(23) P. 174
Matthew 22:1-33	(24) P. 176
Matthew 12:22-45	(25) P. 178
Matthew 12:22-45	(26) P. 181
In Romans 11:25-32	(27) P. 183
Romans 12:3-12	(28) P. 192
Romans 12:13-21	(29) P. 196
Romans 13:1-14	(30) P. 199
Romans 14:1-23	(31) P. 205
Romans 15:1-33	(32) P. 211

Romans 16:1-27	(33)	P. 228
Exodus 34:1-9	(34)	P. 231
Matthew 7:1-6	(35)	P. 233
Titus 2:1-8	(36)	P. 244
Philippians 1:21-25	(37)	P. 245
Isaiah 55:6-13	(38)	P. 246
1 John 5:1-13	(39)	P. 263
Matthew 15:10-11	(40)	P. 264
1 Corinthians 15:57-58	(41)	P. 265
Prov. 22:1-4	(42)	P. 268
Judges 15;16-9	(43)	P. 308
Matthew 26:20-21	(44)	P. 311
Luke 12:22-27	(45)	P. 316
Numbers 11:13-15;	(46)	P. 326
I Sam. 1:9-11;	(47)	P. 325
Psalms 9:9-10;	(48)	P. 328
Matthew 6:28-30	(49)	P. 328
Proverbs 12:25	(50)	P. 333
Matthew 6:24-34	(51)	P. 334
Philippians 2:3	(52)	P. 335
Luke 16:14-17	(53)	P. 336
Ephesians 4:2-16	(54)	P. 336
Ephesians 5:1-2	(55)	P. 338
Romans 5;8-13	(56)	P. 338
II Timothy 3:14-17	(57)	P. 344
James 4:1-10	(58)	P. 346
I John Chapter2	(59)	P. 346
James 4:1-10	(60)	P. 347
Romans 12:1-3	(61)	P. 378
Titus 3:1-8	(62)	P. 378
Psalm 139:17-24	(63)	P. 380
Romans 8:4-9	(64)	P. 381

www.ingramcontent.com/pod-product-compliance
Lightning Source LLC
Chambersburg PA
CBHW060232290526
45789CB00001B/16